Minimal APIs in ASP.NET 9

Design, implement, and optimize robust APIs in C# with .NET 9

Nick Proud

Minimal APIs in ASP.NET 9

Copyright © 2024 Packt Publishing

All rights reserved. No part of this book may be reproduced, stored in a retrieval system, or transmitted in any form or by any means, without the prior written permission of the publisher, except in the case of brief quotations embedded in critical articles or reviews.

Every effort has been made in the preparation of this book to ensure the accuracy of the information presented. However, the information contained in this book is sold without warranty, either express or implied. Neither the author, nor Packt Publishing or its dealers and distributors, will be held liable for any damages caused or alleged to have been caused directly or indirectly by this book.

Packt Publishing has endeavored to provide trademark information about all of the companies and products mentioned in this book by the appropriate use of capitals. However, Packt Publishing cannot guarantee the accuracy of this information.

Group Product Manager: Kaustubh Manglurkar

Publishing Product Manager: Bhavya Rao

Book Project Manager: Sonam Pandey

Senior Editor: Ayushi Bulani

Technical Editor: Simran Ali

Copy Editor: Safis Editing

Indexer: Tejal Soni

Production Designer: Alishon Mendonca

DevRel Marketing Coordinator: Nivedita Pandey

First published: October 2022

Second edition: December 2024

Production reference: 1251024

Published by Packt Publishing Ltd.

Grosvenor House

11 St Paul's Square

Birmingham

B3 1RB, UK

ISBN: 978-1-80512-912-7

www.packtpub.com

To my wife, Kerrie, and my daughter, Neave. You gave me the strength to write, and you waited patiently for me to finish. I love you both with all my heart.

To Chris, Gemma, and Charlotte, my comrades at NexBotix. Thanks for your encouragement and support throughout the whole process.

– Nick

Contributors

About the author

Nick Proud is a software engineer, technology leader, and Microsoft MVP for Developer Technologies, specializing in robotic process automation and .NET. He is currently the director of software engineering at NexBotix an intelligent automation firm, as well as a technical content creator, producing educational video content about C# and Microsoft Azure.

I want to thank the people who have supported me on this journey, especially my family and colleagues at NexBotix. I also want to thank Peter Bull and Daniel Tallentire for their thorough technical review and the LinkedIn/YouTube community for their continued support of my content.

About the reviewers

Daniel Tallentire is a software engineer and engineering manager with two decades of experience developing SaaS software, using the Microsoft development ecosystem. He has a passion for learning and development and has mentored and coached multiple engineers and managers throughout his career. He speaks on these topics at meetups and conferences. Daniel currently works as an engineering manager at Citation Group, supporting multiple teams in developing software in the HR and employment software fields. In his spare time, Daniel likes to walk the hills of the Peak District, read books, and spend time with his family.

Peter Bull is a Microsoft MVP, software developer, presenter, content creator, and Microsoft technology enthusiast. Peter has over three decades of personal software development experience and more than two decades of professional software development expertise, including web, mobile, and desktop. His journey began with BASIC on the Commodore 64, evolving through every major release of .NET to modern .NET, and beyond! Peter, aka RoguePlanetoid, enjoys sharing what he knows with the community, aiming to mentor new or existing developers and inspire them with his tutorials, talks, and workshops with Tutorialr. He is also an avid content creator who enjoys engaging with the tech community through writing, speaking, and his *RoguePlanetoid* podcast.

I want to express my gratitude to those who have inspired and taught me throughout my journey as a software developer. Their support and guidance have been invaluable in helping me reach where I am today. In return, I aspire to inspire and teach others, sharing the knowledge and experiences I have gained. My goal is to help others on their own software developer journey by offering the same encouragement and mentorship I was fortunate to receive.

Table of Contents

Preface   **xiii**

Part 1 - Introduction to Minimal APIs

1

Getting Up and Running with Minimal API Development   3

Technical requirements	4
Understanding minimal APIs	4
Contrasting minimal APIs with traditional API approaches	5
The significance of minimal APIs in modern development	8
Installing required tools and dependencies	8
Installing Visual Studio for Windows	10
Installing Visual Studio Code for Mac and Linux	11
Configuring development environments	12
Creating a project in Visual Studio	12
Creating a project in Visual Studio Code	13
Summary	15

2

Creating Your First Minimal API   17

Technical requirements	17
Project structure and organization	18
Endpoints	18
Models	18
Routes	19
Defining endpoints and routes	20
GET methods	20
POST methods	20
PUT methods	21
PATCH methods	21
DELETE method	22
Building the employee management API	23
Creating the API	23
Creating the first endpoint	25
Handling HTTP requests	28
Summary	30

3

The Anatomy of a Minimal API — 31

Anatomy of a minimal API	31	The API request lifecycle	34
Components of a minimal API application	32	Summary	35

Part 2 - Data and Execution Flow

4

Handling HTTP Methods and Routing — 39

Technical requirements	40	Managing route parameters	45
Handling requests	40	Request validation and error handling	48
Defining endpoints in the Todo API	41	Manual validation	48
Getting todo items	41	Validation with data annotations and model binding	49
Creating Todo items	42		
Updating existing Todo items	43	Summary	54

5

The Middleware Pipeline — 55

Technical requirements	55	Implementing custom middleware	61
An introduction to middleware	56	Terminal middleware	64
Configuring middleware pipelines	58	Handling errors within the middleware pipeline	67
Middleware classes	59	Summary	69
Inline middleware	59		

6

Parameter Binding — 71

Parameter binding sources	71	Route values	72
		Query strings	73

Optional query string parameters	74	Binding parameters through dependency injection	79
Headers	76		
Strongly typed object binding	76	Binding precedence	81
Form values	77	Creating custom binding logic	82
Explicit binding with attributes	78	Summary	85

7

Dependency Injection in Minimal APIs   87

Understanding DI	88	**DI best practices**	100
The DI container	88	Avoiding the service locator pattern	100
The case for DI	88	Registering services with an extension method	101
Configuring DI in minimal APIs	89	Using sensible service lifetimes	102
Setting up a scoped DI project	90	**Summary**	102
Creating a singleton DI project	95		

8

Integrating Minimal APIs with Data Sources   105

Technical requirements	106	and retrieving records	108
Understanding data integration in minimal APIs	106	Inserting Employee records	113
		Executing database transactions from API endpoints	114
Connecting to and integrating with SQL databases	107	**Connecting to MongoDB**	115
Configuring the connection to the database		**Summary**	124

9

Object Relational Mapping with Entity Framework Core and Dapper   127

Technical requirements	128	Configuring Entity Framework in minimal API projects	137
Introduction to ORMs	128		
Configuring Dapper in minimal API projects	129	**Performing CRUD operations with Entity Framework**	141
Performing CRUD operations with Dapper	130		
		Summary	144

Part 3 - Optimal Minimal APIs

10

Profiling and Identifying Bottlenecks — 147

Technical requirements	147	Profiling tools and techniques	149
An introduction to profiling and performance monitoring	147	Profiling in Visual Studio	150
		Benchmarking with BenchmarkDotNet	154
Introducing the profiler	148	Common performance bottlenecks	157
Performance metrics	149	Summary	159

11

Utilizing Asynchronous Programming for Scalability — 161

Technical requirements	162	TAP with async/await	164
Understanding and implementing asynchronous patterns in a minimal API	162	Asynchronous processing pattern	165
		Common pitfalls and challenges	168
		Summary	170
Task-based asynchronous pattern	162		

12

Caching Strategies for Enhanced Performance — 171

Technical requirements	171	Distributed caching strategies	176
Introduction to caching in minimal APIs	172	Response caching	178
		Summary	179
In-memory caching techniques	173		

Part 4 - Best Practices, Design, and Deployment

13

Best Practices for Minimal API Resiliency — 183

Technical requirements	184	The strategy pattern	191
Code organization and structure	184	Error Handling	194
Exploring folder structures	185	Security considerations	196
Feature-based modular structure	185	Authentication	196
Layered modular structure	186	Authorization	197
Design patterns	187	Rate limiting	200
The factory pattern	188	Summary	201
The repository pattern	189		

14

Unit Testing, Compatibility, and Deployment of Minimal APIs — 203

Technical requirements	204	Deploying to Microsoft Azure App Service (cloud deployment)	213
Unit testing and integration testing for minimal APIs	204	Deploying to a Docker container	218
Compatibility and migrating minimal APIs to .NET 9	211	Deploying on-premises with Kestrel	220
Deploying minimal APIs	213	Summary	222

Index — 223

Other Books You May Enjoy — 230

Preface

This book is a comprehensive guide that delves into the world of building streamlined and efficient web services with ASP.NET using minimal APIs.

As the landscape of web development continues to evolve, there is a growing demand for simplicity, speed, and maintainability. I wrote this book to introduce developers—whether experienced or new to the ASP.NET ecosystem—to the power of minimal APIs, an approach that allows for the creation of lightweight and performance-oriented applications.

Why minimal APIs?

With the release of .NET 6 in 2021, Microsoft introduced minimal APIs as a new way to define HTTP APIs with less ceremony and boilerplate code. Minimal APIs focus on reducing the overhead traditionally associated with larger frameworks such as ASP.NET MVC, while still maintaining the robustness of the .NET platform. By stripping away unnecessary complexity, minimal APIs empower developers to rapidly prototype, iterate, and deploy applications that scale with their needs.

In this book, I will walk you through the essentials of minimal APIs, from basic routing and endpoint structure to advanced features such as dependency injection, authentication, and middleware integration.

I'll also introduce you to some core design principles, providing an overview of some best practices designed to keep your minimal APIs maintainable, secure, and scalable over time.

Each chapter is structured to provide hands-on examples, ensuring that by the end, you'll not only understand how to use minimal APIs but also why they matter in modern software development.

At the time of writing, .NET 9 had reached its first release candidate phase (RC1), and .NET 9 was very close to general availability. I've included information throughout the book on new minimal API features in .NET 9.

Who this book is for

The book is intended to serve as an introduction to Minimal APIs, allowing developers with a basic understanding of C# and **object-oriented programming** (**OOP**) to explore the main concepts and begin their Minimal API development journey.

Whether you are an experienced ASP.NET developer looking to leverage new tools or a newcomer seeking to understand web development, this book will guide you step by step. It's ideal for developers seeking to build microservices, start-ups prototyping new ideas, or even established enterprises looking for a more efficient way to handle specific API needs.

What this book covers

Chapter 1, *Getting Up and Running with Minimal API Development*, introduces the world of minimal APIs, helping you to understand their relevance in modern software development and how they differ from traditional API approaches. It also instructs you on how to set up their development environment.

Chapter 2, *Creating Your First Minimal API*, introduces the core elements of a minimal API, such as endpoints, models, and routes, before getting you building endpoints using varying HTTP methods.

Chapter 3, *The Anatomy of a Minimal API*, delves into more detail on the building blocks of a minimal API, outlining the various components found within, along with an overview of the request lifecycle.

Chapter 4, *Handling HTTP Methods and Routing*, focuses on how incoming requests are handled and how this can differ based on different HTTP methods used. It covers the management of route parameters and introduces request validation and error handling in minimal API endpoints.

Chapter 5, *The Middleware Pipeline*, explains the concept of middleware in ASP.NET, before instructing you on how you can configure and implement it in the context of minimal APIs.

Chapter 6, *Parameter Binding*, discusses the ways in which parameters can be sent into minimal API endpoints. The various parameter binding sources are explored, along with examples of how custom bindings can be created.

Chapter 7, *Dependency Injection in Minimal APIs*, introduces dependency injection as a software development concept before exploring its usage in minimal APIs. Best practices for dependency injection are also outlined.

Chapter 8, *Integrating Minimal APIs with Data Sources*, helps you understand how data can be integrated into a minimal API, with examples focusing on SQL Server and MongoDB.

Chapter 9, *Objected-Relational Mapping with Entity Framework Core and Dapper*, takes the learning points from *Chapter 8* further, introducing **object-relational mapping** (**ORM**) frameworks such as Entity Framework Core and Dapper. The chapter provides examples of the configuration of the respective frameworks and how they can be used to create CRUD operations.

Chapter 10, *Profiling and Identifying Bottlenecks*, focuses on managing and optimizing the performance of minimal APIs. Various profiling tools are explored and we explore several common performance bottlenecks.

Chapter 11, *Utilizing Asynchronous Programming for Scalability*, demonstrates the benefits of asynchronous programming in minimal APIs, providing examples of various asynchronous patterns. The chapter also provides examples of common pitfalls and challenges associated with asynchronous execution within minimal APIs.

Chapter 12, *Caching Strategies for Enhanced Performance*, takes the theme of performance further by introducing you to caching and its place within minimal APIs. Various caching techniques are demonstrated, using caching technologies such as ASP.NET's in-memory cache and Redis.

Chapter 13, *Best Practices for Minimal API Resiliency*, turns our attention from performance to resiliency, suggesting ways in which code can be structured in a minimal API to encourage long-term functionality. Topics such as error handling and security considerations are also explored.

Chapter 14, *Unit Testing, Compatibility, and Deployment of Minimal APIs*, closes out the book with topics related to the latter phases of minimal API development. Unit testing and integration testing are demonstrated using xUnit, specific compatibility requirements are outlined, and there are hands-on examples of how minimal APIs can be deployed to various hosting platforms.

To get the most out of this book

You will need to have a basic understanding of OOP languages and C# to understand the examples in this book. You will also need to have a basic understanding of what an API is, as well as how relational databases such as SQL work.

Topics covered in the book	Required Skill Level
C#	.NET 9 SDK (Software Development Kit)
SQL	Microsoft SQL Server
MongoDB Server	Microsoft SQL Server Management Studio
MongoDB Compass	None – setup and configuration for Minimal APIs is covered in the book
Visual Studio 2022	Basic
Visual Studio Code	Basic (if used – Visual Studio can be used alternatively)
Object-Oriented Programming	Basic

As .NET is cross-platform, it is assumed that your operating system is either Windows, MacOS or Linux, all of which are compatible.

> **Readers using MacOS or Linux**
>
> For readers on these operating systems, it is recommended that Visual Studio Code is used as an alternative to Visual Studio 2022.

If you are using the digital version of this book, we advise you to type the code yourself or access the code from the book's GitHub repository (a link is available in the next section). Doing so will help you avoid any potential errors related to the copying and pasting of code.

Download the example code files

You can download the example code files for this book from GitHub at `https://github.com/PacktPublishing/Minimal-APIs-in-ASP.NET-9`. If there's an update to the code, it will be updated in the GitHub repository.

We also have other code bundles from our rich catalog of books and videos available at `https://github.com/PacktPublishing/`. Check them out!

Conventions used

There are a number of text conventions used throughout this book.

`Code in text`: Indicates code words in text, database table names, folder names, filenames, file extensions, pathnames, dummy URLs, user input, and Twitter handles. Here is an example: "In the `Employees` table, we have set the `Id` column as an identity column, meaning that it will be populated by SQL Server on insertion of any record, with the `Id` value incrementing by `1` on each insert."

A block of code is set as follows:

```
app.MapPut("/employees", (Employee employee) =>
{
    EmployeeManager.Update(employee);
    return Results.Ok();
});
```

Any command-line input or output is written as follows:

```
mongodb://localhost:27017/MyCompany
```

Bold: Indicates a new term, an important word, or words that you see onscreen. For instance, words in menus or dialog boxes appear in **bold**. Here is an example: "You can do this by going to **Tools | Manage NuGet Packages | Package Manager Console**."

> **Tips or important notes**
> Appear like this.

Get in touch

Feedback from our readers is always welcome.

General feedback: If you have questions about any aspect of this book, email us at `customercare@packtpub.com` and mention the book title in the subject of your message.

Errata: Although we have taken every care to ensure the accuracy of our content, mistakes do happen. If you have found a mistake in this book, we would be grateful if you would report this to us. Please visit www.packtpub.com/support/errata and fill in the form.

Piracy: If you come across any illegal copies of our works in any form on the internet, we would be grateful if you would provide us with the location address or website name. Please contact us at copyright@packt.com with a link to the material.

If you are interested in becoming an author: If there is a topic that you have expertise in and you are interested in either writing or contributing to a book, please visit authors.packtpub.com.

Share Your Thoughts

Once you've read *Minimal APIs in ASP.NET 9*, we'd love to hear your thoughts! Scan the QR code below to go straight to the Amazon review page for this book and share your feedback.

https://packt.link/r/1-805-12912-0

Your review is important to us and the tech community and will help us make sure we're delivering excellent quality content.

Download a free PDF copy of this book

Thanks for purchasing this book!

Do you like to read on the go but are unable to carry your print books everywhere?

Is your eBook purchase not compatible with the device of your choice?

Don't worry, now with every Packt book you get a DRM-free PDF version of that book at no cost.

Read anywhere, any place, on any device. Search, copy, and paste code from your favorite technical books directly into your application.

The perks don't stop there, you can get exclusive access to discounts, newsletters, and great free content in your inbox daily

Follow these simple steps to get the benefits:

1. Scan the QR code or visit the link below

https://packt.link/free-ebook/978-1-80512-912-7

2. Submit your proof of purchase
3. That's it! We'll send your free PDF and other benefits to your email directly

Part 1 - Introduction to Minimal APIs

In this part, we lay the foundation for understanding minimal APIs. We'll explore how to quickly get started with development and examine the fundamental building blocks that make up a minimal API. Whether you are new to APIs or experienced, this part will ensure you have a solid grasp of the core concepts.

This part has the following chapters:

- *Chapter 1, Getting Up and Running with Minimal API Development*
- *Chapter 2, Creating Your First Minimal API*
- *Chapter 3, The Anatomy of a Minimal API*

1
Getting Up and Running with Minimal API Development

As users, we associate interacting with an application with a **User Interface** (**UI**). This interface consists of interactive elements that allow for interaction between the code and user. You can think of this like the *storefront*, a place where you can browse the available wares or request appropriate action, for example, booking a vacation or adding items to your shopping cart.

If the UI is where customers interact with our *store*, an **Application Programming Interface** (**API**) is the back of the store. This is where we receive deliveries, move goods, process orders, and manage inventory.

Most developers have some experience in interacting with or writing APIs, but what makes **minimal APIs** different?

Minimal APIs were introduced by Microsoft in 2021 with the release of .NET 6. The aim was to empower developers to create APIs with a minimum of boilerplate code, allowing them to focus on the essentials of the business logic in use between requests and responses.

They offer a lightweight solution to API development, which is often a good starting point for projects, as they require much less effort to set them up. This is a key advantage when you're looking to get a system up and running quickly, or where there is a low number of dependencies. It can also mean that performance is better in minimal APIs thanks to the reduced overhead compared to more traditional API formats. In this book, we will learn how to leverage these benefits of minimal APIs.

In this chapter, we're going to cover the following main topics:

- Understanding minimal APIs
- Contrasting minimal APIs with traditional API approaches
- The significance of minimal APIs in modern development
- Installing required tools and dependencies
- Configuring development environments

Technical requirements

To follow the directions in this chapter, you'll need to have the following installed on your Windows, macOS, or Linux machine:

- .NET 9.0 **Software Development Kit (SDK)**
- Visual Studio or Visual Studio Code
- C# extension for Visual Studio Code (if you are using Visual Studio Code)

If you're working in Windows, it's recommended that you use Visual Studio, although Visual Studio Code will still work. If you're a Mac or Linux user, you should use Visual Studio Code. (At the time of writing, Visual Studio for Mac is set to be retired on August 31, 2024.)

The code for this chapter is available in the GitHub repository at: https://github.com/PacktPublishing/Minimal-APIs-in-ASP.NET-9.

Understanding minimal APIs

When it comes to designing and building APIs, we're spoilt for choice with varying styles, approaches, and templates. .NET has proven itself over the years to be a fantastic choice for general-purpose API development. Modern .NET provides us with two main types of API framework, one more traditional than the other. One of the options is, of course, the minimal API, which is still a relatively new feature within .NET compared to its predecessor, the controller-based API.

With minimal APIs, the aim is simplicity. Less code, less ceremony, and less complexity. As a result, minimal APIs are well suited to microservice architectures, where you have lots of small components all requiring a means of transferring data between each other.

Their simplicity also makes them easier to read, as a small block of code can take care of all the classic features of an API, such as receiving HTTP requests, routing, utilizing dependencies, accessing services, and sending responses to clients.

One of the more admirable aspects of minimal APIs is the way they lower the barrier of entry to API development. They provide an alternative means of structuring your code that is more accessible, easier to read, and, in most cases, more performant owing to the decreased overhead.

A simple API can be created using minimal APIs in just four lines of code. Here's the classic *hello world* example:

```
var builder = WebApplication.CreateBuilder(args);
var app = builder.Build();
app.MapGet("/", () => "Hello World!");
app.Run();
```

Congratulations! You just created an API! Let's dig deeper into what's happening in the example:

- On the first line, we create an instance of `WebApplicationBuilder` by calling `CreateBuilder` and passing in any command-line arguments that we might need. Think of this as a blueprint for the API we're creating. The minimal API is an ASP.NET core application like any other, and so it needs a pipeline for it to be run. `WebApplicationBuilder` provides us with this pipeline.

- Then, we call `Build()` on this instance we created, which results in an instance of `WebApplication` that we have called app. This is our API.

- The third line maps any incoming HTTP GET requests on the root path of the application: `("/")`. Following this, we use a lambda statement to indicate the logic that should be executed when the request is received. In this case, we are returning the string `Hello World!`.

- Finally, the fourth line starts the application, making it listen for incoming requests.

Now that you have a high-level understanding of minimal APIs, let's compare them with more traditional API formats.

Contrasting minimal APIs with traditional API approaches

The more traditional API format in .NET compared to minimal APIs is **controller-based APIs**. These are more commonly seen in ASP.NET **Model-View-Controller** (**MVC**) projects, or in ASP.NET web API projects. However, whether you're building an MVC project or not, both API types utilize controllers.

Controllers are simply classes, with many responsibilities within the API, such as the following:

- Handling incoming requests via *actions*, which are interacted with using various HTTP methods, such as `GET`, `POST`, `PUT`, `DELETE`, and `PATCH`.

- Processing data sent in the request via query string parameters or within the request body.

- Interaction with data models and processing of business logic via services.

- Generation of responses to calling clients. These responses could be in JSON, XML, or many other formats.

    Routing of requests to other areas of the application, that is, directing to a page at a specific URL.

When using a controller-based API, each controller tends to be focused on one specific application domain. For example, you may have a controller dedicated to all things *employees*, and another dedicated to *inventory*. This is great for segregating business logic into relevant areas, but requires a lot of ceremony, such as the need to *inherit* from a base *controller* class, the need to add attributes for defining HTTP methods, or management of folder structures for each controller.

Here's an example of an `Employee` controller. Notice the use of attributes for labeling the controller type (`[ApiController]`) and routing. Also observe how the class is required to derive from `ControllerBase`, along with dependency injection managed via a class constructor to get `IEmployeeRepository`, and this is only for *employees*! We'd have to do it all over again in a separate class for our *inventory* controller, and so the ceremony continues:

```
using Microsoft.AspNetCore.Mvc;
using System.Collections.Generic;

namespace EmployeeAPI.Controllers
{
    [ApiController]
    [Route("api/[controller]")]
    public class EmployeesController : ControllerBase
    {
        private readonly IEmployeeRepository
            _employeeRepository;
        public EmployeesController(
            IEmployeeRepository employeeRepository)
        {
            _employeeRepository = employeeRepository;
        }

        [HttpGet]
        public ActionResult<IEnumerable<Employee>>
            GetEmployees()
        {
            var employees =
                _employeeRepository.GetEmployees();
            return Ok(employees);
        }

        [HttpPost]
        public ActionResult<Employee>
            CreateEmployee(Employee employee)
        {
            _employeeRepository.AddEmployee(employee);
            return CreatedAtAction(nameof(GetEmployees),
                new{id = employee.Id }, employee);
        }
    }
}
```

By contrast, you can create a minimal API endpoint directly in the entry point of your application, with routing, dependency injection, and handlers all defined inline, like in the example here:

```
public class Program
{
    public static void Main(string[] args)
    {
        var builder = WebApplication.CreateBuilder(args);

        builder.Services.AddSingleton<IEmployeeRepository,
            EmployeeRepository>();

        var app = builder.Build();

        app.MapGet("/api/employees",
            (IEmployeeRepository employeeRepository) =>
        {
            var employees =
                employeeRepository.GetEmployees();
            return Results.Ok(employees);
        });
        app.Run();
    }
}
```

As you can see, within a much simpler, smaller block of code (and without the need for a separate controller class), we've registered a service for dependency injection, added an HTTP GET endpoint, injected our service, ran the required logic, and returned a result.

> **Dependency injection in minimal APIs versus controllers**
>
> We'll cover dependency injection later in the book, but it's important to know that dependency injection as shown in the example requires more configuration in a controller-based API, as you typically register your dependencies at the startup of the application in Startup.cs. minimal APIs allow you to inject dependencies in a much lighter, straightforward way, wherever they are needed, without the need for Startup.cs. It's also important to note that for the shown examples, you would need to create your own IEmployeeRepository for the code to work.

Having an overall understanding of minimal APIs and how they differ from other development approaches is critical for their optimal use. For more context, let us look at how minimal APIs fit within the context of modern software development.

The significance of minimal APIs in modern development

The concept of creating more lightweight and simple APIs has been around for some time, but the adoption of minimal APIs has increased over the years. Flask and Express.js have historically promoted some elements of minimalism in API development within Python and Node.js, respectively, but compared to its counterparts, .NET's recent entry into the market is specifically designed to exploit the advantages of lightweight, simple APIs.

Now that minimal APIs have arrived and are being used in mainstream development projects, developers are enjoying the benefits of not having to perform lots of setup and configuration. They can have a working API up and running in two minutes and deploy it to the cloud in another two. This provides phenomenal advantages for industries in which getting software to market quickly is critical to success.

In addition, the APIs you write can take advantage of .NET's mature, cross-platform ecosystem, with robust libraries and off-the-shelf security solutions for request validation, **cross-site request forgery** (**CSRF**) protection, and authorization.

So far, we have taken a generic look at minimal APIs and their place within modern software development. Moving forward, we are going to start configuring our environment for building minimal API projects. As with most project setups, the first things to be configured are the tools and dependencies. Follow the steps in the next section to start preparing your development environment.

Installing required tools and dependencies

For us to begin working with minimal APIs, we need to install some tools.

Let us start by installing the .NET 9.0 SDK. Navigate to Microsoft's .NET SDK downloads page at `https://dotnet.microsoft.com/en-us/download/dotnet`. (This can be skipped if you already have the SDK installed.)

At the time of writing, the SDK is available by doing the following:

1. Choose the appropriate build for your operating system and system architecture. For example, if you are running 64-bit Windows, you would download **x64**. Likewise, if you were running a Mac with an ARM CPU, you would select **Arm64** next to **macOS**. Linux tends to be a little different because a package manager is used to obtain the SDK.

If you are a Linux user, follow the relevant Microsoft documentation for your specific Linux distribution:

OS	Installers	Binaries
Linux	Package manager instructions	Arm32 | Arm32 Alpine | Arm64 | Arm64 Alpine | x64 | x64 Alpine
macOS	Arm64 | x64	Arm64 | x64
Windows	Arm64 | x64 | x86 | winget instructions	Arm64 | x64 | x86
All	dotnet-install scripts	

Figure 1.1: Choosing the right installer

Before we move on, let us quickly differentiate between installers and binaries. When software is added to a system, it usually consists of multiple files containing code to be executed when the program runs. These files are binaries: libraries or modules of code that make up the overall application. An installer automatically places all these components in the relevant locations on the host system. Because binaries are managed by installers, if you simply download the binaries, you will not automatically have them placed in specific locations. The configuration that would normally be orchestrated by an installer will not have taken place. This is sometimes necessary if you want to configure an application differently from how an installer would normally do it.

When you download .NET SDKs from Microsoft's website, you usually get the choice between downloading an installer or a binary. The simplest option is to use an installer, as this will configure your .NET development environment for you automatically. It is the version used in examples shown in this book and I recommend you use it also.

2. Once the installer has downloaded, open it and follow the prompts. You will need administrator permissions to install the SDK.

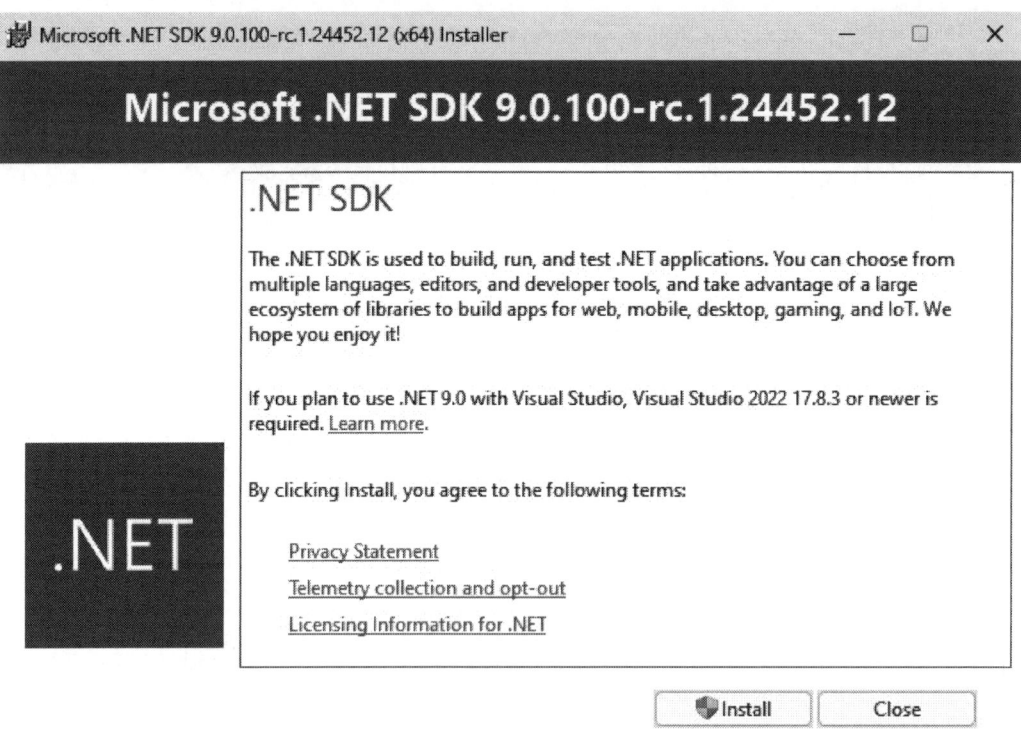

Figure 1.2: The .NET SDK installer

Now that we have the SDK installed, it's time to install Visual Studio (on Windows) or Visual Studio Code (on macOS or Linux). Either application can be obtained from the Visual Studio website at `https://visualstudio.microsoft.com/downloads`.

> **.NET versions**
>
> The version of .NET shown after installation and the version of .NET shown in this example may differ.

Installing Visual Studio for Windows

Follow these steps to install Visual Studio on your device:

1. On the downloads page, choose your desired Visual Studio edition. If you don't have a Visual Studio license, you can select the **Community** edition.
2. Like when using the installer for the SDK, simply follow the prompts in the Visual Studio wizard to install to the desired location on your machine.

Installing required tools and dependencies   11

3. You will be prompted to choose relevant workloads during the setup process. At a minimum, you would need to select **ASP.NET and web development** to develop minimal APIs. Following this, you will be asked about optional additions. None of these will be crucial for minimal API development, so you can simply click **Next** once you have passed the screen shown in *Figure 1.3*.

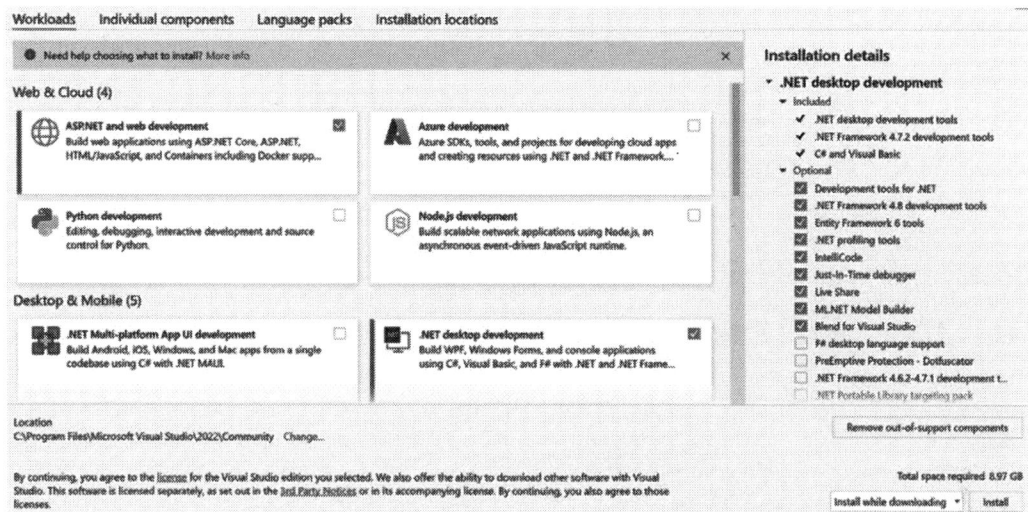

Figure 1.3: Workloads selection when installing Visual Studio

Next, let's install Visual Studio Code.

Installing Visual Studio Code for Mac and Linux

Visual Studio Code is a free application. Simply download the relevant installer for your target operating system. Then, do the following:

1. Once downloaded, run the installer.
2. Open Visual Studio Code and click the **Extensions** button in the left ribbon (or use the keyboard shortcut, *Ctrl + Shift + X*).
3. In the search bar at the top of the extensions pane, search for C#. You will see an extension appear with the same name. This is the **C# for Visual Studio Code** extension, which you will need to program in C# in Visual Studio Code. Click I**nstall**.

Figure 1.4: Microsoft's official C# extension for Visual Studio Code

You now have all the prerequisite tools for writing minimal APIs in .NET installed. Next, we will set up our development environment.

Configuring development environments

We'll start to develop our first minimal API in the next chapter, but before that, let's create the project structure needed for us to start writing code.

To build minimal APIs, we need to be working within an ASP.NET Core project. Depending on whether you are using Visual Studio or Visual Studio Code, there are several ways you can create this type of project.

Creating a project in Visual Studio

Let's begin by creating a project in Visual Studio:

1. Open Visual Studio.
2. The screen shown in the following figure gives you the option to search for the type of project you wish to create. Search for **ASP.NET Core Empty** and select it from the list, before clicking **Next**. (Make sure you choose the C# version of the template. Do not use the F# version, as this is not within the scope of this book.)

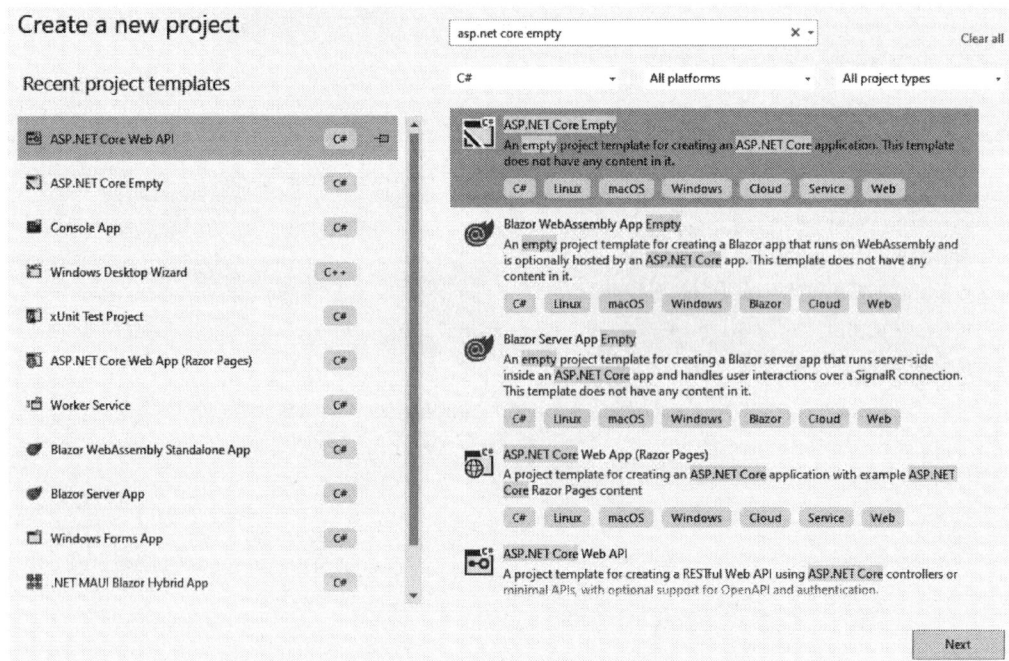

Figure 1.5: Visual Studio's new project creation screen

3. Give your new project a name and choose a folder location in which it should be saved. Then, click **Next**.

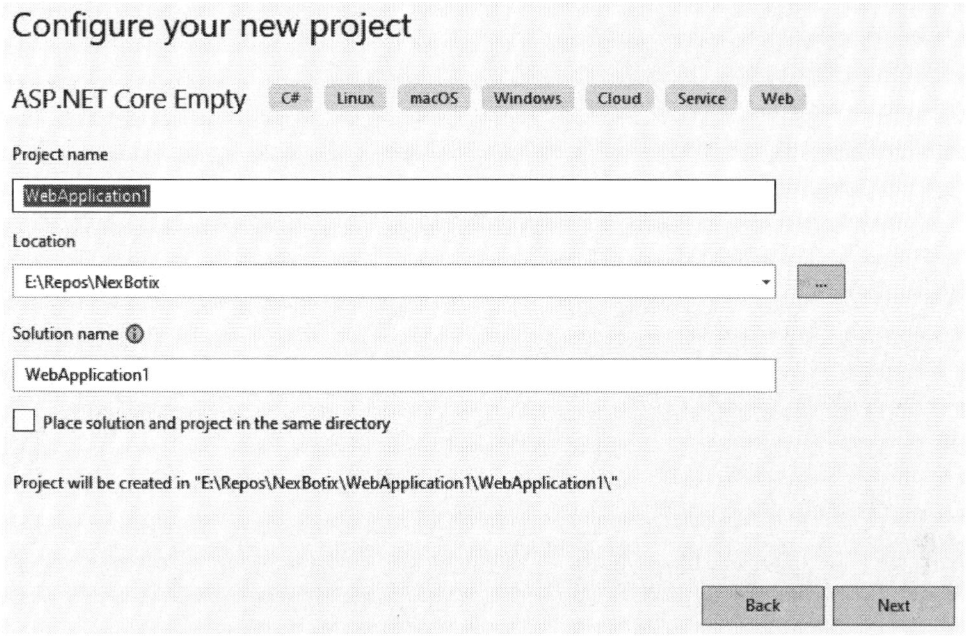

Figure 1.6: Project configuration (ASP.NET Core Empty) in Visual Studio

4. Choose your preferred .NET version. This book uses .NET 9, and we have just installed the .NET 9 SDK, so select this version from the list. **Configure for HTTPS** should be checked by default. This can be left checked. Finally, click **Create**. Your project will then be created.

Visual Studio is arguably the most used IDE for this kind of project. However, it is possible to create minimal API projects in newer IDEs, such as Visual Studio Code. Let us explore how we can set up the same project in Visual Studio Code.

Creating a project in Visual Studio Code

Next, let's create a project in Visual Studio Code in this section:

1. Open Visual Studio Code and open a terminal window by clicking **Terminal** and then **New Terminal Window** (or use the keyboard shortcut, *Ctrl + Shift*).

2. Enter the following commands into the terminal window, replacing MyProjectName with the name of your project:

   ```
   dotnet new web -o MyProjectName
   cd MyProjectName
   code -r ../MyProjectName
   ```

3. When presented with dialog boxes asking whether you want to trust the authors and add required assets to the project, select **Yes**.

Both project configurations will create the same minimal API example that we explored earlier in the chapter, returning `Hello World!` on an HTTP GET endpoint:

```
// A builder is initialized and then built.
var builder = WebApplication.CreateBuilder(args);
var app = builder.Build();

// GET endpoint mapped onto the base URL route, with a
// function body that returns a string.
app.MapGet("/", () => "Hello World!");

//The initialized app is started
app.Run();
```

You now have the basic foundations of a minimal API project.

We can get the output from this example in Visual Studio Code and Visual Studio by clicking the **Play** button. This will run the project in debug mode, opening a browser window that, in the case of this example, simply displays **Hello World!**. This button is in slightly different places depending on which IDE you are using.

In Visual Studio Code it looks like the following:

Figure 1.7: Debugging the project in Visual Studio Code

While the button in Visual Studio looks like *Figure 1.8*:

Figure 1.8: Debugging the project in Visual Studio

Let's recap what we learnt in this chapter!

Summary

In this chapter, you learned about the role of minimal APIs in modern application development, and you should now have a good general understanding of their advantages.

You learned how minimal APIs differ from controller-based APIs in .NET, and gained an understanding of the advantages and disadvantages of these two formats.

You installed the basic required libraries and tools to get started on your journey and learned how to create a new project in Visual Studio or Visual Studio Code.

The key takeaway from this chapter is that minimal APIs promote simplicity, high performance, and maintainability.

In the next chapter, we will start writing our first Minimal API endpoints, which will be able to handle various HTTP methods on different routes. We will minimal build responses to send back to clients and make calls to our API.

2
Creating Your First Minimal API

The convenience of the .NET ecosystem could not be more evident by the steps you took in the last chapter. Minimal APIs in .NET live up to their name by having not only minimal logic and dependencies but also minimal setup requirements.

Just by creating your first project, you have technically already created your first minimal API. It's functional out of the box, with a `GET` endpoint that returns a response.

Obviously, there is more to minimal APIs than what we saw in the `Hello World` example. There are different HTTP request methods, varying endpoints, and more advanced response generation to consider as part of a straightforward API.

In this chapter, we're going to cover the following main topics:

- Project structure and organization
- Defining endpoints and routes
- Building the employee management API
- Handling HTTP requests

By the end of the chapter, you'll have gained experience in defining endpoints for handling HTTP requests. You'll also be able to implement basic HTTP request handling and response generation.

Technical requirements

To follow the directions in this chapter, you'll need to have the following installed on your Windows, macOS, or Linux machine:

- .NET 9.0 **Software Development Kit (SDK)**
- Visual Studio or Visual Studio Code
- C# Extension for Visual Studio Code (if you are using Visual Studio Code)

If you followed the setup guidance in *Chapter 1*, then you are ready to follow the directions in this chapter. However, if you still need to configure the preceding tools, then please follow the *Chapter 1* setup instructions under the *Installing required tools and dependencies* section. The code for this chapter is available in the GitHub repository at: `https://github.com/PacktPublishing/Minimal-APIs-in-ASP.NET-9`.

Project structure and organization

The rules around how a project is structured and organized are not exactly rigid, but it is important to ensure that you are organizing your projects in a cohesive and accessible manner. With minimal APIs in general, we are aiming for simplicity. Project structure and organization in minimal APIs specifically are no different. Therefore, it may not come as a shock that the project structure for minimal APIs outlined in the following examples will be extremely basic.

In the following three subsections, we look at the elements needed to simplify our project structure.

Endpoints

Endpoints are the *open doors* to your API. Each endpoint sits within an area of your domain (e.g., employees or inventory) and is responsible for specific actions within that domain, such as adding, updating, or removing an inventory item.

In ASP.NET `Controller`-based projects, you would usually distribute endpoints for each area of the domain into logical groups called **Controllers**. Each `Controller` is a class containing endpoints that are relevant to that `Controller`'s domain area.

However, in minimal APIs, it is normal for endpoints to simply be defined in the app's entry-point, within `Program.cs`.

Models

Just like in **Model-View-Controller** (**MVC**) projects, a model in minimal APIs can be used to encapsulate domain objects. Models are usually created as their own classes. In the upcoming examples, which demonstrate API endpoint mappings, I will be creating logic for an API that manages employees. Therefore, I will use a model in the form of an `Employee` class.

Using a class to represent domain objects brings many benefits, including the following:

- **Separation of concerns**: Models encapsulate the data for the application, separating it from the business logic, which will be found within the API layer in our case.
- **Reusability**: Model objects can be reused by business logic across the application.
- **Loose coupling**: Thanks to the separation of concerns between data and business logic, changes to the API need not affect the structure of the data inadvertently. This is particularly important in common cases where models mirror a database table's structure through an ORM such as Entity Framework or Dapper (See *Chapter 8*).

> **Staying organized**
> While minimal API project structures can afford to stay very simple, it's still important to keep them organized. It is good practice to keep all models in a dedicated `Models` folder and all endpoints in their own `Endpoints` folder.

For the final piece in the project structure puzzle, we have routes.

Routes

If endpoints are the open door into the API, **routes** are the address of each door. By creating a route, you are defining the URLs that your API will respond to, and which piece of logic will be executed as a result.

Routes can be standalone or contain parameters that will be passed through to the resulting API logic.

In the endpoint on the following pages, you will see routes defined in the form of strings, indicating the text that should be appended onto the application's base URL to access specific endpoints.

For example, if our application is hosted at `getInventoryItem`, the full URL for that endpoint would become `https://adventureworks.com/getInventoryItem`.

We can, however, make our routes more generic. `getInventoryItem` is certainly clear, but it is better practice to, where possible, send different kinds of requests to a generic route, with different logic firing depending on the HTTP method in use.

For example, instead of naming our route `getinventoryitem`, we could apply the generic name `inventoryitems` to as many HTTP methods as is relevant. This means that a `GET` request (we will learn about these methods in the next section) to this route will get an inventory item, but a `POST` to the same route will create one.

This is deemed to be a best practice for naming routes, for several reasons:

- **Consistency**: Since having a generic endpoint has become an API convention, it allows your API to conform to an agreed standard.

- **Intuitiveness**: Most developers consuming an API will work to the same standard. This means that they will be more quickly able to pick up your API.

- **RESTful principles**: Allowing the HTTP method to identify the function of an endpoint rather than the route allows us to conform to RESTful principles, which encourage good use of **CREATE, READ, UPDATE, DELETE (CRUD)** operations, idempotency (during multiple identical requests, the server's state is never changed, and it returns the same results for the same request each time), and the need for full coverage of the standard HTTP methods (`GET`, `POST`, `PUT`, `PATCH`, `DELETE`).

In contrast to the list, if you have API endpoints that support an HTTP method in a very bespoke use case, you can still create routes that are more specific. However, the customary practice is to use the generic route naming convention that we outlined.

Understanding routes is critical to minimal API development in addition to most API frameworks. Let's turn our attention to the way in which routes and their endpoints are defined.

Defining endpoints and routes

Like any other RESTful API framework, minimal API endpoints are accessed using different HTTP methods. Depending on the HTTP method used to contact the API endpoint, a different result will be produced, or an action will be executed.

In the next few sections, we will look at some examples of endpoints being mapped with different HTTP methods.

GET methods

An HTTP `GET` method is a request for information. On successful retrieval, the API endpoint returns a `200 OK` status code, along with the requested data.

The example shows a `GET` endpoint mapped to the `"/employees"` route. It gets the employee ID contained within the URL and uses this to find the relevant employee data before returning it.

For example, if this API were hosted at `constoso.com`, a `GET` call to `contoso.com/employees/24` would retrieve the employee whose ID is `24`:

```
app.MapGet("/employees/{id}", (int id) =>
{
    var employee = EmployeeManager.Get(id);
    return Results.Ok(employee);
});
```

Let's look at `POST` methods now.

POST methods

An HTTP `POST` method is a request to create something. On successful execution, the API endpoint usually returns a `201 Created` status code (this is best practice, although some APIs return the standard `200 OK` code), along with any relevant data.

The following example shows a `POST` method mapped to the `"/employees"` endpoint. It expects to receive an employee payload in JSON format. The endpoint then converts the payload into an object of the `Employee` type, before calling some other back-end code to create an `Employee`, using this object as a parameter.

If everything worked as expected, the endpoint returns a `201 Created` status code, along with the `Employee Created` message.

For example, if this API were hosted at `constoso.com`, a POST call would execute the following code:

```
app.MapPost("/employees", (Employee employee) =>
{
    EmployeeManager.Create(employee);
    return Results.Created();
});
```

Up next, we look at PUT methods.

PUT methods

An HTTP `PUT` method is a request to update something. It's important to remember that `PUT` updates a resource in a particular way compared to the `PATCH` method, which has its own way of updating.

`PUT` methods require a payload that represents the entire resource being updated. So, in the case of our `Employee` API, if you were to use a `PUT` endpoint to update an existing employee, the API endpoint would expect a full `Employee` object to be sent in the request. It would then find the existing employee and replace it with the one sent in the request.

On successful execution, the API endpoint returns the standard `200 OK` status code.

The example shows a `PUT` method mapped to the `"/employees"` route. It expects to receive an employee payload in JSON format. Like in the preceding `POST` example, the endpoint converts this JSON payload into an object of the `Employee` type, before finding the original employee and calling a method to replace it with the updated one

For example, if this API was hosted at `constoso.com`, a PUT call would execute the following code:

```
app.MapPut("/employees", (Employee employee) =>
{
    EmployeeManager.Update(employee);
    return Results.Ok();
});
```

PATCH methods

Like a `PUT` method, an HTTP `PATCH` method is also a request to update something. However, the way it does its update is different. Instead of requiring a payload containing a representation of the entire object, a `PATCH` method only requires that the individual values that need to be changed are sent as part of the request. The API can then take care of updating the relevant properties on the existing object.

On successful execution, the API endpoint usually returns the standard `200 OK` status code.

The example shows a `PATCH` method mapped to the `"/updateEmployeeName"` route. It expects to receive an `Employee` object like `POST` and `PUT`. However, it is only interested in the `Name` and `Id` properties. This means that as long as a JSON payload is sent and it contains these properties, it will work. Using these properties, the code fetches the right object of the `Employee` type based on the given Id. It then updates the name property on the retrieved employee only, without overwriting the whole object.

For example, if this API was hosted at `constoso.com`, a `PATCH` call would execute the following code:

```
app.MapPatch("/updateEmployeeName", (Employee employee) =>
{
    EmployeeManager.ChangeName(employee.Id, employee.Name);
    return Results.Ok();
});
```

The final method we will look at is `DELETE`.

DELETE method

A `DELETE` method is self-explanatory in terms of what it does. Sending an ID for a resource as a parameter in the same way we did for the `GET` endpoint, the API can locate that specific resource and then remove it.

In most cases, on success, a `DELETE` method will usually return the standard `200 OK` status code, but it may instead return `204 No Content`, which is also fine.

The following example shows a `DELETE` method mapped to the `"/employees"` route. The endpoint will use the `Id` parameter to find the corresponding object of the `Employee` type as the target for deletion. After removing the `Employee` object, it returns a `204 No Content` status code to the client.

If this API was hosted at `constoso.com`, a `DELETE` call to `https://contoso.com/employees` would execute the following code:

```
app.MapDelete("/deleteEmployee/{id}", (int id) =>
{
    EmployeeManager.Delete(id);
    return Results.Ok();
});
```

Once you feel you've understood the different HTTP methods available to our API, turn to the next section to start building a basic minimal API based on a simple, real-world use case.

Building the employee management API

Now that we have covered an overview of routing and endpoints, along with the ways in which they support the various HTTP methods, let's start building a new minimal API project, with the use case of employee management.

Our goal in this section will be to create a repository of employees on which our API can operate. The API will then be able to get, create, update, and delete employees.

Creating the API

Follow the next few steps to create the employee management API.

If you haven't followed the steps in *Chapter 1* to create your ASP.NET project in Visual Studio or Visual Studio Code, follow them first, and then continue with the next steps:

1. You may already have this in your project, but if not, ensure that it is present at the top of `Program.cs`. This will build the `WebApplication` instance that hosts the minimal API:

   ```
   var builder = WebApplication.CreateBuilder(args);
   var app = builder.Build();
   ```

2. The two lines in the previous step are enough to build the `WebApplication` instance, but it still needs to be started. Add this line to the bottom of your class to start the instance:

   ```
   app.Run();
   ```

Now you have a runnable app, but no endpoints. Before we define those endpoints, we need some data to work with. We'll come back to `Program.cs` to define the endpoints shortly. But before that, let's create a model of the `Employee` type:

1. In the folder structure of the project, create a new folder called `Models`.
2. Inside the new folder, create a new class called `Employee`.
3. Create these properties in the `Employee` class:

   ```
   public class Employee
   {
       public int Id { get; set; }
       public string Name { get; set; }
       public decimal Salary { get; set; }
       public string Address { get; set; }
       public string City { get; set; }
       public string Region { get; set; }
       public string PostalCode { get; set; }
       public string Country { get; set; }
   ```

```
            public string Phone { get; set; }
    }
```

This model can be used to represent an `Employee` resource, on which the API can perform various CRUD operations. Ordinarily, we would keep this data in a database, such as SQL, but for now, we're going to keep it simple and store the employees in a collection. To do this, the collection needs to be situated somewhere in which it can be accessed by the endpoints we're about to create.

4. At the top level of the project, (the same level as `Program.cs`), create a new class called `EmployeeManager`.
5. We want this class to be available at any time, without the need to instantiate it, so make it a static class.
6. Add a private `List` of the `Employee` type at the top of the class. Your class should look like this:

```
public static class EmployeeManager
{
    private static List<Employee> _employees =
        new List<Employee>();

}
```

Now we have an easily accessible class that can store the employees. As the collection is private, we can now add a set of methods that can be publicly exposed to the endpoints to perform operations.

We're about to create logic for the CRUD actions to be performed on each `Employee` in the collection. As part of this, it will be necessary to look up each employee object in the list. Let's add a private function that will find this for us, for reuse on each CRUD operation. With the private function added, the class now looks like this:

```
public static class EmployeeManager
{
    private static List<Employee> _employees =
        new List<Employee>();
    private static int getEmployeeIndex(int id)
    {
        var employeeIndex =
            _employees.FindIndex(x => x.Id == id);
        if (employeeIndex == -1)
        {
            throw new ArgumentException(
                $"Employee with Id {id} does not exist");
```

```
        }
        return employeeIndex;
    }
}
```

Finally, update the class so that it contains the CRUD methods and functions shown in this code snippet:

```
public static void Create(Employee employee)
{
    _employees.Add(employee);
}
public static void Update(Employee employee)
{
    _employees[_getEmployeeIndex(employee.Id)] =
        employee;
}

public static void ChangeName(int id, string name)
{
    _employees[_getEmployeeIndex(id)].Name = name;
}

public static void Delete(int id)
{
    _employees.RemoveAt(_getEmployeeIndex(id));
}
public static Employee Get(int id)
{
    var employee =
        _employees.FirstOrDefault(x => x.Id == id);
    if (employee == null)
    {
        throw new ArgumentException("Employee Id invalid");
    }
    return employee;
}
```

The `EmployeeManager` class will now enable our API endpoints to perform specific CRUD actions on employees in the collection.

Creating the first endpoint

The first endpoint to add will be the GET endpoint for retrieving a specific `Employee` object by its ID.

Create the following GET endpoint in `Program.cs` right above the final `app.Run()` line you added earlier in the chapter:

```
app.MapGet("/employees/{id}", (int id) =>
{
    var employee = EmployeeManager.Get(id);
    return Results.Ok(employee);
});
```

This code starts by referencing the `WebApplication` instance known as app, calling the `MapGet` method. There are equivalent mapping methods in `WebApplication` named based on the type of HTTP method. Examples include `MapPut`, `MapPost`, and so on.

The first parameter expected on the mapping method will be the route you wish to listen to. In this case, we are mapping to the `"/employees/{id}"` route, which uses a routing parameter (more on this in *Chapter 4*) to capture an employee ID.

This is then followed by a second parameter in the form of a lambda expression, which uses the passed-in ID to execute the intended logic. At this point, the code calls the `Create()` function defined in the `EmployeeManager` class before finally returning the result to the client.

Add the remaining endpoints to `Program.cs` below the GET endpoint we just created and above the `app.Run()` method. `Program.cs` should now look like this:

```
using System.Text.Json;
using WebApplication2;

var builder = WebApplication.CreateBuilder(args);
var app = builder.Build();

app.MapGet("/employees/{id}", (int id) =>
{
    var employee = EmployeeManager.Get(id);
    return Results.Ok(employee);
});

app.MapPost("/employees", (Employee employee) =>
{
    EmployeeManager.Create(employee);
    return Results.Created();
});

app.MapPut("/employees", (Employee employee) =>
{
    EmployeeManager.Update(employee);
```

```
        return Results.Ok();
});

app.MapPatch("/updateEmployeeName", (Employee employee) =>
{
    EmployeeManager.ChangeName(employee.Id, employee.Name);
    return Results.Ok();
});

app.MapDelete("/employees/{id}", (int id) =>
{
    EmployeeManager.Delete(id);
    return Results.Ok();
});

app.Run();
```

You'll notice that all of the subsequent endpoints you've mapped follow a similar pattern to the first GET endpoint you added. Each of them specifies the HTTP method type that is being used, followed by the route, then by any parameters. There is then a body that executes relevant logic before a result is returned.

At this point, the code should compile. (If it does not, check that everything has been typed in correctly.) So, run the application (click the play button in Visual Studio or use the `dotnet run` terminal command in Visual Studio Code) and make some test requests to each of the created endpoints. The POST, PUT, and PATCH endpoints expect an `Employee` object as a parameter, so ensure that you have sent JSON that mirrors the structure of the `Employee` model. Look at this example:

```
{
  "Id": 3,
  "Name": "Happy McHappyson",
  "Salary": 100000.00,
  "Address": "1 Sunny Lane",
  "City": "Happyville",
  "Region": "The Joyful Mountains",
  "PostalCode": "1234565",
  "Country": "Laughland",
  "Phone": "876542-2345-3242-234"
}
```

Having created an endpoint, it is time we test it.

Testing your endpoint using OpenAPI

.NET 9 introduces OpenAPI integration, meaning that you can simply install a package and change the configuration of your API in `Program.cs` to generate a JSON representation of your API and its endpoints. This is useful because you can import it into API tools such as Postman, from which you can then easily test your APIs.

If you wish to test in this manner, follow these steps:

1. Install the `Microsoft.AspNetCore.OpenApi` package via NuGet.
2. Update `Program.cs` so that it uses OpenApi:

   ```
   builder.Services.AddOpenApi();
   var app = builder.Build();
   app.MapOpenApi();
   ```

Run the API and navigate to the `openAPI/v1.json` route. This will provide you with a representation of your API schema, which can be imported into API clients such as Postman for testing.

At this point in the chapter, you've now mapped endpoints with varying HTTP methods, provided them with routes and parameters, created models, and added logic to be executed. The goal of the endpoint is to return a response to the client. We now need to handle the requests by returning a response.

Handling HTTP requests

ASP.NET provides a handy helper object for sending responses back to clients, called `IResult`.

An `IResult` contains properties that can be used to represent standard HTTP responses for many different scenarios. For example, we could use IResult to return a specific status code, return JSON data, or even trigger **ASP.NET Identity** provider functionality such as challenges and sign-in/out.

We can create a new IResult easily using ASP.NET's `Results` factory class. In the preceding examples, you will have seen references to this factory class, where the API has returned status codes by calling `Results.OK()` and `Results.Created()`, to name a few.

Some of these simple HTTP status code methods have optional parameters that allow you to return strongly typed objects as JSON. For example, while you can simply return a 200 result by omitting any parameters in `Results.OK()`, you can also pass an object argument, and it will be sent back to the client. This was done in our Employee API endpoints for the GET endpoint:

```
app.MapGet("/employees/{id}", (int id) =>
{
    var employee = EmployeeManager.Get(id);
    //RETURN 200 OK RESULT WITH THE EMPLOYEE OBJECT
    return Results.Ok(employee);
});
```

The ability to pass strongly typed .NET objects such as Employee back to the client in a helper method is one of the most powerful aspects of minimal APIs.

There'll be more detailed examples of handling HTTP requests in *Chapter 4*. For now, here are some examples of how Results can be used to return common HTTP responses:

```
//200 OK
return Results.Ok();

//201 CREATED
return Results.Created();

//202 ACCEPTED
return Results.Accepted();

//204 NO CONTENT
return Results.NoContent();

//400 BAD REQUEST
return Results.BadRequest();

//401 UNAUTHORIZED
return Results.Unauthorized();

//403 FORBIDDEN
return Results.Forbid();

//404 NOT FOUND
return Results.NotFound();

//409 CONFLICT
return Results.Conflict();
```

After exploring Results, let's take a look at one of its alternatives.

Typed Results

An alternative to using Results to return specific HTTP status codes is TypedResults, which is similar to Results but where the example responses using Results return an IResult each time, TypedResults returns a strongly typed object representing the status code.

TypedResults implements a factory returning the appropriate strongly typed object that implements IResult for the specified status (e.g., returning OK<string> for a 200 OK result).

You can use `TypedResults` in virtually the same way you use `Results`. Here's an example:

```
//200 OK
return TypedResults.Ok();

//201 CREATED
return TypedResults.Created();

//202 ACCEPTED
return TypedResults.Accepted();

//204 NO CONTENT
return TypedResults.NoContent();
```

NET 9 also introduces support for `500 INTERNAL SERVER ERROR` responses in `TypedResults`:

```
//204 NO CONTENT
return TypedResults.InternalServerError();
```

At this point, you should now have a decent understanding of how to handle HTTP requests, returning the relevant HTTP status codes and strongly typed objects back to the client. Let us sum up everything we have covered in this chapter.

Summary

In this chapter, we covered most of the introductory aspects of creating simple minimal APIs, and you created your first minimal API project.

You learned how to define endpoints, and how they act as doors into the API, each of them sitting on their respective routes. Using the example of the `Employee` API, you gained insight into how to structure your project, splitting endpoints and data to achieve the benefits of loose coupling and reusability.

You explored the concept of models as data structures that describe the domain objects in use by the API, and you built a simple CRUD system for manipulating data during requests.

Finally, you gained a basic understanding of how to handle HTTP requests in a minimal API, using ASP.NET helper logic to compose and return responses to clients.

Armed with your foundational knowledge, turn to the next chapter, where we will explore the anatomy of a minimal API. We'll delve deeper and more scientifically into the key components that make up minimal APIs, and you'll be introduced to some of the various architectural and design patterns that can be adopted to fully realise their potential.

3
The Anatomy of a Minimal API

To understand how minimal APIs work, it makes sense to learn how they are put together in the context of an ASP.NET application. In ASP.NET project types such as **Model-View-Controller** (**MVC**) and **Web API**, various components are tied together to create the overall application, and minimal APIs are no different.

By the end of this chapter, you will have learned how minimal APIs fit within the ASP.NET ecosystem and how the various components are combined to make them possible.

The aim here is to ensure you have a deeper understanding of the wider context surrounding minimal APIs, which will inform the way you design and implement them in future projects.

In this chapter, we are going to cover the following main topics:

- Anatomy of a minimal API
- Components of a minimal API Application
- The API request lifecycle

Let's get into the chapter!

Anatomy of a minimal API

When referring to the *anatomy* of a minimal API, what we are really talking about is the pieces of the puzzle that fit together to bootstrap the application. Before ASP.NET Core, bootstrapping involved two classes: `Program.cs` and `Startup.cs`. The former stayed at the high level of the project, setting up an HTTP pipeline before calling the startup class to add components and features to the pipeline.

ASP.NET Core majorly changed this by making it possible to configure the application in a single file. This simplified the process, paving the way for native support of minimal APIs. So, in the most recent iterations of .NET, we now only need `Program.cs` for bootstrapping an ASP.NET application.

The minimum that `Program.cs` does to create a minimal API is to build and run an instance of `WebApplication`. This `WebApplication` instance is built using another class, called `WebApplicationBuilder`. As you can see in the upcoming code, `WebApplication` uses a *factory* in the form of the `CreateBuilder` method to create an instance of `WebApplication` called app. You will have seen this code in code examples in the previous chapter:

```
WebApplicationBuilder builder = 
    WebApplication.CreateBuilder(args);
var app = builder.Build();
```

The result of this code is an instance of `WebApplication` on which endpoints can be mapped, using functions such as `MapGet` and `MapPost`.

`WebApplication` embodies the overall API and is created using a builder pattern implementation via a `WebApplicationBuilder` object. This object allows configuration to be specified while building the `WebApplication` instance. For example, services can be registered for dependency injection (we will learn about dependency injection in *Chapter 7*) while the `WebApplication` is being built via the `WebApplicationBuilder` object.

An example of this initial setup of dependencies can be seen in the next code, where we use `AddScoped` to register the `PayrollRunner` type for dependency injection before the line of code on which the app is finally built using `builder.Build()`:

```
WebApplicationBuilder builder = 
    WebApplication.CreateBuilder(args);
builder.Services.AddScoped<PayrollRunner>();
var app = builder.Build();
```

A minimal API does not have its own dedicated project template in Visual Studio. Think of a minimal API as an option within an ASP.NET project, rather than its own project type. The reason for this is that minimal APIs are more often than not a part of another kind of project, although it is certainly common to have small ASP.NET projects consisting exclusively of minimal API endpoints.

By default, an ASP.NET project creates a set of minimal API endpoints. You can see this using the `ASP.NET Core (Empty)` project template in Visual Studio. Despite the name, the template's resulting project generates an example minimal API endpoint, as we saw in the *Hello World!* example in *Chapter 1*.

Components of a minimal API application

There are several components that go together to create a minimal API project, most of which are applicable to any ASP.NET web application.

At the top level, the application is represented by an instance of `WebApplication`. This class holds together all the pieces that form the API system. Think of it like the application's body.

Components that live inside `WebApplication` include the following:

- **Application Lifecycle**: As the application runs, various events will occur, such as application startup and shutdown, and thrown exceptions. `WebApplication` contains several **hooks** that can be used to handle these events. For example, you could execute specific functions or methods when the application starts up or change the way specific exception types are handled when caught.

- **Services**: Your APIs will no doubt have reusable aspects that could be used across multiple use cases and different areas of the application. Creating *services* allows you to package up these reusable aspects into components that can be passed to various parts of your API using dependency injection. For example, several of your endpoints may rely on retrieving data from a SQL database, so it would not be good practice to write the code to access the database multiple times. Instead, a service can be written once and then injected into any classes that need to communicate with SQL.

- **Routing**: We talked about routing in the previous chapter. In the context of a minimal API's anatomy, routing is a key component; it is responsible for ensuring that traffic is sent to the appropriate destination based on the endpoint URL and the HTTP method being used.

- **Middleware**: In ASP.NET, middleware is a pipeline that allows developers to interrupt the API flow with code that is executed during requests. The middleware pipeline is a chain of components executing any required logic. Examples of common middleware use cases include handling or modifying requests, authenticating clients, caching, and logging. Middleware can be a reusable component that is added to the pipeline or custom code.

    Once a middleware component has finished running, the next component in the pipeline executes, until all components are finished. This is particularly useful because it can be applied globally, running on all incoming requests. It's important to note that the pipeline can run both when the request comes in and when the response is sent back to the client, the difference being that the order of the middleware components in the pipeline is reversed when the response makes its way back to the client.

- **Configuration**: Most applications, including minimal APIs, require configuration to be specified, through connection strings for databases, authentication tokens, a flag to indicate whether the API is in developer mode, and so on. Think of these like environment variables. These variables are stored in an accessible location for use throughout the application's lifecycle. For example, if you have a SQL database that several of your API endpoints need to work with data, they will need the relevant connection string to initiate the SQL connection. This can be stored as a configuration setting for any of these endpoints to obtain when they need it.

So far, we have covered, at a basic level, the various components within an ASP.NET web application, including ones set up to host minimal API endpoints. To better understand the anatomy of a minimal API, it helps to also understand how a request travels through an ASP.NET API.

The API request lifecycle

APIs share one thing in common, irrespective of the underlying technology – the conversation between client and server. The lifecycle of this conversation is visualized in *Figure 3.1*.

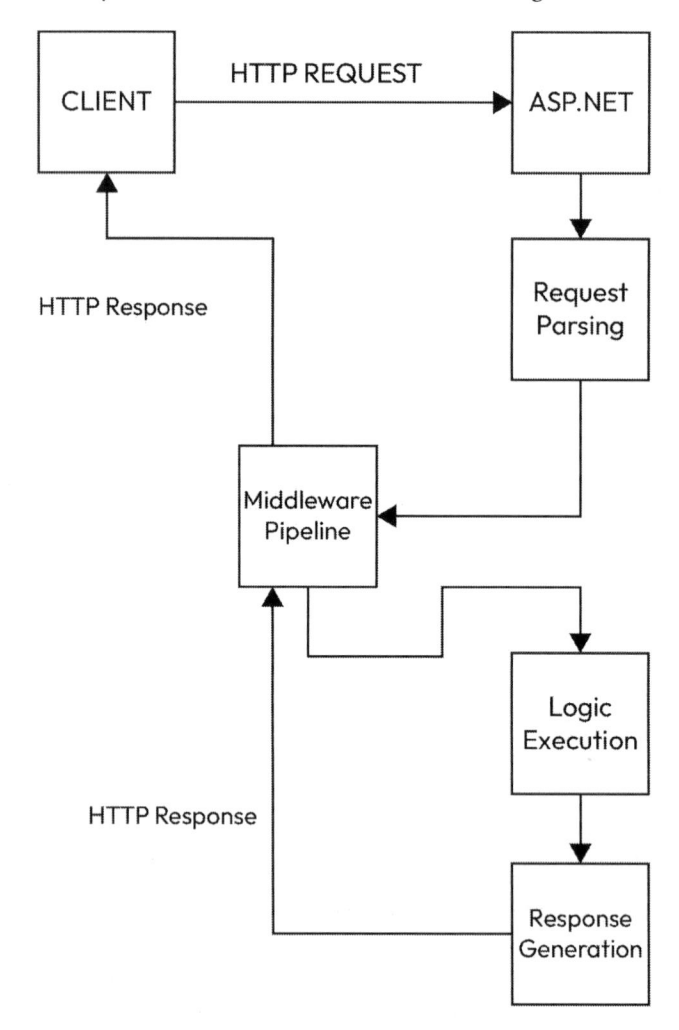

Figure 3.1: The journey of an HTTP request

Let's explore this lifecycle in more detail. Specifically, for ASP.NET, and therefore minimal APIs, the steps we outline next are taken from the point a client makes a request, to the point a response is received:

1. **The request is parsed** – On receipt of the request, ASP.NET takes the incoming data and extracts critical information, such as the HTTP method in use (GET, POST, PUT, etc.). The URL is extracted, along with the request's headers and body.

2. **The middleware pipeline is executed** – Middleware sitting in the chain is processed, with each middleware component operating on the request as configured. For example, authentication middleware could check that the sender of the request is authenticated, custom middleware could alter the structure of the request, and logging middleware could reference the request in logs that it writes to various data sources.

3. **Routing** – Now that the application has parsed the request and processed it through any relevant middleware, it can match the extracted URL and HTTP method against the routes configured in the API. This allows the request's content to be routed to the appropriate endpoint for handling. Routing is just another example of a middleware component. As such, its order of execution can be altered within the pipeline.

4. **Dependency injection** – Once the request has been routed to the correct request, the dependency injection container will resolve any dependencies required to process the request and inject them into the components containing the endpoint, making them available during processing.

5. **Request handling** – The request is effectively now *inside the endpoint*, as in, it is being processed by the logic a developer has written inside the body of a minimal API endpoint they have written. Parameters passed in can be used within the endpoint body to process the required logic.

6. **Response generation** – Once the logic defined within the body of the endpoint has finished executing (or if an exception is thrown), a response will be generated. The response contains any expected data for the HTTP method on the endpoint, such as JSON or a simple string. It also has a status code appropriate to the processing result, for example, `200 OK`, `400 Bad Request`, or `500 Internal Server Error`. Once generated, the response is sent back to the client, and the HTTP conversation is over.

Now that we have explored the journey of a request, let's review what we have covered in this chapter.

Summary

The chapter has detailed the different components that ASP.NET employs to construct an application capable of hosting minimal API endpoints. It explained how the **WebApplication** instance is configured using the **WebApplicationBuilder**. The chapter also described the integration of elements like routing, services, dependency injection, and middleware into the application. Additionally, it emphasized the importance of the application lifecycle and how lifecycle events can be managed through hooks. The journey of an HTTP request from the client to minimal API endpoints and back was also discussed. Finally, the chapter outlined the steps involved in matching incoming requests with the appropriate logic, and the process of handling the request in preparation for a client response.

In the next chapter, we will move away from the conceptual and back to the practical with a more advanced guide on handling HTTP requests and routing.

Part 2 - Data and Execution Flow

This part delves into the crucial aspects of how data flows through minimal APIs. You'll learn how to handle various HTTP methods, set up routing, customize middleware pipelines, and integrate with different data sources. These chapters cover everything from dependency injection to working with databases using **Object-Relational Mapping(ORM)** tools.

This part has the following chapters:

- *Chapter 4, Handling HTTP Methods and Routing*
- *Chapter 5, The Middleware Pipeline*
- *Chapter 6, Parameter Binding*
- *Chapter 7, Dependency Injection in Minimal APIs*
- *Chapter 8, Integrating Minimal APIs with Data Sources*
- *Chapter 9, Object Relational Mapping with Entity Framework Core and Dapper*

4
Handling HTTP Methods and Routing

In *Chapter 2*, we discussed ways that you can define endpoints and use routing within a minimal API. That was from a high level.

However, in this chapter, we will discuss in more detail how routes and endpoints can be configured for the handling of incoming requests. We will go into more detail about how you can use route parameters to be more specific about the required parameters received by each endpoint, and we will also explore examples of request validation, wherein we ensure that the request is properly formed, issuing the relevant response as necessary.

Finally, no API can be deemed reliable if its endpoints do not adequately recover from receiving invalid data so we will also explore ways in which validation errors can be handled gracefully.

To gain a better understanding of these topics, we will use an example application for managing tasks. The application is part of a productivity suite, which has an API for managing to-do lists and projects. By building elements of this API, you will gain a more in-depth understanding of how requests are received by minimal APIs and how they are handled.

In summary, this chapter will cover the following main topics:

- Handling requests
- Defining endpoints in the Todo API
- Managing route parameters
- Request validation and error handling

Technical requirements

The code for this chapter is available in the GitHub repository at: `https://github.com/PacktPublishing/Minimal-APIs-in-ASP.NET-9`.

You can of course follow along and write the code yourself as you read the chapter if you have Visual Studio 2022 / Visual Studio Code installed with .NET 9.

Handling requests

To handle incoming requests, we first need a set of minimal API endpoints for those requests to be sent to. Let's recap what we explored in *Chapter 2*, around creating minimal API endpoints with varying HTTP methods (`GET`, `POST`, `PUT`, `DELETE`, and `PATCH`). We can refresh our memories by creating some static *mock* data that will represent the task entities our API is handling. Then, we can define some simple endpoints that manipulate or query that data.

Let's create the mock data first. We'll do this by creating a simple `TodoItem` class, and a static list for instances of this class to reside in:

```
public class TodoItem
{
    public int Id { get; set; }
    public DateTime StartDate { get; set; }
    public DateTime DueDate { get; set; }
    public string Title { get; set; }
    public string Description { get; set; }
    public string Assignee { get; set; }
    public int Priority { get; set; }
    public bool IsComplete { get; set; }
}
```

The `TodoItem` class can stay quite simple for the time being. It can be expanded upon later with more specific properties as we understand our needs further. The same approach can be taken with the next piece of code, which for now will be a list of `TodoItem`, simply called `ToDoItems`. In this list, we store instances of `TodoItem` to be handled by endpoints during requests. Let's place this list in `Program.cs`:

```
List<TodoItem> ToDoItems = new List<TodoItem>();
```

Now that we have our temporary data storage solution in the form of a list, we can focus on creating endpoints for handling requests and managing todo items.

Defining endpoints in the Todo API

It's advisable to start as simple as possible in creating a minimal API. After all, the name *minimal API* connotes simplicity. This isn't just simplicity for simplicity's sake though. For now, our API only needs to cover one area: todo items. Sure, the scope might expand further in the future, and minimal APIs can still be crafted in such a way that they are expandable and therefore somewhat future-proofed, but until more requirements become apparent (for example, assigning to-do items to users, adding to-do items to specific projects, etc.), the aim is minimalism. With this in mind, we will, for now, keep our endpoints in `Program.cs`.

We should now ask ourselves a simple question: *What do I want to do in this API?*

By this, I mean the actions that the API will need to facilitate. For example, fetching todo items, updating todo items, deleting todo items, and so on.

In understanding the *verbs* that are part of the actions of your API, we can identify the required HTTP methods. Consider the basic actions required for todo items. We will certainly want to *retrieve* todo items. That will require an HTTP GET method. Moreover, we will also want to *create* a `TodoItem` object. This will require an HTTP POST method. Let's start with the first example, retrieving some todo items, and then build up from there.

Getting todo items

If you've read through *Chapter 2*, you will have already seen examples of how an HTTP GET method can be created as an endpoint in minimal APIs. For this project, we will first create an endpoint that simply retrieves the contents of `List<TodoItem>`, which we created previously.

To achieve this, we need to *map* an HTTP GET method onto the instance of `WebApplication` on which our minimal API is running. There are several functions within `WebApplication` that achieve this. Each of them is prefixed with the word `Map` and followed by the relevant method verb. In this example, we'll use `MapGet()`:

```
app.MapGet("/todoitems", () =>
{

});
```

In this code, an HTTP GET method has been mapped to the `/todoitems` route, meaning that should a user request the API's base URL, followed by `/todoitems`, this endpoint would be reached.

For example, if our URL is hosted at `https://example.org/reallysimpletodoapi`, accessing `https://example.org/reallysimpletodoapi/todoitems` will reach this endpoint.

Now we can get to the handling of the request, which happens in the function body. Notice that the endpoint we've created has a lambda expression after the route definition. The expression body is currently empty. It is within this expression body that we will handle the request by retrieving the requested data and responding to the client.

In this case, because we are simply returning the contents of the `ToDoItems` list, the data is readily available, but how do we get that data back to the client? ASP.NET provides us with a helper object in the form of `IResult`, whose `Results` object exposes various methods for responding to requests. This takes care of the fundamental aspects of returning a response, such as the status code, response body, and so on.

For this simple HTTP `GET` method, we can return an HTTP `200 OK` response along with the requested data by simply returning the result of `Results.OK(ToDoItems)`. This function generates the relevant status code and takes an argument of type `object`, representing the data that should be returned to the client. Once added, the endpoint should look like this:

```
app.MapGet("/todoitems", () =>
{
    return Results.Ok(ToDoItems);
});
```

So far, the focus has been on routing requests into the API for the purposes of retrieving data. We will also need to create new data in the system; so, let us turn our attention to the creation of todo items.

Creating Todo items

Let's now look at another critical operation for APIs: creating an entity. To create a new `TodoItem`, we would use an HTTP `POST` method.

The mapping of an HTTP `POST` method is similar to the code we've just written for mapping a `GET` method. Once again, we use a method prefixed with the word `Map`. This method is `MapPost()`. However, there is a slight difference in the syntax compared to our `GET` method, as we now need to receive a data structure. In the case of creating a `TodoItem`, we will require the client to send an object of type `TodoItem`, represented in JSON format on the client-side. ASP.NET will then take care of parsing the JSON into a strongly typed instance of `TodoItem`, which we can use whilst handling the request.

To allow the method to receive an object as part of the incoming request, we can take the parentheses at the beginning of the lambda expression within the endpoint's body and add the object to it. For example, notice how the previous endpoint we created, which retrieves a `TodoItem`, has these empty parentheses:

```
app.MapGet("/todoitems", () =>
```

The handling of our minimal API endpoints is represented by a lambda expression. Lambda expressions open with an input in the form of parameters, which are passed in through these empty parentheses, as shown in the following code. This means that for our HTTP POST endpoint, we can add a parameter of type `TodoItem` to the `MapPost()` method we are adding, like so:

```
app.MapPost("/todoitems", (TodoItem item) =>
{

});
```

Now, we have an HTTP POST endpoint, sitting on the `/todoitems` route, just like our HTTP GET endpoint. The difference is that not only does it respond to a different HTTP verb, but it also requires the client to send a JSON payload mirroring the structure of `TodoItem`.

We don't yet have anything inside the lambda expression within the endpoint, meaning that nothing will happen when a client sends a request. Let's finally handle the request by adding the incoming `TodoItem` to the list and then returning the relevant response:

```
app.MapPost("/todoitems", (TodoItem item) =>
{
    ToDoItems.Add(item);
    return Results.Created();
});
```

Just like in the GET example, we are using `Results` to form a response and send it back to the client. However, we have opted for a slightly different response in this case. As the request is intended to create an entity, it is appropriate to return an `HTTP 201 CREATED` status code on successful creation, hence the use of `Results.Created();`.

Updating existing Todo items

When it comes to updating a `Todoitem`, we have a couple of HTTP methods at our disposal. Let's start with an HTTP PUT method.

An HTTP PUT requires the client to send a full copy of the entity being updated. It will then replace the entity with the copy. It is a *full update*. Therefore, we need to create an endpoint that receives a `TodoItem` as part of the request, before finding the relevant item in our list and then replacing it with the incoming `TodoItem`. First, we'll create an empty PUT endpoint sitting on the `/todoitems` route that expects the item as an object parameter:

```
app.MapPut("/todoitems", (TodoItem item) =>
{

});
```

Next, the request should be handled by finding the `TodoItem` that we intend to update. We can do this using a **Language Integrated Query (LINQ)** query to find the item by its unique ID, with `FindIndex();`.

> **LINQ queries**
>
> A LINQ query with lambda expressions in C# lets you easily search and manipulate data in collections such as lists. You start by defining your data source, then use methods such as `Where` to filter the data and `Select`" to choose what you want from the data. Each method takes a lambda expression, which is a simple function that defines your criteria. In our example, we're using a LINQ query to find the index of an item in a list that shares the same ID as a given item.

Once found, `TodoItem` can be replaced with the incoming item:

```csharp
app.MapPut("/todoitems", (TodoItem item) =>
{
    var index = ToDoItems.FindIndex(x => x.Id == item.Id);
    if (index == -1)
    {
        return Results.NotFound();
    }
    ToDoItems[index] = item;
    return Results.NoContent();
});
```

Notice how we did not return `Results.OK` again in this example. Because we're simply updating a resource, the client is not expecting content to be returned; so, we indicate success by returning an HTTP 204 NO CONTENT status code using `Results.NoContent();`.

Updating `TodoItem` via HTTP PATCH is handled slightly differently. Unlike PUT, we handle the request by once again finding the relevant item, but this time, we only change specific properties of the item, as dictated by the request parameters. This is usually used in scenarios where you want to create an endpoint on a route that is for a specific update. So, in this case, we will no longer create the endpoint on the `/todoitems` route. Instead, we will be specific about what we want to change by mapping the PATCH method to the `/updateTodoItemDueDate` route. In this example, we are creating an endpoint intended for a single purpose – to change the due date on the target `TodoItem`:

```csharp
app.MapPatch("/updateTodoItemDueDate/{id}",
    (int id, DateTime newDueDate) =>
{
    var index = ToDoItems.FindIndex(x => x.Id == id);
    if (index == -1)
    {
```

```
            return Results.NotFound();
    }
    ToDoItems[index].DueDate = newDueDate;
    return Results.NoContent();
});
```

The code looks like the PUT method we created, but you can see that the parameters are quite different. Instead of requiring the full ToDoItems object to be sent in by the client, we instead ask for two parameters, an int parameter (to find the target item by ID) and a DateTime parameter containing the new due date. It is then possible to find the target item with another LINQ query, and then only update its DueDate property.

So far, we've handled scenarios wherein we need to get all items, create an item, and update items. We will next look at scenarios in which we intend to get single items and delete items. However, to do this, we first need to explore the concept of route parameters.

Managing route parameters

Route parameters give us the ability to capture values from the URL of an API endpoint. This is useful in many scenarios where we need to target specific entities, such as when requesting a TodoItem by its ID.

Route parameters are quite simple to add, and work using curly braces to define the parameters to be captured from the URL.

Let's use a GET request as an example. In this request, the client requests a TodoItem with the ID:

```
app.MapGet("/todoitems/{id}", (int id) =>
{
    var index = ToDoItems.FindIndex(x => x.Id == id);
    if (index == -1)
    {
        return Results.NotFound();
    }
    return Results.Ok(ToDoItems[index]);
});
```

Like the generic GET request we created to fetch all todo items, this endpoint is sitting on the /todoitems route. However, it has an extra section appended to this route in the URL. The client is expected to also add an ID value as an extra URL section. This is shown by the presence of {id} in the route.

This use of parameters within curly braces is how ASP.NET handles dynamic content in the route URL. Using a form of templating, it can replace the section of the URL where we added {id} with the value specified by the client.

Another example of this can be seen in an HTTP DELETE endpoint. Again, when deleting TodoItem, we want to delete a specific item so we will once again need to pass in an ID for the target to be deleted. Let's write the code for this in which we will map a new HTTP DELETE method to the /todoitems route. On the route, we'll add a route parameter to pass the ID for the TodoItem to be deleted:

```
app.MapDelete("/todoitems/{id}", (int id) =>
{
    var index = ToDoItems.FindIndex(x => x.Id == id);
    if (index == -1)
    {
        return Results.NotFound();
    }
    ToDoItems.RemoveAt(index);
    return Results.NoContent();
});
```

On receiving a DELETE request on the /todoitems route, if an int has been appended to the URL, it will be stripped out and used within the request as a parameter. The subject of parameter data type is an important one. In the DELETE example, we passed an int as an ID parameter because that is the data type used on the ID property of the TodoItem class (our model).

What if someone sends a different data type as the parameter, such as a string? We would need to handle this of course, but we shouldn't have to ensure that the incoming ID is an int within the code. There is a better way of ensuring that the request only hits the route if the parameters being sent are of the correct data type: **route parameter constraints**.

Adding a constraint to a route parameter makes it so that the incoming parameter must be formed in a particular way for the route to be found and the request received. In our DELETE endpoint, we can use a parameter constraint to dictate that the parameter must be an integer.

Adding a constraint to the parameter is very simple. We just append a : character to the parameter, followed by the constraint. Let's add a constraint to our DELETE endpoint to ensure the route is only used when the id parameter is of type int:

```
app.MapDelete("/todoitems/{id:int}", (int id) =>
{
    var index = ToDoItems.FindIndex(x => x.Id == id);
    if (index == -1)
    {
        return Results.NotFound();
    }
    ToDoItems.RemoveAt(index);
    return Results.NoContent();
});
```

Now that we have the constraint in place, if a request was received that could not be treated as an `int`, the API would return a `404 NOT FOUND` response. It does this because the constraint stops ASP.NET from attempting to use the parameter as an ID, because it has already evaluated the data type thanks to the constraint. The result is that no other suitable route is found. (Unless there is a route on the `/todoitems` URL that can receive a string and is also an HTTP `DELETE` method.)

Parameter constraints are not limited to data types. Parameters can be constrained by string length, numerical ranges, regex patterns; the list goes on.

Let's constrain the `DELETE` range even further by adding a range constraint. We'll make it so that the route can only delete the first 100 IDs. We can add multiple constraints to a single route like so:

```
app.MapDelete("/todoitems/{id:int:range(1,100)}",
    (int id) =>
{
    var index = ToDoItems.FindIndex(x => x.Id == id);
    if (index == -1)
    {
        return Results.NotFound();
    }
    ToDoItems.RemoveAt(index);
    return Results.NoContent();
});
```

By chaining another constraint onto the existing one, we have now enforced that the `Id` parameter must be an `int` and that its value must be between `1` and `100`.

Table 4.1 shows some other constraint examples:

Constraint Type	Route Example	Constraint Detail
Length	`/users/{username:length(3,20)}`	The username string must be between three and twenty characters long
Length	`/users/{username:length(8)}`	The username string must be exactly eight characters long
Min Length	`/users/{username:minlength(5)}`	The username string must be at least five characters long
Max Length	`/users/{username:maxlength(30)}`	The username string must be no more than thirty characters long
Regular Expression	`/addNewCreditCard/{cardNumber:regex(^3[47][0-9]{{13}}$)}`	The credit card number must conform to the pattern of an American Express card number

Table 4.1: Examples of parameter constraints in minimal APIs

Now that we are more focused on how parameters are passed into our requests, we can focus our attention on the request body, in which we do the main handling of the request. A major part of handling any request is validation. Minimal APIs, like any other API, will receive data within requests, which must suit the conditions needed to handle the request. Let's look at some validation techniques we can use to manage the request flow and handle any errors that may arise as a result of any violations of validation rules.

Request validation and error handling

There are several different methods of validation at our disposal. We're going to look at two of them in this section: **manual validation** and **data annotation** and **model binding validation**.

Manual validation

This kind of validation is the simplest, as you are writing code inside the route handler (the body of the lambda expression within an endpoint) that validates the request and decides on the appropriate response.

We've already applied manual validation in some parts of the todo items API. For example, the PATCH method we created to update the due date on items first checks for the Todo item with the target ID. It *could* just assume that TodoItem exists in the list, but instead, we check first to see if it exists and then return a 404 NOT FOUND status code if this is the case:

```
app.MapPatch("/updateTodoItemDueDate/{id}",
    (int id, DateTime newDueDate) =>
{
    var index = ToDoItems.FindIndex(x => x.Id == id);
    if (index == -1)
    {
        return Results.NotFound();
    }
    ToDoItems[index].DueDate = newDueDate;
    return Results.NoContent();
});
```

By adding this manual check, we are actively validating and handling an exceptional scenario. Having validation in an API endpoint is not just best practice, it is critical. Manual validation is the most basic form of validation. The problem is it relies on the intuition of a human; the developer writing the code. This is a subject of some debate because a lot of validation methods have gaps, but relying solely on manual validation can result in fragile APIs.

To mitigate this, we can also adopt a more standardized framework for validation, one provided by ASP.NET: validation with data annotations.

Validation with data annotations and model binding

As demonstrated by the simple API example we've built in this chapter, models are an important aspect of minimal APIs. They allow us to represent the entities that incoming requests retrieve, move, and transform. In the todo items API, we created a `TodoItem` class as a model, and then stored the entities in `List<TodoItem>`.

It is possible to validate a request's data by the way it binds to specific models. For example, in the `TodoItem` model, it is reasonable to expect that the `Title` field should be populated when `TodoItem` is created.

We can specify a field's requirements by annotating it with an attribute. Attributes are handy pieces of metadata that allow us to apply constraints to code. One of the most common uses of attributes in this case is the `[Required]` attribute.

The attributes we need are part of the `System.ComponentModel.DataAnnotations` namespace.

> **Required namespace for validation**
>
> As in the Todo class, `System.ComponentModel.DataAnnotations` must also be added to `Program.cs` for validation to be performed.

Add this namespace to the top of the `TodoItem` class, followed by the `[Required]` attribute above the `Title` field:

```
using System.ComponentModel.DataAnnotations;

namespace TodoApi
{
    public class TodoItem
    {
        public int Id { get; set; }
        public DateTime StartDate { get; set; }
        public DateTime DueDate { get; set; }
        [Required]
        public string Title { get; set; }
        public string Description { get; set; }
        public string Assignee { get; set; }
        public int Priority { get; set; }
        public bool IsComplete { get; set; }
    }
}
```

Adding a `[Required]` attribute is not enough on its own to trigger validation. We still need to invoke validation within our requests. However, we can do this once within the request, and then all items requiring validation will be validated, according to the attributes we applied. Here's how we can invoke validation of our model from the `POST` request we created earlier:

```
app.MapPost("/todoitems", (TodoItem item) =>
{
    var validationResults = new List<ValidationResult>();
    var validationContext = new ValidationContext(item);
    bool isValid = Validator.TryValidateObject(
        item, validationContext, validationResults, true);

    if (!isValid)
    {
        return Results.BadRequest(validationResults);
    }

    ToDoItems.Add(item);
    return Results.Created();
});
```

In this example, we have initialized a new collection, a list of `ValidationResult`. This will contain information about the success or failure of validation. We will return this collection to the client if validation fails.

We also create a new `ValidationContext`, passing in the item that is to be validated. Because we want to validate the `TodoItem` instance that is sent as a payload, we pass this into `ValidationContext`.

We can then invoke validation by calling `Validator.TryValidateObject()`, passing in the item as the validation target, the context we created that will be validated against, and the collection into which results will be saved, followed by a Boolean value of `true`, to state that all properties should be validated.

Now, when a request is sent that omits a `Title` field from the payload, the following error JSON is automatically generated and sent back to the client:

```
[
    {
        "memberNames": [
            "Title"
        ],
        "errorMessage": "The Title field is required."
    }
]
```

This validation and error handling all happen automatically, thanks to the use of attributes and the built-in validator.

The error message shown is automatically generated because of the `[Required]` attribute. This can be overridden by adding a parameter to the attribute.

Here is the updated code on the `TodoItem` model, with a custom error message:

```
public class TodoItem
{
    public int Id { get; set; }
    public DateTime StartDate { get; set; }
    public DateTime DueDate { get; set; }
    [Required(ErrorMessage =
        "You need to add a title my dude!")]
    public string Title { get; set; }
    public string Description { get; set; }
    public string Assignee { get; set; }
    public int Priority { get; set; }
    public bool IsComplete { get; set; }
}
```

Now, we can see the custom error message in the generated error response JSON:

```
[
    {
        "memberNames": [
            "Title"
        ],
        "errorMessage": "You need to add a title my dude!"
    }
]
```

`[Required]` is just one of many validation attributes that data annotations have to offer. There are many other constraints you can add. Some examples of these include the following:

- `[EmailAddress]`: This ensures the value conforms to the format of an email address.
- `[AllowedValues]`: This forces the use of specific values.
- `[DeniedValues]`: This is the opposite of `[AllowedValues]`, denying the use of specific values.
- `[StringLength(x)]`: This requires that a string value be of a certain length.
- `[CreditCard]`: The annotated value must be a valid credit card format.

These are just a few of the many attributes that can be used to validate incoming responses, returning appropriate errors as needed.

Managing HTTP methods and handling requests are critical aspects of minimal APIs, as it is in any API implementation.

Validation with filters

You can also apply more specific validation rules with filters. `IEndpointFilter` is an interface that can be implemented to perform validation of the incoming request information before it hits the logic within an endpoint.

There is a handy extension method, `AddEndPointFilter<T>`, which allows you to attach a class implementing `IEndpointFilter` to an endpoint.

Let's explore an example of this against a `POST` endpoint on our todo API. We'll create a rule where a todo item cannot be assigned to anyone named Joe Bloggs:

1. Create a class that implements `IEndpointFilter`. This class will be required to define a function called `Invoke`, returning `ValueTask<object?>`. The function takes `EndPointFilterInvocationContext` and `EndpointFilterDelegate` as parameters in order to carry out the validation logic:

    ```
    public class CreateTodoFilter : IEndpointFilter
    {
        public async ValueTask<object?> InvokeAsync(
            EndpointFilterInvocationContext context,
            EndpointFilterDelegate next)
        {
        }
    }
    ```

2. `EndPointFilterInvocationContext` will contain the incoming `TodoItem`, as it represents the context of the endpoint we are validating. Inside `InvokeAsync`, define logic to gain access to the incoming `TodoItem` from the endpoint's context and then validate that we are not attempting to assign it to Joe Bloggs. If we are, return the appropriate response so that validation fails:

    ```
    var todoItem = context.GetArgument<TodoItem>(0);
    if(todoItem.Assignee == "Joe Bloggs")
    {
        return Results.Problem(
            "Joe Bloggs cannot be assigned a todoitem");
    }
    ```

3. Finally, for validation that passes, we want to pass the flow of execution back to the original endpoint (or any other chained logic attached to it, a bit like we do for a middleware pipeline). Do this by returning a call to `EndpointFilterDelegate`, which we received as a parameter, passing in the endpoint context:

```
return await next(context);
```

4. Finally, add the filter validation to the endpoint as shown:

```
app.MapPost("/todoitems", (TodoItem item) =>
{
    ToDoItems.Add(item);

    return Results.Created();

}).AddEndpointFilter<CreateTodoFilter>();
```

5. Alternatively, if you want to define the endpoint filter inline, you can do so by passing in an anonymous function instead of a type after `AddEndpointFilter`:

```
app.MapPost("/todoitems", (TodoItem item) =>
{
    ToDoItems.Add(item);

    return Results.Created();

}).AddEndpointFilter(async (context, next) =>
{
    var toDoItem =
        context.GetArgument<TodoItem>(0);
    if (toDoItem.Assignee == "Joe Bloggs")
    {
        return Results.Problem(
            "Joe Bloggs cannot be assigned todo
            items");
    }
    return await next(context);
});
```

Now that you've gained some insight into the various ways we can achieve validation for different API endpoints, let's recap the things we've learned in this chapter.

Summary

In this chapter, we took a high-level view of HTTP methods and how they are handled. We explored in further detail the way in which requests can be routed, allowing essential parameters to be lifted out of route definitions with routing parameters.

We also delved into the basics of validation, firstly by placing constraints on our API routes to ensure that the data received is formatted in an appropriate manner. Following this, we learned how to handle validation in different ways, including manual validation, and the use of data annotations in models to invoke validation in a centralized fashion within the endpoint body.

Throughout the chapter, we saw examples of how errors can be captured through validation techniques, and how informative error responses should be handed back to clients to inform their debugging strategies.

By now, you should be capable of putting together a basic yet functional minimal API project. In the next chapter, we will learn how to introduce custom functionalities to our application pipelines in the form of middleware.

5
The Middleware Pipeline

APIs are collections of commands that can be triggered on request. When a request is received, we can execute logic that is bespoke to the use case of that request. However, a request does not instantly hit our endpoints as soon as it is received. There is a pipeline that is first traversed before our logic can be executed and the request is eventually returned to the client. This pipeline is called the middleware pipeline, and it is a feature set within ASP.NET that allows us to extend our APIs in a way that separates concerns, optimizes performance, and promotes reusability.

In this chapter, we are going to explore the following:

- An introduction to middleware
- Configuring middleware pipelines
- Implementing custom middleware

Technical requirements

You are encouraged to write and extend the code examples shown in this chapter to improve your practical understanding. However, if you wish to gain access to the source code, you can obtain it from the following GitHub link: `https://github.com/PacktPublishing/Minimal-APIs-in-ASP.NET-9`.

An introduction to middleware

Middleware as a concept was introduced to ASP.NET in ASP.NET Core. Replacing the older HTTP pipeline model, which used HTTP modules and HTTP handlers, it offers a simpler and more flexible way to manage the way HTTP requests are handled by APIs.

If you think of an API application as a pipeline with requests traveling through it, the concept becomes more straightforward.

Middleware is a component that sits on the pipeline before a request is handled by an endpoint. It is executed on every request and is part of a sequence, with components executing in the order in which they were registered.

Each middleware component has a role to play, with the ability to affect the request irrespective of the endpoint it has requested. Each middleware component can be built in, such as routing, for example, or custom middleware, written for specific purposes such as logging or authentication, to name a couple.

Once a middleware component has completed its work, it passes the request to the next middleware component in the pipeline, until all middleware components have been traversed. Then the request can hit the endpoint holding the code written, which has logic specific to that endpoint.

> **Middleware progression**
>
> It's worth noting that while it is true that middleware components pass requests on to each other in a chain, they only do this unless there is a reason for the request to be terminated, with an exception being returned. Depending on the context, a middleware pipeline can end prematurely by design.

As you have seen in the previous chapters, endpoints must send some form of response to their clients. Once request handling has been completed, endpoints then send the response back to the client via the middleware pipeline, where it travels once again through each middleware component in reverse order.

Here is a visualization of an example request pipeline:

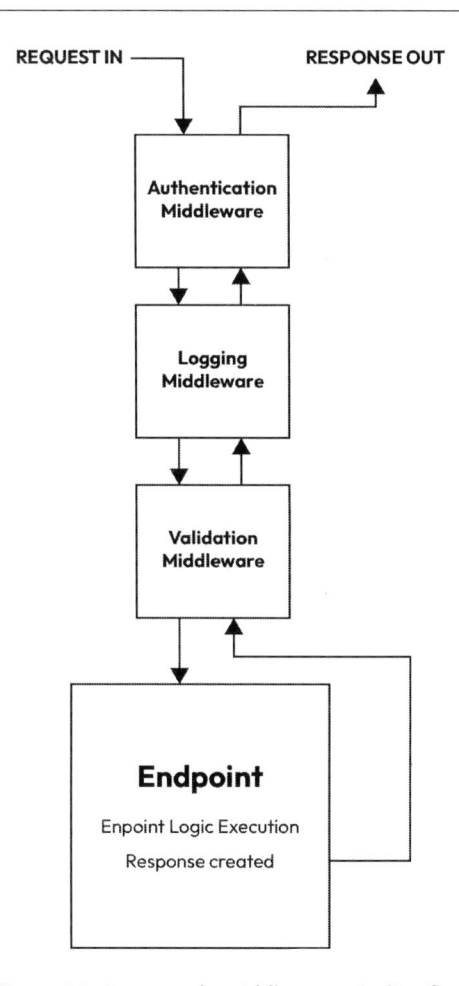

Figure 5.1: An example middleware pipeline flow

Middleware is a very important aspect of not just minimal APIs but ASP.NET in general, with widespread use in web API and MVC projects. It provides developers with a way of registering custom behavior at the application level, as a design pattern that decouples this behavior from endpoint-specific logic.

For example, there are certain logs that might need to be captured every time a request is received. This could be a log stating that a resource such as a SQL database was accessed as part of a request, or an error log if the request should not have been made.

It would be inefficient to include the logging code in every endpoint as they are written, and the developer would have to remember to include the logic to capture the log message. This is, as you can imagine, not sustainable and is a violation of the **don't repeat yourself** (**DRY**) principle. Using a logging middleware component means that the required log messages will be captured every time a request is received, and it only has to be configured once.

This is not to say that middleware components *must* be general in their execution. They are classes or methods like any other and have access to the incoming request in the form of an `HttpContext` object. As a result, they can scrutinize the request just like an endpoint can and execute any custom logic applicable to that request before the endpoint is reached.

Let's look at a basic example of a middleware component that is created as a class. The component simply writes to the console before calling the next component in the sequence:

```
public class MySuperSimpleMiddlewareClass
{
    private readonly RequestDelegate _next;

    public MySuperSimpleMiddlewareClass(
        RequestDelegate next)
    {
        _next = next;
    }

    public async Task InvokeAsync(HttpContext context)
    {
        Console.WriteLine(
            "Request handled by middleware component");

        await _next(context);

        Console.WriteLine(
            "Response handled by middleware component");
    }
}
```

This middleware class has a constructor that receives an object of type `RequestDelegate` when the class is instantiated. This delegate is a representation of the next middleware component in the pipeline. The `_next()` delegate can be used to call the next middleware component and continue the sequence.

Understanding how the pipeline passes control flow between each component is critical, but it's worth nothing if we don't know how to build our own components. We'll now move on to explore how you can create and configure middleware within your pipeline.

Configuring middleware pipelines

You can structure a middleware component in different ways depending on its purpose. The previous example demonstrated the creation of a simple middleware component using a class. Let's explore this type of component in more detail before looking at other ways of building and registering them.

Middleware classes

Middleware classes need to have an `Invoke` or `InvokeAsync` method so that they can be triggered when it is their turn. Notice how, in the example we saw in the previous section, we have a method called `_next()`, passing in the `HttpContext` object that the same method received. This is where the middleware component calls the next component in the pipeline.

Once you've created a middleware component, you will need to add it to the pipeline. In a minimal API, the setup of the API takes place in `Program.cs`, with the creation of a `WebApplication` object.

Remember in the previous chapters when we created an instance of `WebApplication` and called it app? This app object has a method called `UseMiddleware<T>()`. This allows us to tell the `WebApplication` object that it should use a middleware component of a specific type. If we wanted to register our `MySuperSimpleMiddleware` class as middleware, we would do it before we start the `WebApplication` object with `app.Run()`:

```
WebApplicationBuilder builder =
    WebApplication.CreateBuilder(args);

var app = builder.Build();
app.UseMiddleware<MySuperSimpleMiddlewareClass>();
app.Run();
```

Now that the middleware has been added to our `WebApplication` object. it will be invoked within the pipeline.

Writing middleware in a class has its advantages and disadvantages. On one hand, it might make sense to use a class to be keep middleware tidy and decoupled from the `WebApplication` object. You might also want to use a factory design pattern to produce and register appropriate middleware classes. On the other hand, the use of a class may be overkill. After all, we are building *minimal APIs*, where, most of the time, it is favorable to keep logic small and simple.

In the spirit of minimalism, there is an alternative to middleware classes in the form of inline middleware.

Inline middleware

This is a lot simpler than using classes. When creating middleware inline, we create and register the component with our `WebApplication` object in one block of code. Once again, considering our instance of `WebApplication` called app, we will still be passing in an `HTTPContext` object and `RequestDelegate` object, but instead of a constructor, private field, and `InvokeAsync()` method, everything will happen inside the body of the endpoint.

Let's look at how we could rewrite `MySuperSimpleMiddlewareClass` into an inline middleware component:

```
app.Use(async (context, next) =>
{
    Console.WriteLine(
        "Request handled by inline middleware component");
    await next(context);
    Console.WriteLine(
        "Response handled by inline middleware component");
});
```

In this example, we add `app.UseMiddleware<MySuperSimpleMiddlewareClass>()` with the much more generic `app.Use()`. Instead of specifying a type, we are now passing an asynchronous anonymous function that will be registered to the pipeline. The body of the lambda expression shown in the example is the equivalent of `InvokeAsync()` found within `MySuperSimpleMiddlewareClass`.

Just like before, we are writing a console message on the incoming request, followed by a call to the `RequestDelegate`, object which passes to the next component. We then have another console message, which will be executed on the request response as it travels back through the pipeline on its way to the client.

The beauty of registering middleware inline is its consistency with the endpoints you create. If you were to register small middleware components in this way, before constructing endpoints by mapping them onto the `WebApplication` object, your project would indeed be minimal in the way minimal APIs were designed to be.

We have covered the basics of configuring pipelines in the previous section, but there are some pitfalls that you should be aware of to ensure you are getting the benefits of middleware.

Maintaining order

As we discussed in the first part of the chapter, middleware resides as a sequence of components within a pipeline in which a request travels between the client and server.

This sequence of components is linear, meaning that the order in which individual components are executed is critical, depending on their respective goals.

The order of execution is determined by the order in which the components are registered, and how they are registered is determined by the way they are constructed – that is, class-based or as inline middleware.

Each of these components can modify the request and the response within the pipeline. As you can imagine, this makes it easy to produce unexpected results if caution is not taken. For example, as part of your pipeline, you may need to add a field to the payload. This is fine, but if you have another middleware component within the pipeline that references that new field, you have created a dependency between components.

If the component that references the new field was to be registered before the component that created it, the pipeline would hit an exception because a property that does not yet exist will have been referenced.

Therefore, when writing middleware, it is essential that you verify that the request is hitting each component in the correct order.

Go ahead and run the project containing these middleware examples. You will see the order in which the middleware is executing in the logs shown in the **Output** tab accessible from the bottom left of the window in Visual Studio.

Default middleware

There are built-in middleware components that ASP.NET automatically registers for minimal API projects depending on the way they have been configured.

If the hosting environment is set to `Development`, `UseDeveloperExceptionPage` middleware will be registered. This component displays a page showing error responses from the pipeline when they occur, which is very useful for debugging.

The routing that we depend on and worked with in the previous chapter is itself a middleware. It is added automatically by ASP.NET if endpoints exist. ASP.NET will not add it automatically if you add `UseRouting()` manually.

After `UseRouting`, ASP.NET will also add `UseAuthentication` if `IAuthentication-SchemeProvider` is detected in the service provider. Like `UseRouting`, if you add the component manually, ASP.NET will skip adding `UseAuthentication`. The same is true for `UseAuthorization()` with `IAuthorizationSchemeProvider`. Most default middleware will not be noticed by the developer unless there is a need to override it.

Now that we've explored middleware as a concept, we should move on to discuss how we can extend minimal APIs by writing our own custom middleware.

Implementing custom middleware

Custom middleware is any middleware component that either you have written yourself or is not part of the default middleware components registered by ASP.NET.

Custom middleware affords us a lot of flexibility in the way we extend the functionality of our API outside of request endpoints.

Some examples of custom middleware might be the following:

- **Logging middleware**: Capture events and store logs as requests are received
- **Error-handling middleware**: Have specific ways that errors are treated within the pipeline
- **Validation middleware**: Check that data is in a specific state on receipt or response.

- **Request-timing middleware**: Record the time a request takes for the purposes of monitoring and telemetry
- **IP-blocking middleware**: Check the IP address of the request's remote host and check to see if it is in the ban list

Let's write some custom middleware using the example of logging. In this example, we'll keep things simple and minimal by writing the middleware as an inline middleware component.

Open `Program.cs` and start by creating a new blank middleware component; that is to say, create a `Use()` method receiving an `HttpContext` object and a `RequestDelegate` object with nothing in the body of the accompanying lambda expression:

```
app.Use(async (context, next) =>
{

});
```

Now we have a blank canvas for a simple middleware component, we can add some logic to log some content. In this example, we're going to log the content to the console.

The question is, *what* do we want to log?

The useful thing about having the request passed into the component as a `HttpContext` instance, is that we can access the individual properties of the request via this object. This means we can access the target HTTP method, the target route, and so on.

Let's start by logging some content from the request as it is received, before passing the control flow on to the next component in the pipeline. To do this, update the body of the lambda expression so that it reflects this updated example here:

```
app.Use(async (context, next) =>
{
    Console.WriteLine(
        $"Request: {context.Request.Method}
        {context.Request.Path}");
    await next(context);
});
```

Now our middleware is accessing data from the request and using string interpolation, arranging the data into a string that can be logged to the console. This gives our API the benefit of being auditable (easy to track and review historical events) and easier to maintain. On top of this, because we've used a custom middleware, we've not had to repeat ourselves by writing the same log for each endpoint we create.

Remember, the middleware components on the pipeline don't just execute for the incoming request. The outgoing response also traverses the middleware pipeline in reverse on its way back to the client.

If we wanted to log the contents of the response to the console as it travels back through the pipeline, we could simply add another `Console.WriteLine()` statement underneath our call to `next()`. The `Response` member of the `HttpContext` object should provide us with up-to-date data for the outgoing response, which we can log, as in the example shown here:

```
app.Use(async (context, next) =>
{
    Console.WriteLine(
        $"Request: {context.Request.Method}
        {context.Request.Path}");
    await next(context);
    Console.WriteLine(
        $"Response: {context.Response.StatusCode}");
});
```

As a reminder, this was an inline middleware component, meaning that it was created using a lambda expression in `Program.cs`. For the sake of consistency, here is an example of how the same middleware component could be written in a class:

```
public class LoggingMiddleware
{
    private readonly RequestDelegate _next;

    public LoggingMiddleware(RequestDelegate next)
    {
        _next = next;
    }

    public async Task InvokeAsync(HttpContext context)
    {
        Console.WriteLine(
            $"Request: {context.Request.Method}
            {context.Request.Path}");
        await _next(context);
        Console.WriteLine(
            $"Response: {context.Response.StatusCode}");
    }
}
```

Here is how the `Program` class would look after registering the class-based middleware:

```
var builder = WebApplication.CreateBuilder(args);
var app = builder.Build();

app.UseMiddleware<LoggingMiddleware>();
```

```
app.MapGet("/", () => "Hello World!");

app.Run();
```

Logging is a straightforward example of middleware's ability to take action before routes are hit. For more complex use cases, it might be necessary to **short-circuit** the pipeline. This would stop other components in the pipeline from executing and can be easily achieved by omitting the call to the `RequestDelegate` object.

Short-circuiting is simple enough, but what if our middleware has a level of complexity that means it might have to block routing from taking place? This would mean the middleware stops the request from reaching the intended endpoint, or any endpoints at all.

To understand this concept further, we need to look at a style of middleware component called **terminal middleware**.

Terminal middleware

Classic middleware components such as the ones we have worked with in this chapter all have one thing in common – the requests that pass through them on the pipeline will eventually reach an endpoint, and then the endpoint will handle sending the requests back through the pipeline to the client.

However, there are scenarios where we would not want a request to reach the endpoint. For example, if we had implemented a banned IP list, in which IP addresses for malicious or suspicious hosts were listed, we would want to achieve the following with middleware:

1. Identify the IP address of the remote host sending the request
2. Determine whether the IP address is on the list of banned IPs
3. If it is a banned IP address, send a response back to the client from the middleware, stating that the host is forbidden from proceeding further

Let's write our own middleware component that checks incoming IP addresses and blocks the request from going any further if needed.

First, create a *scaffold* of a middleware class:

```
public class IPBlockingMiddleware
{
    private readonly RequestDelegate _next;

    public IPBlockingMiddleware(RequestDelegate next,
        IEnumerable<string> blockedIPs)
    {
        _next = next;
```

```
        }

        public async Task InvokeAsync(HttpContext context)
        {
            await _next(context);
        }
}
```

At the moment, our middleware doesn't do anything, other than simply passing control to the next component in the pipeline.

Looking back at the three goals of our IP-blocking middleware, the first goal is to identify the IP address of the requesting host. This information can be retrieved from the `HttpContext` object as shown here:

```
var requestIP =
    context.Connection.RemoteIpAddress?.ToString();
```

Next, we need to identify whether the requesting IP address is a banned IP. To do this, we need to add a collection to store the banned list, and then a check against the incoming IP address.

Add a private `HashSet<string>` field under the `RequestDelegate` field. We'll use this as our banned list:

```
private readonly HashSet<string> _blockedIPs;
```

This list can be passed to the middleware when it is registered via its constructor.

Update the constructor to reflect this:

```
public IPBlockingMiddleware(RequestDelegate next,
    IEnumerable<string> blockedIPs)
    {
        _next = next;
        _blockedIPs = new HashSet<string>(blockedIPs);
    }
```

Now all that remains is to act against the offending request. We can write messages into the response to the client via the `HttpContext` object. Here, we can include a message to inform the client that their IP address is blocked. Following this, we can use a `return` statement to stop the request in its tracks:

```
public async Task InvokeAsync(HttpContext context)
    {
        var requestIP =
            context.Connection.RemoteIpAddress?.ToString();
```

```csharp
            if (_blockedIPs.Contains(requestIP))
            {
                context.Response.StatusCode = 403;
                Console.WriteLine(
                    $"IP {requestIP} is blocked.");
                await context.Response.WriteAsync(
                    "Your IP is blocked.");
                return;
            }
            Console.WriteLine($"IP {requestIP} is allowed.");
            await _next(context);
        }
```

Once all these changes have been added, we will have a fully functioning custom middleware class that is able to detect banned IP addresses for incoming requests and block them from reaching the endpoints we've configured.

Your `IPBlockingMiddleware` class should now look like this:

```csharp
public class IPBlockingMiddleware
{
    private readonly RequestDelegate _next;
    private readonly HashSet<string> _blockedIPs;

    public IPBlockingMiddleware(RequestDelegate next,
        IEnumerable<string> blockedIPs)
    {
        _next = next;
        _blockedIPs = new HashSet<string>(blockedIPs);
    }

    public async Task InvokeAsync(HttpContext context)
    {
        var requestIP =
            context.Connection.RemoteIpAddress?.ToString();

        if (_blockedIPs.Contains(requestIP))
        {
            context.Response.StatusCode = 403;
            await context.Response.WriteAsync(
                "Your IP is blocked.");
            return;
        }
```

```
        await _next(context);
    }
}
```

In the preceding middleware example, we have a constructor parameter in the form of a list of blocked IPs. This means that when registering the middleware in `Program.cs`, the list would have to be created beforehand, and then passed in during registration:

```
//Create the list of blocked Ips
private readonly List<string> _blockedIPs =
    new List<string> { "192.168.1.1", "203.0.113.0" };
app.UseMiddleware<IPBlockingMiddleware>(_blockedIPs);
```

You could test the `IPBlocking` functionality by adding the loopback address to the blacklist. This should return a response with a `403` status code:

```
app.UseMiddleware<IPBlockingMiddleware>(
    new List<string> { "::1" }
);
```

Gradually, we're starting to introduce more complex logic into our minimal API with custom and default middleware components. As complexity increases, so does the probability that errors will occur. As we know, all potential errors must be handled to maintain system continuity.

Middleware can also be used to achieve this. Let's explore how we can write a component that catches and handles unexpected behavior and errors that may occur within the pipeline.

Handling errors within the middleware pipeline

In this example, we will stick with a class-based middleware component structure, as it offers a clean structure with types that can be swapped out as needed. (This is more of a personal preference than good practice.)

A dedicated error handling component can be useful, as it ensures that you are always able to review and address errors as they occur, rather than facing the problematic and often embarrassing situation where an unhandled exception crashes the application completely.

Here is an example of a basic exception-handling middleware component:

```
public class ExceptionHandlingMiddleware
{
    private readonly RequestDelegate _next;

    public ExceptionHandlingMiddleware(
        RequestDelegate next)
```

```csharp
{
    _next = next;
}

public async Task InvokeAsync(HttpContext context)
{
    try
    {
        await _next(context);
    }
    catch (Exception ex)
    {
        Console.WriteLine(
            $"Exception caught: {ex.Message}");
        context.Response.StatusCode = 500;
        await context.Response.WriteAsync(
            "An unexpected error occurred.");
    }
}
}
```

Notice how, in this code, the `try catch` block in `InvokeAsync()` doesn't do much at all in the `try` body. It simply passes execution to the next component. This is because this middleware will be the first component in the pipeline to be registered. It is the first because we are not interested in handling errors at the first component in the pipeline, but we are for all other components. By placing our logic in the `catch` body, any errors that happen later in the pipeline will *bubble up* to this component and be caught, allowing us to handle them and then update the response to the client accordingly.

It also covers us for the handling of any exceptions during the execution of middleware components on the return journey (the response) as the flow of execution is heading back toward this component. As the component was the first to be registered, it will be the last to execute on the return journey.

In the `catch` statement, we can do whatever is needed to handle the exception. In this example, we simply write the value of the caught exception's `Message` field to the console. Then we set the status code of the request to `500 INTERNAL SERVER ERROR` and write a message into the response. All of this happens via the `HttpContext` object that travels through the pipeline.

If you wanted to force one of these exceptions to see an example of the output, you could create a dedicated example endpoint that simply throws an exception:

```csharp
app.MapGet("/employees/exceptionexample", () =>
{
    throw new NotImplementedException();
});
```

Calling this endpoint while in `Debug` mode will display the exception details in the browser.

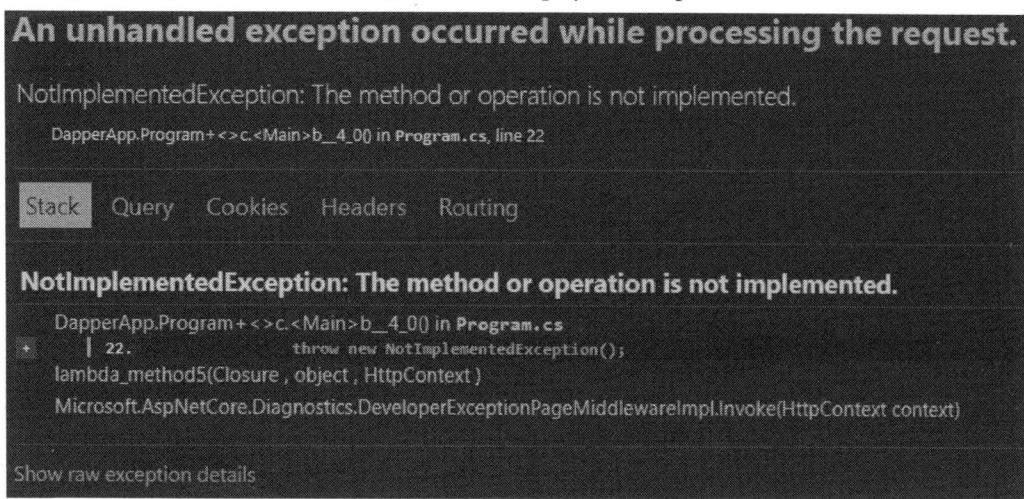

Figure 5.2: Exception details shown in the browser for debugging purposes

In this chapter, we've delved deep into the intricacies of middleware and pipeline customization in minimal APIs. By understanding the concepts and practical implementations of middleware, we've laid the groundwork for creating more robust, maintainable, and flexible API applications. Let's summarize the key points and skills we've covered.

Summary

In this chapter, we explored the essential role that middleware plays in the ASP.NET Core minimal APIs. Middleware components are pivotal in the request-response lifecycle, enabling developers to handle key areas of a system such as logging, authentication, error handling, and more.

We started by introducing the concept of middleware and explaining how it fits into the overall architecture of minimal APIs. Middleware components act as intermediaries that can inspect, modify, or terminate HTTP requests and responses. This modular approach promotes a clean separation of concerns and enhances the maintainability of the application.

Next, we delved into configuring middleware pipelines, illustrating how the order of middleware registration affects the processing of requests. Middleware components are executed in the order they are added to the pipeline, and the response travels back through the pipeline in reverse order. This sequential processing model is critical for ensuring that each middleware component functions correctly and efficiently.

We then moved on to implementing custom middleware, providing examples such as logging and IP blocking. These examples demonstrated how custom middleware can be tailored to meet specific application requirements.

We highlighted the importance of error-handling middleware, showing how it can be used to catch and manage exceptions centrally, thereby simplifying error management and improving application robustness.

Middleware is a fantastic way of extending the functionality of minimal APIs, but they are useless if their requests don't have data that can be reviewed, manipulated, and transformed. In the next chapter, we'll explore how data traveling through an API can be mapped for it to be processed optimally and accurately.

6
Parameter Binding

Context is a critical aspect of any API. The client has their own understanding of how data is structured, as does the server. For example, as the client, you will view API documentation that tells you to format a request payload in JSON format. You therefore create the JSON payload as per the API requirements.

When the API receives your payload, it is not guaranteed that the object you transmitted will remain as JSON (especially in an ASP.NET API), and a mechanism will often be in place to bind the JSON object to a strongly typed .NET object that the API can manipulate more easily within its own context.

Let us take another example. You (still as the client) make a GET request for all logs corresponding to a *job* with a particular ID. However, you want to restrict the number of logs returned to 100, which the API allows you to do. According to the API documentation, you can do this by including the job ID in the route, and an option in the query string specifying how many logs you wish to return.

When receiving this request from you as the client, the API will need to know where to look to retrieve these parameters, so that they can be used in the context of the request handler. This type of transformation of data between client and server during requests is known as **parameter binding**, and we are going to explore it in detail in this chapter.

In this chapter, we will explore the following:

- Parameter binding sources
- Binding precedence
- Creating custom parameter bindings

Parameter binding sources

Out of the box, ASP.NET supports several different parameter binding types. Each binding type has a source from which it can bind. Additionally, each binding source is situated in a different location within the request, with various ways in which they can be bound to data structures in the API.

Let's start with one of the most common binding sources, the route value.

Route values

A **route value** is simply a section of an API route. Look at a typical route and imagine it is split into sections delimited by each occurrence of the / character. Each of these resulting sections is a value within the route.

Take this example: /todoitems/2. It would be split into two route value sections: todoitems and 2.

In this context, 2 is the route value we are interested in, because it is the ID of a TodoItem entity. So, how can we access this within an endpoint?

```
app.MapGet("/todoitems/{id}", (int id) =>
{
    TodoItem item = GetById(id);
    if(item != null)
    {
        return Results.Ok(item);
    }
    return Results.NotFound();

});
```

In this code, we can see that the incoming route has been modified to add a value surrounded by curly braces. This id value is a placeholder for an integer value that will be passed in its place from the client's perspective.

In the parameter of the lambda expression that follows the route, we declare that we are passing in an integer parameter, called id. We can do this thanks to ASP.NET's routing module, which detects the route value placeholder and parses out the actual value, converting it to the data type needed for the lambda expression, which in this case is an integer.

On the client's side, the requested route might look like this: https://myTodoAPI/todoitems/2

It is important to remember that in this example, if an item with an id value of 2 does not exist, the binding will not match, and the endpoint won't hit at all, instead returning 404 NOT FOUND.

By declaring a route parameter in the endpoint, the id value of 2 found at the end of this route will be automatically detected and bound to the integer parameter declared in the lambda expression, allowing it to be used within the request.

Route values do not have to be automatically bound to the lambda expression parameters. They can be manually accessed within the request by passing an HttpRequest object as the parameter instead. On HttpRequest, there is a RouteValues collection that will be populated with the values you need for binding.

This is useful if you have multiple types of parameter bindings and you want to make the request more readable. Here's an example that passes in an `HttpRequest` parameter. This does not require any change on the client side, as it is already present. By adding it as a parameter, we are allowing the endpoint to access it:

```
app.MapGet(
    "/todoitems/{id}",
    (HttpRequest request) =>
{

    if(int.TryParse(
        request.RouteValues["id"].ToString(),
        out var id) == false)
    {
        return Results.BadRequest(
            "Could not convert id to integer");
    }
    TodoItem item = GetById(id);
    return Results.Ok(item);
});
```

When making requests to an API, there are times when you need to be more granular about the state or the conditions of a query you're making. In these situations, query strings can be added to the endpoint URL. This allows you to pass more specific parameters to the API.

Query strings

In the case of route values, they are often a direct route to data. Requesting something by an ID using a route value, on its own, produced a predictable result. However, data comes in many different forms, meaning that we often need to specify specific conditions that will transform the data we are retrieving in the required shape. **Query strings** allow us to achieve this. They sit at the end of a route, and they have their own notation that defines them, starting with a ? character.

> **Checking for the presence of query string parameters**
>
> The benefit of checking for the query strings before using them only if they exist is that we can make query string parameters optional (more on that in the next section). Otherwise, our code would assume that the client is always going to send query string values, therefore making them mandatory parameters for the endpoint. This is fine when intended, but in the examples shown in this chapter, the aim is to ensure that the client has the choice to either filter the data or not, using query string values.

As we can see in this route, `https://myTodoAPI/todoitems?pastDue=true&priority=1`, the query string starts at the end of the route values with a ? character. After this, a collection of key-value pairs is specified.

The purpose of the query string in the route is to pass a series of variables into the API, which can be used to filter the data that will be returned. In this case, the client is requesting any `TodoItem` that is past its due date, but also has a priority with a value of `1`.

Optional query string parameters

You can make it so that a parameter passed in is optional. It's very simple; you just make the query string parameter you added to the endpoint nullable by affixing a ? character to it. Then, in the body of your endpoint, you can check for the existence of an optional value. If the optional value is not null, you can use it.

Here's an example of an optional parameter used on an endpoint that fetches a todo item by ID. It allows the client to specify that the assignee must be a certain value. If the assignee value is not null and does not match the assignee value on the item, you can send a different response, such as `404 NOT FOUND`:

```
app.MapGet(
    "/todoitems/{id}",
    (int id, string? assignee) =>
{

    var index = TodoItems.FindIndex(x => x.Id == id);
    if (index == -1)
    {
        return Results.NotFound();
    }
    var todoItem = TodoItems[index];
    if (assignee != null)
    {
        if(todoItem.Assignee != assignee)
        {
            return Results.NotFound();
        }
    }
    return Results.Ok(ToDoItems[index]);
});
```

On the server side, the query string parameters are bound as per the following example. In this example, we are also checking for the existence of certain query string key-value pairs and building the relevant query for the data based on the specified query string values, using `IQueryable`:

```
app.MapGet("/todoItems", (HttpRequest request) =>
{
    bool pastDue = false;
    int priority = 0;

    var todoItemsQuery = ToDoItems.AsQueryable();

    if (request.Query.ContainsKey("pastDue"))
    {
        var parsedDueDate = bool.TryParse(
            request.Query["pastDue"],
            out pastDue
        );
        if (parsedDueDate) {
            todoItemsQuery = todoItemsQuery.Where(
                x => x.DueDate <= DateTime.Now
            );
        }
    }
    if (request.Query.ContainsKey("priority"))
    {
        var parsedPriority = int.TryParse(
            request.Query["priority"],
            out priority
        );
        if (parsedPriority) {
            todoItemsQuery = todoItemsQuery.Where(
                x => x.Priority == priority
            );
        }
    }

    var result = todoItemsQuery.ToList();
    return Results.Ok(result);
});
```

We've spent most of our time so far passing parameters within the URLs of our requests. Let us explore parameters that exist outside of this, starting with headers.

Headers

Headers are a classic component of general API architecture, providing important metadata about the request. They are like query strings in the sense that they are defined by a key-value structure, but the syntax used when applying them differs.

Like query strings and route values, they can also be accessed from an `HttpRequest` object:

```
app.MapGet("/todoItems", (HttpRequest request) =>
{
    var customHeader = request.Headers["SomeCustomHeader"];
    var result = todoItemsQuery.ToList();
    return Results.Ok(result);
});
```

Another critical parameter type that exists outside of the URL is the request body, sometimes referred to as the *payload*. ASP.NET has a clever feature that allows the payload's contents to be automatically converted into a strongly typed object defined in the project. The feature is known as **object binding**.

Strongly typed object binding

When representing objects in a request payload, it is extremely common for that object to be structured as JSON when the client creates the request. ASP.NET provides a convenient way of automatically binding incoming JSON parameters to a strongly typed object so that it can be easily used when handling the request.

We have seen examples of this already in previous chapters, where we send a JSON payload representing a `TodoItem` object.

If the JSON object can be parsed, ASP.NET allows you to implicitly declare that the request parameter is an object of type *x* – *x* in our example being a `TodoItem` object.

To use implicit binding in this manner, simply declare a parameter of the type you wish to receive as a parameter in your endpoint, as shown in the following example, where we receive a new `TodoItem` to be created via a `POST` method:

```
app.MapPost("/todoitems", (TodoItem item) =>
{
    var validationContext = new ValidationContext(item);
    var validationResults = new List<ValidationResult>();
    var isValid = Validator.TryValidateObject(
        item, validationContext, validationResults, true);
    if (isValid)
    {
        TodoItems.Add(item);
```

```
        return Results.Created();
    }
    return Results.BadRequest(validationResults);
});
```

Object binding is initiated thanks to the client sending a data structure represented by a string, within the body of the request. This is often the result of a developer formatting the payload after the data was gathered, before sending it to the API. However, if the data was gathered by a user, who could be entering the data in the **Graphical User Interface** (**GUI**) via a form, the process can be streamlined further, thanks to form values.

Form values

API endpoints take in data and do something with it. What better use case can there be for data submission than a form? Minimal APIs support the receipt of **form values**, making them a suitable option for handling submissions from forms within a GUI.

Like the previous parameter examples, form values can be retrieved from their own dedicated member within an HttpRequest object, where they also exist in a key-value structure within an IFormCollection collection. The following code shows the retrieval of form values within a PATCH request:

```
app.MapPatch(
    "/updateTodoItemDueDate",
    async (HttpRequest request) =>
{
    var formData = await request.ReadFormAsync();
    var id = int.Parse(formData["Id"]);
    var newDueDate =
        DateTime.Parse(formData["newDueDate"]);

    var index = TodoItems.FindIndex(x => x.Id == id);

    if (index == -1)
    {
        return Results.NotFound();
    }
    TodoItems[index].DueDate = newDueDate;
    return Results.NoContent();
});
```

So far, we've made some good progress exploring the various types of parameters that can be bound to API endpoints. In each of the previous examples, a lot is assumed about how these parameters should be bound. The location of the parameters, whether they be in the URL as query strings or in the request body, is *implicit*; it does not require definition, instead occurring automatically. Inversely, there will be times when we will need to be *explicit* about how parameters are bound. This explicit binding can be achieved with **attributes**.

Explicit binding with attributes

All the previous examples have something in common – they are accessible using keys from collections that exist within an `HttpRequest` object.

There is another way of binding these parameter types without needing to inject `HttpRequest` or its parent, `HttpContext` – attributes.

The benefit of this is that we can make the code more readable and arguably improve the structure of the request, because the parameters can be bound from within the parentheses of the endpoint's lambda expression, leaving the expression body dedicated exclusively to handling the request. As shown in the previous examples, we are using the parentheses to receive parameters but then performing explicit binding in the body, as well as executing handling logic, which can be somewhat messy.

Parameter binding with attributes is simpler because you are explicitly stating that you have a parameter that should be bound from a specific location in the request.

Let us take query strings as an example. In the code block in the *Query strings* section, we were accessing query strings from within the endpoint body by index on `IQueryCollection` within the `HttpRequest` object.

The following code block demonstrates how this endpoint can be refactored to obtain query string values using attributes, reducing the amount of code and making it easier to read:

```
app.MapGet(
    "/todoItems",
    ([FromQuery(Name = "pastDue")] bool pastDue,
     [FromQuery(Name = "priority")] int priority  ) =>
{
    var todoItemsQuery = ToDoItems.AsQueryable();
    if (pastDue)
    {
        todoItemsQuery = todoItemsQuery.Where(
            x => x.DueDate <= DateTime.Now
        );
    }
    if (priority > 0)
    {
        todoItemsQuery = todoItemsQuery.Where(
            x => x.Priority == priority
        );
```

```
    }
    var result = todoItemsQuery.ToList();
    return Results.Ok(result);
});
```

If you were to change the [FromQuery] attributes in this code slightly by removing the argument, for example, to Name = "priority", the API would still match the query values, assuming that the name was specified in the query string.

All the parameter binding methods demonstrated previously in this chapter can be extracted in this way – by specifying in an attribute where the parameter should be bound from and then providing an object with the appropriate data type in which it can be bound.

Let us update another of our previous POST examples by checking the headers in this manner. For the purposes of demonstration, let us assume that when a client posts a new TodoItem, they can indicate whether another process should be triggered in the background by using a custom header.

The header can be explicitly bound using an attribute, as shown here:

```
app.MapPost(
    "/todoitems",
    (TodoItem item,
      [FromHeader(Name ="TriggerBackgroundTask")]
      bool triggerBackgroundTaskHeader ) =>
{
    if ( triggerBackgroundTaskHeader)
    {
        // do something else in the background
    }

    ToDoItems.Add(item);
    return Results.Created();
});
```

We're ready to step into more advanced territory now, in which we can explore parameters that have been *injected* from a catalog of previously registered **services**.

Binding parameters through dependency injection

Parameters can be bound to an endpoint that was not necessarily sent by the client. One example of this is dependencies. Where an API has dependencies registered for injection, they can be explicitly bound as parameters. Let us explore an example of this by rewriting the GET request example from the first code block in the *Explicit binding with attributes* section.

First, as you can see in the code on GitHub, we've created a service called `TodoItemService`:

```
public class TodoItemService
{
    List<TodoItem> todoItems = new List<TodoItem>();
    public TodoItem GetById(int id)
    {
        return todoItems.FirstOrDefault(x => x.Id == id);
    }

    public List<TodoItem> GetTodoItems(
        bool pastDue, int priority)
    {
        var todoItemsQuery = todoItems.AsQueryable();
        if (pastDue)
        {
            todoItemsQuery = todoItemsQuery.Where(
                x => x.DueDate <= DateTime.Now
            );
        }
        if (priority > 0)
        {
            todoItemsQuery = todoItemsQuery.Where(
                x => x.Priority == priority);
        }
        return todoItemsQuery.ToList();
    }
}
```

This service has been registered for dependency injection as a singleton service in `Program.cs`:

```
builder.Services.AddSingleton<TodoItemService>();
```

This means that we can now access this service from within an endpoint using the `[FromServices]` attribute:

```
app.MapGet(
    "/todoItems",
    ([FromQuery(Name = "pastDue")] bool pastDue,
     [FromQuery(Name = "priority")] int priority,
     [FromServices] TodoService todoItemService) =>
    {
```

```
        var todoItemsQuery =
            todoItemService.TodoItems.AsQueryable();
        if (pastDue)
        {
            todoItemsQuery = todoItemsQuery.Where(
                x => x.DueDate <= DateTime.Now
            );
        }
        if (priority > 0)
        {
            todoItemsQuery = todoItemsQuery.Where(
                x => x.Priority == priority
            );
        }
        var result =
            todoItemService.GetTodoItems(todoItemsQuery);
        return Results.Ok(result);
});
```

In this code, binding a service registered for dependency injection is demonstrated using a [FromService] attribute. This allows API endpoints to leverage reusable components easily.

So far, we have looked at examples of various parameter types and how they are bound to API endpoints. Hopefully, it is clear that ASP.NET is taking care of the heavy lifting when it comes to resolving these parameters before binding. It is also important to understand the order in which this resolution of parameters happens. This is known as **binding precedence**.

Binding precedence

ASP.NET has its own defined order in which it will bind parameters, known as its **order of precedence**. Using this order keeps resolution consistent and ensures that ASP.NET is resolving in a predictable way, starting with the most specific parameters to the least.

Figure 6.1 outlines the official order ASP.NET uses, which is useful to know as a developer, as it can help you anticipate any potential binding issues depending on the parameters in use.

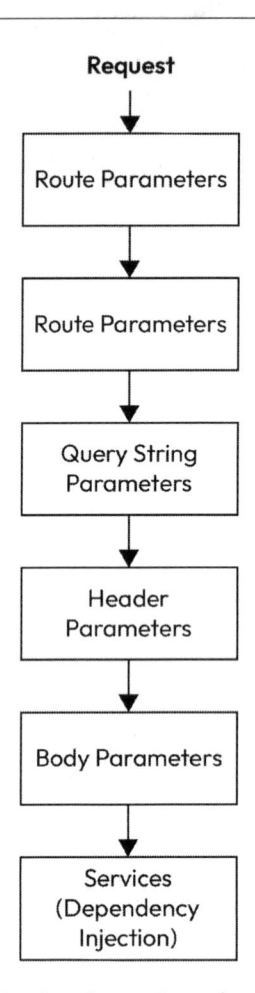

Figure 6.1: ASP.NET order of precedence for parameter binding

Let us look at a working example of how we can create custom binding logic, giving us more control over the way binding is executed on incoming parameters.

Creating custom binding logic

In this example, we are going to change the way we bind an incoming `TodoItem`, adding validation logic that will occur at the point of binding.

To implement this kind of custom binding, we need to implement a function within `TodoItem`. This function is static and is called `BindAsync()`.

`BindAsync()` allows us to interrupt the binding process for an object and apply our own logic. Let us start by adding `BindAsync()` to the `TodoItem` class.

In `TodoItem`, add the following static function below the property definitions:

```
public static async ValueTask<TodoItem> BindAsync(
    HttpContext context, ParameterInfo parameter)
{
}
```

Next, we need to add a `try/catch` block so that we can perform JSON validation logic, catching any errors in the process. We are expecting to see exceptions of type `JsonException` if the validation fails, so we will explicitly catch this exception type in our `try/catch` block:

```
public static async ValueTask<TodoItem> BindAsync(
    HttpContext context, ParameterInfo parameter)
{
    try
    {

    }
    catch (JsonException)
    {

    }
}
```

Now, we can start by accessing the body of the request and deserializing the raw JSON to a `TodoItem` instance. We will add options to ensure case is not factored into validation, and then check to see whether deserialization was successful. If it was not, the incoming parameter cannot be bound and the request is invalid, so we will return a `400 Bad Request` response. Update the `try` block with this code, shown here:

```
    var requestBody = await new StreamReader(
        context.Request.Body
    ).ReadToEndAsync();
    var todoItem = JsonSerializer.Deserialize<TodoItem>(
        requestBody,
        new JsonSerializerOptions
        {
            PropertyNameCaseInsensitive = true
        }
    );

    if (todoItem == null)
    {
        context.Response.StatusCode = 400;
        await context.Response.WriteAsync("Invalid JSON");
```

```
        return new TodoItem();
}
```

At this point, we have now checked the validity of the JSON to be bound. In *Chapter 5*, we explored an example of validation middleware for verifying that objects were created according to specific rules. We used `ValidationContext` along with the static type, `Validator`, to return a list of `ValidationResult`, which would determine the validity of the model.

We can use this same logic in `BindAsync()` to implement validation of the object as part of the parameter binding process.

Add this logic to the `try` block to complete the custom binding logic:

```
var validationResults = new List<ValidationResult>();
var validationContext = new ValidationContext(
    todoItem,
    serviceProvider: null,
    items: null
);
if (!Validator.TryValidateObject(
    todoItem,
    validationContext,
    validationResults,
    validateAllProperties: true
))
{
    context.Response.StatusCode = 400;
    var errorMessages = string.Join(
        "; ",
        validationResults.Select(x => x.ErrorMessage)
    );
    await context.Response.WriteAsync(errorMessages);
    return new TodoItem();
}
return todoItem;
```

Finally, we need to add the following basic logic to the `catch` block to handle any exceptions of type `JsonException` that are caught:

```
context.Response.StatusCode = 400;
await context.Response.WriteAsync("Invalid JSON");
return new TodoItem();
```

Refer to this chapter's code in the accompanying GitHub repository to see the finished class: https://github.com/PacktPublishing/Minimal-APIs-in-ASP.NET-9

Custom parameter binding is a good example of ASP.NET's flexible feature set. Minimal APIs may be labeled as such but that doesn't mean they restrict custom configurations. Let us review what we have covered in this chapter.

Summary

The binding of parameters is a fairly broad subject, and we have certainly covered the bulk of it in this chapter.

We started by looking at how the different parameter types are bound, from route values and query strings right up to headers and the automatic binding provided for strongly typed objects.

We then explored some alternative binding methods for these parameter types in the form of explicit attribute binding and the order of binding precedence, before looking at how dependency injection can be leveraged within requests to add parameters that may not have been received from the client.

Finally, we worked through an example of custom parameter binding, adding custom validation to the binding logic of the `TodoItem` model.

This chapter is not the last we have seen of dependency injection in minimal APIs. In the next chapter, we will explore the topic in more detail.

7
Dependency Injection in Minimal APIs

In any software project, developers rarely craft the application entirely from scratch. At some level, generic libraries and toolsets will be absorbed into the application to accelerate and optimize the project. **ASP.NET** as a framework is no different. In fact, it requires that developers take on dependencies; third-party or independently created code that plays a key role in the smooth running of the system.

The result is a (hopefully) finely tuned and well-designed architecture, formed of modules and components, some of which run code that was written by developers on the project, and the rest being more generic, boilerplate code that was written and pre-compiled before the project started.

Keeping track of dependencies is one of the classic problems facing software developers, and the problems that arise from this can progress to a point that results in what the industry refers to as **dependency hell** – a nightmarish scenario in which developers are retracing their steps, trying to figure out where a dependency was introduced, and finding ways that they can overcome the challenge of conflicting dependencies across a potentially massive code base.

Dependency injection (**DI**) is a way of standardizing and simplifying the experience of consuming dependencies in software projects.

In this chapter, we are going to cover the following main topics:

- Understanding DI
- Configuring DI in minimal APIs
- DI best practices

By the end of the chapter, you will have improved your understanding of DI principles, as well as the benefits they can bring to minimal APIs and ASP.NET projects in general.

You will also have gained practical experience in the configuration of DI containers and registration of services.

Let us start by improving our understanding of DI.

Understanding DI

DI started out as a design pattern in software development, aimed at centralizing common dependencies and making them available to consumers in a consistent manner.

Using this approach, common development tasks such as testing, swapping out dependencies, modification of dependency logic, centralization of dependencies, and so on, can be easily achieved through one straightforward system.

Over time, .NET made DI more of a feature rather than just a design pattern. In ASP.NET, there is a robust DI toolset that is simple to use and understand.

Developers can register their dependencies in a centralized location, making them available to *inject* into the constructors of classes as arguments when they are instantiated.

With DI, dependencies live within a *container*, making them centrally available to consuming classes. But what is a container?

The DI container

On the startup of your application, dependencies are registered in the container. The **container** is simply a group of dependencies that have been registered for DI. Each of the dependencies has a lifetime specification that defines how they are instantiated when injected into a consuming class. We'll explore dependency lifetimes in more detail later in the chapter.

When a class that has a dependency is instantiated, it reaches out to the container, which takes care of the business of resolving the dependency and instantiating it according to the lifetime setting that was configured when the dependency was registered.

It might sound like this is an extra layer of complexity for something as simple as using a class within another, but there is good reason for mandating the use of DI as a best practice. Let us explore this in more detail.

The case for DI

Think back to your career to date as a software engineer. Whether you're still at the beginning, or you've been doing this for a while, you may have spent considerable time *newing up* dependencies in the form of classes.

Let's say you're building an API endpoint that needs to reach into a SQL database. (I'm deliberately not using Entity Framework for this example for simplicity.) You may have already created a class that abstracts away the specifics (we'll call it SqlHelper), such as creating an instance of SqlConnection, opening the connection, building SqlCommand, and so on. What do you think you'll need to do each time you realize that you need this SqlHelper class?

The first thing you'll notice is that you have to create a new instance of SqlHelper at any point that the need for interaction with your SQL Server arises. On the face of it, this sounds harmless enough, but from a design perspective, it's problematic. Let's look at the potential pitfalls of this approach a little more closely:

- **Tight coupling**: Without DI, you create a concrete implementation of SqlHelper each time you use it. Whenever you have a concrete implementation of a class, you run the risk of being forced to change each class that consumes it if you need to significantly change SqlHelper. This means that your consuming classes become tightly coupled to SqlHelper.

- **Difficulties in testing**: Being able to mock dependencies is critical to effective testing. Without DI, you will have to be more hands-on in ensuring that dependencies are properly instantiated, mocked, and then accessible for each test. The added need for manual instantiation increases the potential for mistakes in setting up the tests. This is problematic because it can make your tests unreliable.

- **Resource management issues**: When dependencies are using resources as SqlHelper is (it will have a connection to a SQL Server), there is always the risk that those resources are not managed effectively. In the case of something like a SQL connection, spinning up a lot of these connections over time without adequate disposal could exhaust the connections, leading to performance issues.

- **Violation of single responsibility, open-closed principle, Liskov substitution, interface segregation principle, dependency inversion principle (SOLID) principles**: We've not yet explored SOLID principles in this book, but they are an important part of any object-oriented software system. One of the guiding principles of SOLID is *single responsibility*, in which we are expected to ensure that classes have a primary responsibility. In the case of a class consuming SqlHelper, their primary responsibility is to the logic that is requesting or manipulating data. Forcing the class to instantiate SqlHelper means you're giving it a new responsibility; a responsibility of managing its own dependencies. DI removes this added responsibility, simply passing the dependencies into the class when the class is constructed.

Hopefully, this breakdown has painted a picture of how not using DI can make your code base inconsistent and messy. Now, let us explore how DI is achieved in ASP.NET.

Configuring DI in minimal APIs

As standard, ASP.NET offers a way for us to declare that a class we have created can be registered as a service. Converting a class into a service means it can be reused via DI. For example, say you've got a piece of logic that calculates overtime pay for any given employee. That logic is the same, but you'll need it in many other areas of the code base. To avoid writing the same logic again, it's obvious that you would simply call on the same logic, but as we've already discussed, creating a new instance of the class to get to this logic whenever you need it is messy; so, by registering the class as a service, we can cleanly inject it into any other class that needs it.

Moreover, DI allows us to control the life cycle of the service when it is injected. In essence, we can dictate how the dependency is instantiated on each injection and how long it should exist.

There are three built-in lifetime options in ASP.NET:

- **Singleton**: The service is created once, as a single instance. This instance is then shared across the code base. This can be useful when you need to maintain state on a global scale. Logging is a good use case for this, as all log entries can be channeled through one single service that has access to the relevant output resource. For example, a logging service that creates logs in a file.
- **Scoped**: The service is created once for every incoming request. This means that when a client makes a request to the API, a service is created when needed and that instance is in use for the duration of the request. This is ideal when you need to manage state within a request. It is also favorable if you do not want to share the same service between different requests.
- **Transient**: The service has an instance created every time it is injected. This means that regardless of the request being made to the API, each time a service is injected, that service will be a new instance. This is ideal for scenarios where state does not need to be maintained.

Let's set up a new minimal API project to use as an example of how we can benefit from DI.

Please note, if you haven't read them already, refer to the first two chapters to understand how you can create a new minimal API project. This will allow you to follow along with the examples in this chapter.

Setting up a scoped DI project

For our new API project, we're going to use the example of an order-processing API. It will contain a series of products or services that can be put together to create an order.

First, we need models to represent products and orders. Create two classes, `Product` and `Order`. In the first code, we create the `Product` class:

```
public class Product
{
    public int Id { get; set; }
    public string Name { get; set; }
    public string Description { get; set; }
    public float RRP { get; set; }
}
```

In the following code, we create the `Order` class:

```
public class Order
{
    public int Id { get; set; }
    public List<Product> Products { get; set; }
    public decimal DiscountAmount { get; set; }
    public DateTime DeliveryDate { get; set; }
}
```

We need to be able to refer to a collection of available products. Ordinarily, we would store this information in a database and then use either `SqlConnection` or an **Object Relational Mapping (ORM)** framework, such as Microsoft's Entity Framework, to access the database, mapping the data to the models (`Product` and `Order`) we've created. However, database connections are not within the scope of this chapter and will be covered later in the book.

For now, and for simplicity, we will simply create a JSON file containing an array of objects that can be read into the project as text and deserialized into the strongly typed object, `Product`. I've created an example of five products that can be saved in JSON format, in the following code. Feel free to copy my examples or create your own. Whatever you do, save the products in a file called `Products.json` in an accessible location. Ensure that each project is a JSON object contained within a single JSON array and that the values you use match the data types of the properties in `Product`; otherwise, it will not be possible to deserialize the JSON:

```
[
    {
        "Id": 1,
        "Name": "Laptop",
        "Description": "A high-performance laptop suitable
                    for all your computing needs.",
        "RRP": 999.99
    },
    {
        "Id": 2,
        "Name": "Smartphone",
        "Description": "A latest generation smartphone with
                    a stunning display and excellent
                    camera.",
        "RRP": 799.99
    },
    {
        "Id": 3,
        "Name": "Headphones",
        "Description": "Noise-cancelling headphones with
```

```
                        superior sound quality.",
        "RRP": 199.99
    },
    {
        "Id": 4,
        "Name": "Smartwatch",
        "Description": "A smartwatch with fitness tracking
                        and health monitoring features.",
        "RRP": 299.99
    },
    {
        "Id": 5,
        "Name": "Tablet",
        "Description": "A lightweight tablet with a vibrant
                        display, perfect for entertainment
                        on the go.",
        "RRP": 399.99
    }
]
```

Now, let's create a means of bringing these objects into memory when they are needed. (Again, not the most efficient example as we're not using a database, but we will be covering database usage later in the book.)

For this example, we'll do this by creating a class, called `ProductRepository`. This class can be used to access a list of objects of type `Product`.

Add the `ProductRepository` class as per the example here:

```
public class ProductRepository
{
    public List<Product> Products { get; private set; }
}
```

As you can see, this is a very simple class that just holds a list of `Product`. We need to somehow populate this list with the JSON objects we've saved as text. We could very easily just fetch the items when we instantiate the class, but we want to do this using an injected service, so we'll come back to `ProductRepository` shortly. Before that, let's create a service that will have the responsibility of retrieving the products from the text file. We'll call it `ProductRetrievalService`:

```
public class ProductRetrievalService
{
    private const string _dataPath =
        @"C:/Products.json";
```

```
            public List<Product> LoadProducts()
            {
                var productJson = File.ReadAllText(_dataPath);
                return JsonSerializer
                    .Deserialize<List<Product>>(
                        productJson
                    );
            }
        }
```

This simple service reads the contents of the JSON file and uses the `JsonSerializer` class found within `System.Text.Json` to convert, or deserialize, the JSON content into the strongly typed `Product` type, putting each `Product` into the list.

> **Permissions on C:/**
>
> If you have trouble writing or reading from `C:/`, you may not have permission to do so. You can work around this by creating a folder in a location to which you do have read/write permissions, and then change the path in the code to match the new one.

At this point, the products have been retrieved. This means that we can simply call `LoadProducts()` and we will always get the latest data. However, how do we access `ProductRetrievalService` to do this? Our `ProductRepository` class will need this logic in order to populate its `Product` list.

Here is where DI becomes useful. We can inject an instance of `ProductRetrievalService` any time we use `ProductRepository`. To make this possible, we first need to register `ProductRetreivalService` as a service.

The following code demonstrates registration of this service for DI within `Program.cs`:

```
public static void Main(string[] args)
{
    var builder = WebApplication.CreateBuilder(args);
    builder.Services.AddScoped<ProductRetrievalService>();
    var app = builder.Build();


    app.Run();
}
```

By adding `ProductRetrievalService` as a scoped service, an instance will be created for the duration of the incoming request. Now that it is registered, we can inject `ProductRetrievalService` into `ProductRepository` when we instantiate it, via its constructor. Let us look at an example of this in an API endpoint example.

Create a new HTTP GET method, mapped onto the `getProductById` route, as shown in the following code:

```
app.MapGet("/getProductById/{id}", (int id) =>
{


});
```

The endpoint takes an integer parameter in the form of the product ID. We can now use this to get the product with the matching ID. First things first, let's add a new instance of `ProductRepository` to the endpoint:

```
app.MapGet("/getProductById{id}", (int id) =>
{
    var productRepository = new ProductRepository();

});
```

We have a `ProductRepository` instance now, which has a list of `Product`, but this list is empty. We need to modify `ProductRepository` to inject `ProductRetreivalService`, to populate that list. The following code shows an example of how the service can be injected into `ProductRepository` via the constructor before being used to populate the products held within a `List<Product>`:

```
public class ProductRepository
{
    public List<Product> Products { get; private set; }

    public ProductRepository(
        ProductRetrievalService productRetrievalService
    )
    {
        Products = productRetrievalService.LoadProducts();
    }
}
```

Now, we should be able to use some logic in the endpoint to get the relevant product from `ProductRepository`. However, we have a problem. If we try to instantiate a new instance of `ProductRepository` in the endpoint, we will see an error.

The reason we see an error is that we have changed the way `ProductRepository` is instantiated. It now requires a `ProductRetrievalService` to be passed as an argument to the constructor, but how are we supposed to get hold of this?

This is where minimal APIs allow us to, within an endpoint, take advantage of services registered within the DI container.

`ProductRetreivalService` can be passed as an argument within the parameters we pass into the lambda expression within the body of the endpoint. This makes it the same as the ID parameter passed in by the client, except it's not coming from the client, it's coming from the DI container.

To make this possible, you need to prefix the `ProductRetrievalService` argument with an attribute that indicates that it was injected. This attribute is `[FromServices]`.

Injecting `ProductRetrievalService` with this attribute will now allow us to pass the required `ProductRetrievalService` to the constructor of `ProductRepository`, as shown here:

```
app.MapGet("/getProductById/{id}",
    (
        int id,
        [FromServices] ProductRetrievalService
            productRetrievalService
    ) =>
    {
    var productRepository = new ProductRepository(
        productRetrievalService
    );
    return Results.Ok(
        productRepository.Products
            .FirstOrDefault(x => x.Id == id)
    );
});
```

It is also worth noting that the instance of `ProductRepository` we created in this example could itself be injected into the class using DI.

Let's move on to our next example now.

Creating a singleton DI project

Let's look at another example, but this time, we'll use a different life cycle for the dependency. In this use case, we will create an endpoint for creating an order. The incoming `Order` object will have a list of `Product` that can be used to submit a new customer order into the system. However, we also need to establish a delivery date.

> **Note**
> To avoid repeating ourselves, we can for this example, simply use a collection such as `List<DateTime>` rather than feeding them in from a JSON file.

Let's imagine that there is a feed of upcoming available dates that are centrally managed. We could create a service that has the available context to be able to choose the next available date. This decouples the logic from the endpoint and can be reused in other endpoints.

The code shows an example of this kind of service:

```csharp
public class DeliveryDateBookingService
{
    private ConcurrentQueue<DateTime>
        _availableDates = new ConcurrentQueue<DateTime>();

    public DeliveryDateBookingService()
    {
        _availableDates.Enqueue(DateTime.Now.AddDays(1));
        _availableDates.Enqueue(DateTime.Now.AddDays(2));
        _availableDates.Enqueue(DateTime.Now.AddDays(3));
        _availableDates.Enqueue(DateTime.Now.AddDays(4));
        _availableDates.Enqueue(DateTime.Now.AddDays(5));
    }

    public DateTime GetNextAvailableDate()
    {
        if(_availableDates.Count == 0)
        {
            throw new Exception("No Dates Available");
        }
        var dequeuedDate = _availableDates
            .TryDequeue(out var result);
        if (dequeuedDate == false)
        {
            throw new Exception("An error occured");
        }
        return result;
    }
}
```

This service allows requests to get the next available date, throwing an exception if there is no date available. We have a queue to hold the available dates so they can be removed as they are retrieved to ensure that the same date is not offered twice.

Configuring DI in minimal APIs

We also must consider thread safety here. You could have multiple requests all trying to get an available date, which is very likely to lead to a race condition, where two requests end up dequeuing the same available date. To avoid this, we are using `ConcurrentQueue`, which will handle the business of ensuring thread safety between requests.

We now need to register this as a service that can be injected into the endpoint that posts the order. With multiple requests in mind, we want to ensure that all requests are retrieving dates from the same list. Therefore, we will register the service using `AddSingleton()`, which will ensure that only one instance of the service is used between threads and requests during injection.

Once the service has been registered in this way, `Program.cs` should look like the code shown here:

```
public class Program
    {
        public static void Main(string[] args)
        {
            var builder = WebApplication
                .CreateBuilder(args);
            builder.Services
                .AddScoped<ProductRetrievalService>();
            builder.Services
                .AddSingleton<DeliveryDateBookingService>()
                ;
            var app = builder.Build();

            app.MapGet("/getProductById/{id}",
                (int id,
                [FromServices] ProductRetrievalService
                productRetreivalService) =>
            {
                var productRepository = new
                    ProductRepository(
                        productRetreivalService
                );
                return Results.Ok(
                    productRepository.Products
                        .FirstOrDefault(
                            x => x.Id == id)
                );
            });
```

```
            app.Run();
        }
    }
```

Now that the API has our second service registered, it is time to create the endpoint for creating an order.

Seeing as we are creating a new record, we should use a `POST` method to achieve our goal. The `POST` method will take in a JSON object, which is implicitly parsed into an `Order` object within the endpoint parameter.

Following this, we indicate that we are injecting `DeliveryDateBookingService` into the request.

Once this is done, we can complete the endpoint by adding the relevant logic to the body of the lambda expression.

The endpoint with logic for fetching the next delivery date is shown here:

```
app.MapPost(
    "/order",
    (Order order,
     [FromServices] DeliveryDateBookingService
     deliveryDateBookingService) =>
{
    order.DeliveryDate =
        deliveryDateBookingService.GetNextAvailableDate()
        ;

    // save order to repository
});
```

Whilst we created a repository for `Product`, we have not yet created one for `Order`. Furthermore, we did not demonstrate saving entities to their respective repositories.

This kind of logic will be covered later in the book as we explore design patterns (such as the repository pattern) and data sources, but for now, here is an example of how you can save the new order in the preceding endpoint:

1. Create an `OrderRetreivalService` class so we stay consistent in using a service to retrieve entities (as we did for products):

```
public class OrderRetrievalService
{
    private const string _dataPath =
        @"C:/Orders.json";
    public List<Order> LoadOrders()
    {
```

```
            var ordersJson = File.ReadAllText(_dataPath);
            return JsonSerializer
                .Deserialize<List<Order>>(ordersJson);
    }
}
```

2. Register `OrderRetrievalService` as a scoped service in the DI container within `Program.cs`:

    ```
                    builder.Services
                        .AddScoped<OrderRetrievalService>();
    ```

3. Create an `OrderRespository` class that follows the same style as `ProductRespository`. The added difference is that a `SaveOrder()` method is added to allow for saving the `Order` from the `POST` endpoint. Also, the collection being used to hold the orders is `ConcurrentQueue<Order>` rather than a list. This is because we expect orders to be saved from multiple concurrent requests and we need to allow for thread safety:

    ```
    public class OrderRepository
    {
        public ConcurrentQueue<Order>
            Orders { get; private set; }
        public OrderRepository(
            OrderRetrievalService orderRetrievalService)
        {
            var retrievedOrders =
                orderRetrievalService.LoadOrders();
            foreach (var order in retrievedOrders)
            {
                Orders.Enqueue(order);
            }

        }

        public void SaveOrder(Order order)
        {
            Orders.Enqueue(order);
        }
    }
    ```

4. Register `OrderRepository` as a singleton service in `Program.cs` so that we can always add to it on a single instance regardless of how many requests are saving orders:

    ```
                    builder.Services
                        .AddSingleton<OrderRepository>();
    ```

5. The `POST` endpoint can now be updated to inject `OrderRepository` and to use it for saving the incoming order:

```
app.MapPost(
    "/order",
    (Order order,
     [FromServices] DeliveryDateBookingService
     deliveryDateBookingService,
     [FromServices] OrderRepository
     orderRepository) =>
    {
        order.DeliveryDate =
            deliveryDateBookingService
                .GetNextAvailableDate();
        orderRepository.SaveOrder(order);
    });
```

Now that you have some experience creating dependencies as services and registering them for injection, let's go over some basic best practices for using DI in minimal APIs.

DI best practices

DI is integral to most ASP.NET projects, and minimal APIs are often particularly reliant on them. As a result, it's important to ensure that we are following best practices when it comes to dependencies and the methods of accessing them.

There are some simple rules of thumb when it comes to implementing DI in minimal APIs. We look at these rules in the next few sections.

Avoiding the service locator pattern

There is an anti-pattern in minimal APIs known as the **service locator pattern**. In this pattern, instead of explicitly injecting your dependency, you inject `IServiceProvider` containing the dependency, and then you fish the service out of it within the body of your method or function.

An example of the service locator pattern is shown in the following code, in which the `POST` method we made for creating orders is altered to use `IServiceProvider`:

```
app.MapPost(
    "/order",
    (Order order,
     IServiceProvider provider) =>
    {
```

```
            var deliveryDateBookingService =
                provider.GetService
                    <DeliveryDateBookingService>();
            order.DeliveryDate =
                deliveryDateBookingService
                    .GetNextAvailableDate();

        // save order to repository in same way we did for
        // Product using ProductRepository
    });
```

A significant drawback to this practice is that it makes the code harder to read. It is less obvious from the parameter that you are injecting specific services, and you have to write extra lines of code to get the service of `IServiceProvider`.

It also makes it more difficult to write unit tests for your endpoints, because it is less clear which objects you need to instantiate for mocking.

Probably the most destructive aspect of this anti-pattern is the potential for runtime failures to be hard to diagnose. When injecting `IServiceProvider`, the compiler doesn't know if the service you actually need is registered, whereas if you attempt to explicitly inject your service and it isn't registered, it will become apparent much more quickly, allowing for easier debugging.

Registering services with an extension method

You can make your code more readable by creating an extension method on `IServiceCollection`. This means that within `Program.cs`, you can register all your services with just one line of code or group your services together in an appropriate way and register each group.

Here is an example of how you can write such an extension method:

```
public static class ServiceCollectionExtensions
{
    public static IServiceCollection AddMyServices(
        this IServiceCollection services)
    {
        services.AddScoped<IMyService, MyService>();
        services.AddSingleton<IOtherService,
            OtherService>();
        return services;
    }
}
```

After implementing the extension method, you can simply write the following in `Program.cs` to register all services:

```
builder.Services.AddMyServices();
```

Using sensible service lifetimes

When registering services, it is important to consider the lifetime you are assigning to them. Here are some examples of when you would use each service lifetime:

- **Transient**: Use this lifetime if your service is lightweight, stateless, and is only to be used for a short period of time.
- **Scoped**: Use this lifetime when your service must maintain state within a single request, and the state needs to be unique to the current request.
- **Singleton**: Use this lifetime when your service must maintain state across the whole application. It is also useful for situations where you need to create heavy services that are costly to create. Creating them once reduces the overhead.

Making the effort to follow best practices when creating and managing dependencies is a long-term investment, and is a selfless act, ensuring that the code base is easy to maintain for other developers in the future.

Let's summarize what we've covered in this chapter.

Summary

We started the chapter by exploring DI from a high level, gaining an understanding of the benefits it brings to minimal APIs by encouraging good design, loose coupling, and reusability across the code base.

We then looked at how dependencies can be created in the form of services, before being registered for injection, using the example of an order processing API.

It was demonstrated that parameter attributes can be used within a minimal API endpoint to inject services into the scope of an endpoint's execution, and we covered the various lifetimes available to services when they are registered.

Finally, some best practices were outlined, helping you to ensure that your use of DI is productive, efficient, sustainable, and testable, whilst also being easy to read for other developers who may be less familiar with the project.

DI is a fundamental aspect of not only minimal APIs but software engineering in general. Having a good grounding in it will be essential for your success as a developer.

In this chapter, we also used some pretty unorthodox methods of storing and reading in data for use within the example API endpoints. There is good reason for this. Normally, we would use more standardized data sources to host and retrieve entities, which is something we are going to explore in detail in the next chapter.

8
Integrating Minimal APIs with Data Sources

Despite us working with minimal APIs, an API would have to be even more minimal not to work with an external state, which is not to say that it doesn't happen. For example, an API might be in place to simply perform a calculation or validate data, which, on their own, are not necessarily use cases that require some kind of managed data.

However, it is fair to say that a wide range of production APIs have some element of **create, read, update, delete** (**CRUD**) functionality. In the examples shown in previous chapters, such as the `Employee` API and the `Todo Item` API, we have referred to entities or objects, all of which would be potentially created, updated, deleted, or retrieved. The examples we explored stored these domain objects in memory, meaning that they would disappear with the application when it is stopped. It is now time to move that data into an external data source, where it can be persisted and managed separately from the minimal APIs we write.

We will explore two fundamental methods of moving data between data sources in this book. Firstly, in this chapter, we will explore direct database connections with the `SqlConnection` type in addition to MongoDB Driver for SQL and NoSQL database types, respectively. The next chapter will cover the second method, which is **object-relational mapping** (**ORM**). Each method has its own configuration requirements.

In this chapter, we're going to cover the following main topics:

- Understanding data integration in minimal APIs
- Connecting to SQL Server with `SQLConnection`
- Connecting to a NoSQL database with a MongoDB Driver

Technical requirements

This chapter is quite hands-on, using several different technologies. As a result, you will need the following to be installed on your machine:

- Visual Studio 2022
- Microsoft SQL Server 2022 Developer Edition
- Microsoft SQL Server Management Studio
- MongoDB Community Server
- MongoDB Compass

You will need to download and install all of the listed software. Installation for all products is wizard-based, so follow each of the wizards until you have them installed.

You might already have Visual Studio 2022 installed if you have been following along with the code examples in previous chapters.

If you have been using Visual Studio Code, it is recommended that you now switch to Visual Studio 2022.

Alternatively, you can host your SQL and MongoDB servers on a cloud platform, such as Microsoft Azure or **Amazon Web Services** (**AWS**). Please note that the configuration and deployment of these data sources in the cloud are outside of the scope of this book.

The code for this chapter is available in the GitHub repository at: `https://github.com/PacktPublishing/Minimal-APIs-in-ASP.NET-9`

Understanding data integration in minimal APIs

In the first chapter, we defined APIs and their purpose. It is worth reiterating this definition in relation to data sources. APIs act as a gateway to a system, offering programmatic access to that system.

In many cases, the objective of a client connecting to a system via an API is to work with data. That data has to be stored somewhere – preferably a source separate from the API itself so that it can be externally managed and persistent.

minimal APIs offer various connection methods to data sources. For the purposes of this chapter, we are going to focus on the most common persistent data storage types, those being **SQL** and **NoSQL**.

> **SQL versus NoSQL**
> It's highly likely that as a reader of this book, you are at least somewhat familiar with SQL and NoSQL, but by way of a brief primer, SQL databases are relational databases, meaning that data is stored in a collection of tables, with records represented by rows and columns in each table. NoSQL is less structured than SQL in that the data can be stored in various formats, including documents, key-value pairs, column families, or graphs. Data is stored in these various formats in collections of entities.

There are many SQL and NoSQL products to choose from, with the mainstream ones outlined in *Table 8.1*:

Relational Databases	NoSQL Databases
MySQL	Mongo DB (document store)
PostgreSQL	Cassandra (column family store)
Microsoft SQL Server	Redis (key-value store)
Oracle Database	DynamoDB (key-value store)
SQLite	CouchDB (document store)
MariaDB	Cosmos DB (multi-model database)

Table 8.1: Examples of mainstream database platforms

Regardless of whether the data stores are SQL- or NoSQL-based, there are numerous ways that minimal APIs can access them, with different design patterns that can be adopted to ensure the consistency and integrity of the data being managed between the database and the API.

We're going to start exploring data sources via minimal APIs with a direct connection to a SQL database.

Depending on your use case, the data connection method you choose is really important for optimal performance and security resilience, as is the way you manage connection lifetimes, the way queries are written, and how you pass parameters into commands and queries.

Direct SQL commands offer a lot of flexibility, as they act in the same way as they would if you had a database IDE open and you were writing queries in them. A connection is initiated to a database, a query or command is executed, and then the connection is disposed of.

Let us start by exploring direct connection methods. We will continue to use the example of the `Employee` API, first connecting to a Microsoft SQL database, and then connecting to a MongoDB instance (NoSQL).

Connecting to and integrating with SQL databases

We will start with an example that uses Microsoft SQL. First, open SQL Server Management Studio and create a database called `MyCompany`, with one table, `Employees`.

You can use the SQL script in the following code block to create the table with the relevant columns and data types for this example:

```
CREATE TABLE dbo.Employees
    (
    Id int NOT NULL IDENTITY (1, 1),
    Name varchar(MAX) NOT NULL,
```

```
    Salary decimal(10, 2) NOT NULL,
    Address varchar(MAX) NOT NULL,
    City varchar(50) NOT NULL,
    Region varchar(50) NOT NULL,
    Country varchar(50) NOT NULL,
    Phone varchar(200) NOT NULL,
    PostalCode varchar(10) NOT NULL
    )
```

In the `Employees` table, we have set the `Id` column as an identity column, meaning that it will be populated by SQL Server on insertion of any record, with the `Id` value incrementing by 1 on each insertion.

We now have everything we need to set up a connection to the database from our minimal API project.

Let us go back into the `Employee` API and set up the database connection.

Configuring the connection to the database and retrieving records

SQL databases use a **connection string** to allow access from a code base. In this case, I am using Windows Authentication with my local SQL server, so I can use a simple connection string that assumes the currently logged-in Windows user is able to access my SQL server. Alternatively, if you are using a SQL server, you will need to generate a slightly different connection string. The simplest way to form the connection string is to use the guides for Microsoft SQL servers found at https://connectionstrings.com, where (based on your authentication type) you can generate the appropriate string. The following code shows some simple examples of connection strings for each authentication type:

```
//Windows Auth (Trusted Connection)
Server=myServerAddress;
Database=myDataBase;
Trusted_Connection=True;
// SQL Server Authentication
Server=myServerAddress;
Database=myDataBase;
User Id=myUsername;
Password=myPassword;
```

Now that we have a connection string, we can store it somewhere within the API where it can be easily retrieved. A good place to do this would be in a configuration file, which is, by default, offered to us in the form of `appsettings.json`.

Open `appsettings.json` and add your connection string as shown (I am using SQL authentication in my JSON example, but you will need to add your Windows Authentication connection string if appropriate):

```
{
  "ConnectionStrings": {
      "DefaultConnection":
          "Server=localhost;Database=MyCompany;
          User Id=your_user;Password=your_password;"
  }
}
```

Your `appsettings.json` file may have extra template values when you create your project. For simplicity, when following this example, it might be best to overwrite the content of the existing `appsettings.json` file with the example content shown in the preceding code.

Next, we will create a service that will manage the interactions with the database. This service will be injected into our API endpoints using dependency injection (see *Chapter 7* for more details on dependency injection).

We will register the service as a **singleton**. Doing this allows us to cleanly specify that there should only be one instance of the service, meaning that any requests coming into the API will share that service. Let us first get started with the creation of this database service by creating a new interface called `IDatabaseService`. This interface will lay out the **contract** for any services that are created for the purposes of speaking to a database:

```
public interface IDatabaseService
{
    Task<IEnumerable<Employee>> GetEmployeesAsync();
    Task AddEmployeeAsync(Employee employee);
}
```

Don't worry if you see an error at this point stating that `Employee` isn't a known type. When it is created later, this error will clear.

We can now create our service in the form of a concrete class that implements `IDatabaseService`. Create the class, calling it `SQLService`.

Once the `SQLService` class has been created, add a constructor that receives `IConfiguration` as a parameter, saving its value to a local `readonly` field.

> **More on IConfiguration**
>
> `IConfiguration` is already registered for dependency injection in an ASP.NET application. It represents the content of `appsettings.json`.

This field will contain the connection string, and will allow it to be referenced in all queries and commands executed by the service, as shown here:

```
public class SqlService : IDatabaseService
{
    private readonly string _connectionString;

    public SqlService(IConfiguration configuration)
    {
        _connectionString =
            configuration.GetConnectionString(
                "DefaultConnection"
            );
    }
}
```

Next, we're going to finish off this service by adding the ability to add and retrieve employee records from the database.

We will use the same `Employee` class that we added in the examples from previous chapters. As a convenient reminder, this code block shows the `Employee` class that will act as the model for the database records:

```
public class Employee
{
    public int Id { get; set; }
    public string Name { get; set; }
    public decimal Salary { get; set; }
    public string Address { get; set; }
    public string City { get; set; }
    public string Region { get; set; }
    public string PostalCode { get; set; }
    public string Country { get; set; }
    public string Phone { get; set; }

}
```

You will be seeing errors by now (in the Visual Studio error list, and in the form of red lines under the code) stating that the class does not fully implement the `IDatabaseService` interface. We should add the two functions specified in the interface to the `SqlService` class to correct this.

Let's start with `GetEmployeesAsync()`. The aim of this function is to return a list containing all the employees in the database. Start by creating the function definition and, in the body, instantiate a new `Employee` list:

```
public async Task<IEnumerable<Employee>>
    GetEmployeesAsync()
{
    var employees = new List<Employee>();
}
```

Before going further, make sure you add the `Microsoft.Data.SqlClient` NuGet package, as this will be required. You can do this by going to **Tools | Manage NuGet Packages | Package Manager Console**, and then typing the following:

```
dotnet add package Microsoft.Data.SqlClient
```

Next, we will open a new connection to SQL Server using `SqlConnection`. By wrapping the instance in a `using` statement, we are ensuring that once the control flow has exited the body of the `using` statement, the connection is automatically disposed of, thanks to `SqlConnection` implementing `IDisposable`:

```
using (var connection = new
    SqlConnection(_connectionString))
{
    await connection.OpenAsync();
}
```

At this point, you have a connection open that will be automatically disposed of. This is good because we're responsibly managing the use of an external resource.

Next, inside the `using` statement, another `using` statement is added, but this time, for the creation of a `SqlCommand` object. This `SqlCommand` object represents the query we wish to execute, targeting the connection we now have open:

```
using (var command = new
    SqlCommand("SELECT * FROM Employees", connection))
{

}
```

Following this, we nest another `using` statement inside this one. This creates `SqlDataReader`, reading any returned rows from the query in `SqlCommand`, creating a new `Employee` instance for each record, and adding it to the list:

```
using (var reader = await command.ExecuteReaderAsync())
{
```

```csharp
        while (await reader.ReadAsync())
        {
            var employee = new Employee
            {
                Id = reader.GetInt32(0),
                Name = reader.GetString(1),
                Salary = reader.GetDecimal(2),
                Address = reader.GetString(3),
                City = reader.GetString(4),
                Region = reader.GetString(5),
                PostalCode = reader.GetString(6),
                Country = reader.GetString(7),
                Phone = reader.GetString(8)
            };
            employees.Add(employee);
        }
    }
```

Finally, we can finish the function by returning the list of type `Employee`, meaning the finished function looks like the following:

```csharp
public async Task<IEnumerable<Employee>>
    GetEmployeesAsync()
{
    var employees = new List<Employee>();

    using (var connection = new
        SqlConnection(_connectionString))
    {
        await connection.OpenAsync();

        using (var command = new SqlCommand(
            "SELECT * FROM Employees", connection))
        {
            using (var reader = await
                command.ExecuteReaderAsync())
            {
                while (await reader.ReadAsync())
                {
                    var employee = new Employee
                    {
                        Id = reader.GetInt32(0),
                        Name = reader.GetString(1),
                        Salary = reader.GetDecimal(2),
```

```
                        Address = reader.GetString(3),
                        City = reader.GetString(4),
                        Region = reader.GetString(5),
                        PostalCode = reader.GetString(6),
                        Country = reader.GetString(7),
                        Phone = reader.GetString(8)
                    };

                    employees.Add(employee);
                }
            }
        }
    }

    return employees;
}
```

Take a look at the `SqlCommand` usage in the previous code. Notice how we don't build the SQL command string using concatenation, passing in the values from `Employee` as part of the string being put together. Instead, the best practice is to use SQL parameters. Parameterized queries allow us to guard against a security vulnerability called SQL injection.

In a SQL injection attack, a malicious value is passed in as a value, which can alter the originally intended behavior of a command. By passing in parameters, we avoid this, with parameters represented by the @ character in the command string and added to the `SqlCommand` after the string is formed (we see this in the next section).

Inserting Employee records

We have now completed our first connection to SQL with a transaction. Armed with this knowledge, we can also create the `AddEmployeeAsync()` function. The connection method is the same but the command is different, with `INSERT` being used instead of `SELECT`:

```
public async Task AddEmployeeAsync(Employee employee)
{
    using (var connection = new
        SqlConnection(_connectionString))
    {
        await connection.OpenAsync();

        using (var command = new SqlCommand(
            "INSERT INTO Employees (Name, Salary, " +
            "Address, City, Region, Country, Phone, " +
            "PostalCode) VALUES (@Name, @Salary, " +
```

```
                    @Address, @City, @Region, @Country, " +
                    @Phone, @PostalCode)", " +
                    connection))
            {
                command.Parameters.AddWithValue(
                    "@Name", employee.Name);
                command.Parameters.AddWithValue(
                    "@Salary", employee.Salary);
                command.Parameters.AddWithValue(
                    "@Address", employee.Address);
                command.Parameters.AddWithValue(
                    "@City", employee.City);
                command.Parameters.AddWithValue(
                    "@Region", employee.Region);
                command.Parameters.AddWithValue(
                    "@Country", employee.Country);
                command.Parameters.AddWithValue(
                    "@Phone", employee.Phone);
                command.Parameters.AddWithValue(
                    "@PostalCode", employee.PostalCode);

                await command.ExecuteNonQueryAsync();
            }
        }
    }
}
```

Let us now turn our attention to the minimal API endpoints.

Executing database transactions from API endpoints

These endpoints will need to have the SQL service injected into them in order for them to be used in the endpoint body.

Go back to `Program.cs` and register the service as a singleton:

```
var builder = WebApplication.CreateBuilder(args);
builder.Services.AddSingleton<IDatabaseService,
SqlLService>(); var app = builder.Build();
```

Because we have created a service for managing interaction with the SQL server and we have made it easily available through dependency injection, getting and creating employees from minimal API endpoints is very easy. Simply add a `GET` endpoint for retrieval and a `POST` endpoint for creation, adding calls to the appropriate functions we created in `SqlService`:

```
app.MapGet(
    "/employees",
    async (IDatabaseService dbService) =>
{
    var employees = await dbService.GetEmployeesAsync();
    return Results.Ok(employees);
});

app.MapPost(
    "/employees",
    async (IDatabaseService dbService,
        Employee employee) =>
{
    await dbService.AddEmployeeAsync(employee);
    return Results.Created(
        $"/employees/{employee.Id}", employee);
});
```

Give the new endpoints a try. If successful, you should be able to retrieve the employees in the data source as a list or add new employees via the API.

As alluded to earlier in the chapter, because we have created an interface, we should be able to swap out the service for one that uses a different data source without having to change the endpoint. This leads us nicely to an example of a database connection to a NoSQL database.

Connecting to MongoDB

For demonstrative purposes, we will connect to **MongoDB**, a widely used NoSQL database platform.

Before we create the service, we should first add some data to a MongoDB database. As per the technical requirements, you should have installed a MongoDB server, along with **MongoDB Compass**, a **graphical user interface** (**GUI**) for MongoDB.

Start by opening MongoDB Compass and creating a connection to your installed MongoDB server instance. If you've installed MongoDB locally without modifying the installation, you should be able to just click **Connect**:

Integrating Minimal APIs with Data Sources

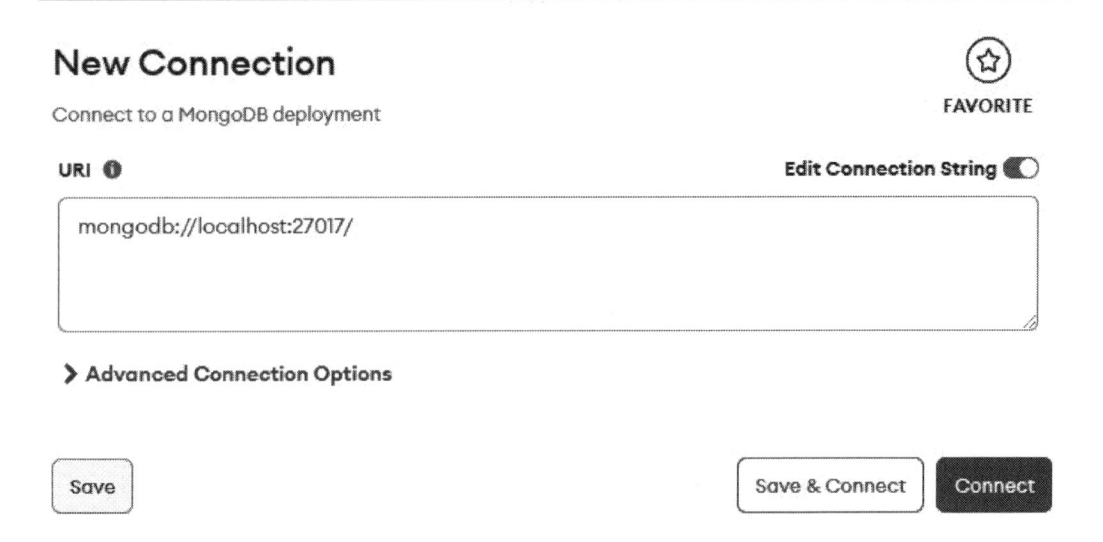

Figure 8.1: Creating a new MongoDB connection

Once connected, you will be able to see the existing databases on your server:

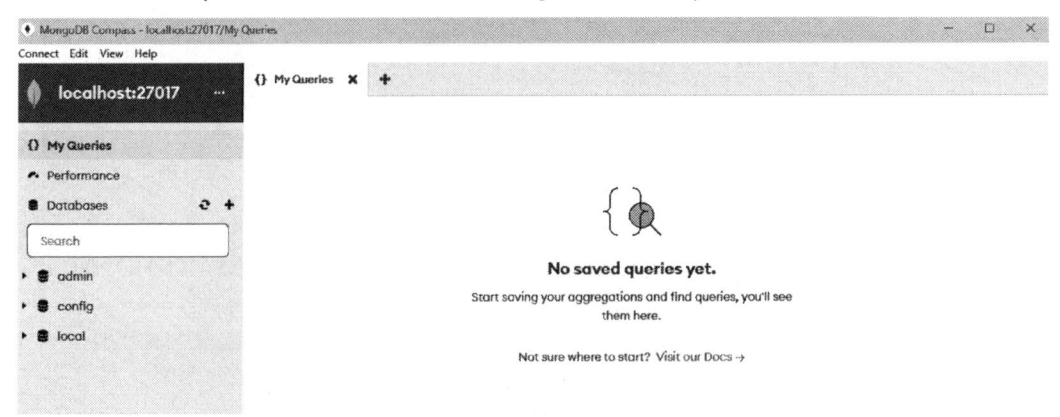

Figure 8.2: View of existing MongoDB connections

In the navigation bar on the left-hand side, click the plus icon to add a new database. Once again, we will call the database `MyCompany`. Compass will also require you to create a collection. Just as we created an `Employees` table in our SQL database, we will create an `Employees` collection in MongoDB:

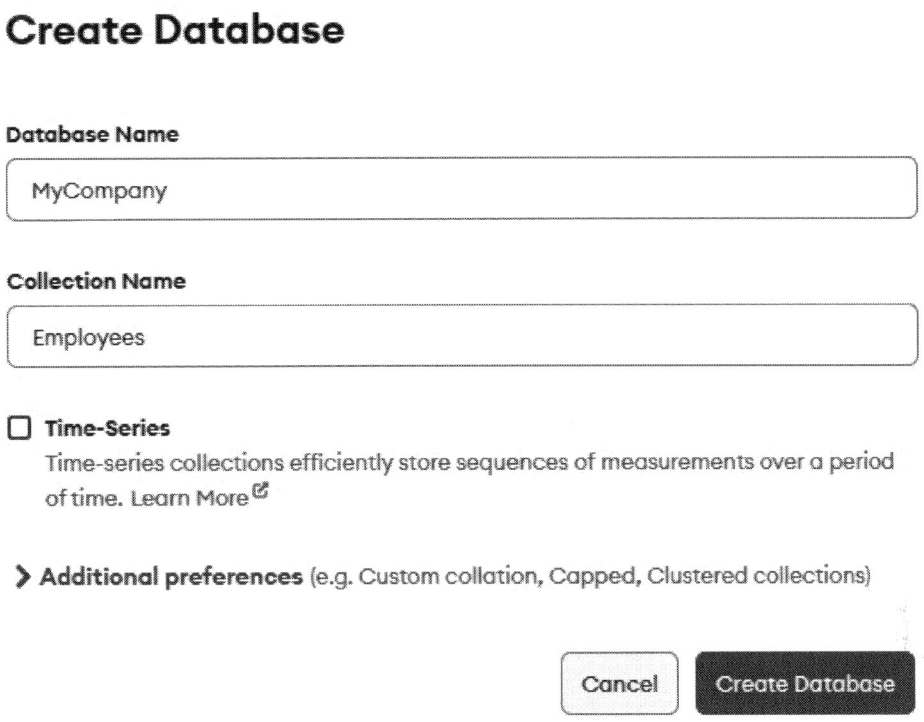

Create Database

Database Name

MyCompany

Collection Name

Employees

☐ **Time-Series**
Time-series collections efficiently store sequences of measurements over a period of time. Learn More

> Additional preferences (e.g. Custom collation, Capped, Clustered collections)

Cancel   Create Database

Figure 8.3: MongoDB Database creation in Compass

Notice how we haven't been specified a schema for the `Employees` collection. This is because the collection is document-based. We can import data in JSON format, which mirrors the `Employee` class in our API.

Create a couple of fake employees and save them to a local JSON file. Here is some example JSON to get you started:

```
[
    {
        "Id": 1,
        "Name": "John Doe",
        "Salary": 55000.75,
        "Address": "123 Elm Street",
        "City": "Springfield",
        "Region": "IL",
        "PostalCode": "62701",
        "Country": "USA",
        "Phone": "555-1234"
    },
```

```
    {
        "Id": 2,
        "Name": "Jane Smith",
        "Salary": 62000.50,
        "Address": "456 Oak Avenue",
        "City": "Metropolis",
        "Region": "NY",
        "PostalCode": "10001",
        "Country": "USA",
        "Phone": "555-5678"
    }
]
```

Once you've saved the JSON file, you can import it into the `Employees` collection in MongoDB Compass:

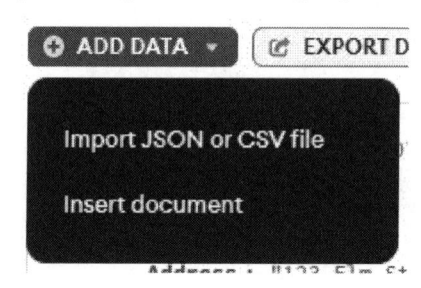

Figure 8.4: Importing data into a MongoDB database in Compass

Our MongoDB collection is now set up with example data. Let us turn our attention back to the minimal API, where we will write a new service to interact with this NoSQL database.

First, we'll need to install the MongoDB driver in order to support interactions with a MongoDB database. You can do this via the **Package Manager Console** in Visual Studio:

```
dotnet add package MongoDB.Driver
```

Create a new class called `MongoDbService`, implementing the `IDatabaseService` interface. Make sure you reference `MongoDB.Bson` and `MongoDB.Driver`:

```
using MongoDB.Bson;
using MongoDB.Driver;
using System.Collections.Generic;
using System.Threading.Tasks;

public class MongoDbService : IDatabaseService
{

}
```

Next, we will create a constructor that, as before, receives an injected `IConfiguration` object containing the database connection string, before initiating the connection with an instance of `MongoClient`.

Following this, a reference to the collection of type, `Employee` can be retrieved and stored in a `private` field:

```
private readonly IMongoCollection<Employee>
    _employeesCollection;

    public MongoDbService(IConfiguration configuration)
    {
        var connectionString =
            configuration.GetConnectionString(
                "MongoDbConnection");
        var mongoClient = new
            MongoClient(connectionString);
        var mongoDatabase =
            mongoClient.GetDatabase("MyCompany");
        _employeesCollection =
            mongoDatabase.GetCollection<Employee>(
                "Employees");
    }
```

Next, complete the implementation of the `IDatabaseService` interface by adding the required functions. These functions can simply utilize the `Employee` collection for querying and inserting records:

```
public async Task<IEnumerable<Employee>>
    GetEmployeesAsync()
    {
        return await _employeesCollection
            .Find(new BsonDocument())
            .ToListAsync();
    }

    public async Task AddEmployeeAsync(Employee employee)
    {
        await _employeesCollection
            .InsertOneAsync(employee);
    }
```

The connection string needs to be changed to point to the MongoDB server and database. MongoDB connection strings are fairly simple in format. By default, the server should be running on port `27017`. Here is how a default connection string would look for this configuration:

```
mongodb://localhost:27017/MyCompany
```

This connection string can then be added to the `ConnectionStrings` object in `appsettings.json`. We should also add a Boolean flag to the JSON that allows us to specify whether MongoDB should be used, or whether the default SQL connection should be adopted.

Once complete, the `ConnectionStrings` section of `appsettings.json` should look like the example shown here:

```json
"UseMongoDB": true,
"ConnectionStrings": {
    "DefaultConnection":
        "Server=.\\SQLEXPRESS;Database=MyCompany;
        Trusted_Connection=True;
        TrustServerCertificate=True;",
    "MongoDbConnection":
        "mongodb://localhost:27017/MyCompany"
}
```

Having added a new data source connection string and an option to switch from the default source to MongoDB, we must register the new `MongoDbService` class for dependency injection. We will, however, also need to specify a new rule for how the dependency is resolved depending on whether the `UseMongoDB` flag is enabled or not.

Back in `Program.cs`, register the new `MongoDbService` class

```csharp
builder.Services.AddSingleton<MongoDbService>();
```

Next, add the following singleton registration for `IDatabaseService`, along with logic that checks the MongoDB flag in `appsettings.json` before resolving the correct database service to be used:

```csharp
builder.Services.AddSingleton<IDatabaseService>(sp =>
{
    var config = sp.GetRequiredService<IConfiguration>();
    var useMongoDB = config.GetValue<bool>("UseMongoDB");

    if (useMongoDB)
    {
        return sp.GetRequiredService<MongoDbService>();
    }
    else
    {
        return sp.GetRequiredService<SqlService>();
    }
});
```

You might not have realized it yet if you haven't run the code, but we have a problem.

The aim of using an interface for `IDatabaseService` was to ensure that we could easily switch between data sources by modifying a Boolean flag in `appsettings.json`.

This would be fine if the data structures in the two data sources had identical schemas. Unfortunately, they don't because, in SQL Server, `Id` is an `int` type, whereas, in MongoDB, the equivilent identifier is called `_id` and its data type is a string.

This means that as it exists currently, `Employee` is interchangeable between the two sources. This means that if we switch to MongoDB and try to deserialize data to `Employee`, it will fail with `FormatException` due to the differing data type.

To fix this, we should create separate models for different data sources. This sounds like it goes against the idea of having a flexible system, but we can still ensure that we don't have to modify existing endpoints for different data sources by using another interface.

Create a new interface called `IEmployee`. It does not require any fields at the moment:

```
public interface IEmployee
{
}
```

We can use this interface to represent an employee model generically, regardless of whether it is a SQL Server model or a MongoDB model.

Create a new model called `EmployeeMongoDb` and set it up as shown here:

```
using MongoDB.Bson;
using MongoDB.Bson.Serialization.Attributes;

{
    public class EmployeeMongoDb : IEmployee
    {
        [BsonId]
        [BsonRepresentation(
            MongoDB.Bson.BsonType.ObjectId)]
        public string Id { get; set; }
        public string Name { get; set; }
        public decimal Salary { get; set; }
        public string Address { get; set; }
        public string City { get; set; }
        public string Region { get; set; }
        public string PostalCode { get; set; }
        public string Country { get; set; }
        public string Phone { get; set; }
    }
}
```

By adding the attributes shown in the previous code to the `Id` field, we are mapping `Id` to the string-based `_id` field in the MongoDB collection. We have also implemented `IEmployee`.

We will treat `Employee` as the default model, seeing as SQL Server is the default connection string in `appsettings.json`. Ensure that it also implements `IEmployee`.

Now, we must change any area in the MongoDB service or SQL service that returns a concrete class to instead return `IEmployee`. You'll also need to change any code that receives `Employee` as an argument. This then requires the service to cast `IEmployee` to a compatible concrete implementation, such as `EmployeeMongoDb` for the MongoDb service.

Changes to both `SqlServerService` and `MongoDbService` can be seen in the following code:

```
private readonly IMongoCollection<EmployeeMongoDb>
    _employeesCollection;

public MongoDbService(IConfiguration configuration)
{
    var connectionString =
        configuration.GetConnectionString(
            "MongoDbConnection");
    var mongoClient = new MongoClient(connectionString);
    var mongoDatabase =
        mongoClient.GetDatabase("MyCompany");
    _employeesCollection =
        mongoDatabase.GetCollection<EmployeeMongoDb>(
            "Employees");
}
```

Continuing the previous code, we add the `GetEmployeesAsync()` and `AddEmployeeAsync()` methods using MongoDB. Notice how, in the `AddEmployeeAsync()` method, we can still take in `IEmployee` but then simply convert it to an `EmployeeMongoDb` object so that MongoDB can take care of generating a `string` ID, unlike the `int` ID used in SQL Server:

```
public async Task<IEnumerable<IEmployee>>
    GetEmployeesAsync()
{
    var result = await _employeesCollection
        .Find(new BsonDocument())
        .ToListAsync();
    return result;
}

public async Task AddEmployeeAsync(IEmployee employee)
```

```
{
    var employeeToAdd = new EmployeeMongoDb
{
    Name = employee.Name,
    Salary = employee.Salary,
    Address = employee.Address,
    City = employee.City,
    Region = employee.Region,
    PostalCode = employee.PostalCode,
    Country = employee.Country,
    Phone = employee.Phone
};
    await _employeesCollection
        .InsertOneAsync(employeeToAdd);
}
```

The following method shows the same code using SQL Server:

```
// GetEmployeesAsync only needs the return type to be
// changed
public async Task<IEnumerable<IEmployee>>
    GetEmployeesAsync()



public async Task AddEmployeeAsync(IEmployee employee)
{

    var employeeToAdd = (Employee)employee;
    using (var connection = new
        SqlConnection(_connectionString))
    {
        await connection.OpenAsync();

        using (var command = new SqlCommand(
            "INSERT INTO Employees (Name, Salary, " +
            Address, City, Region, Country, Phone, " +
            PostalCode) VALUES (@Name, @Salary, " +
            @Address, @City, @Region, @Country, " +
            @Phone, @PostalCode)", " +
            connection))
        {
            command.Parameters.AddWithValue(
                "@Name", employeeToAdd.Name);
```

```
                    command.Parameters.AddWithValue(
                        "@Salary", employeeToAdd.Salary);
                    command.Parameters.AddWithValue(
                        "@Address", employeeToAdd.Address);
                    command.Parameters.AddWithValue(
                        "@City", employeeToAdd.City);
                    command.Parameters.AddWithValue(
                        "@Region", employeeToAdd.Region);
                    command.Parameters.AddWithValue(
                        "@Country", employeeToAdd.Country);
                    command.Parameters.AddWithValue(
                        "@Phone", employeeToAdd.Phone);
                    command.Parameters.AddWithValue(
                        "@PostalCode", employeeToAdd.PostalCode);

                    await command.ExecuteNonQueryAsync();
                }
            }
        }
```

Because `Employee` and `EmployeeMongoDb` both implement `IEmployee`, the endpoint logic no longer has to change. We are preserving genericness at the highest level of abstraction, while dealing with more concrete classes lower down the abstraction layer within the services.

> **Open-closed principle**
>
> The changes we have made using interfaces help us adhere to the open-closed principle, where we aim to allow new data sources to be added in the future without having to alter the original code base invasively. We will discuss this principle in more detail in *Chapter 13*.

This was quite an intense chapter, so let's review what we've covered before moving on.

Summary

In this chapter, we have covered some basic examples of direct communication with a database from minimal API endpoints.

We started by defining the different kinds of databases, with examples of various SQL- and NoSQL-based database platforms.

Following this, we talked about how using services with dependency injection can allow minimal API projects to seamlessly provide minimal API endpoints with interoperability with our chosen data source.

Summary

We created a service that interacts with a SQL Server database, using `appsettings.json` to define the specific properties of our data source for use in the service. We leveraged the functionality of `SqlConnection` and `SqlCommand` to execute commands and queries against the SQL Server database containing relational employee data.

Next, we created a counterpart service that interacts with MongoDB, demonstrating the differences between `SqlCommand` and the MongoDB driver.

Finally, we modified the project using interfaces to make differing data source models interchangeable, while preserving the generic style of the API endpoint code.

In the next chapter, we will take our exploration of data sources further by implementing two ORMs within the `Employee` API – Dapper and Entity Framework Core.

9
Object Relational Mapping with Entity Framework Core and Dapper

In the previous chapter, we used direct connections to SQL and NoSQL databases to create and retrieve data, a staple of most APIs.

In reality, a large segment of APIs based on .NET favor the use of **Object Relation Mapping** (**ORM**) to converse with databases over the direct connection method. This is because ORMs offer another layer of abstraction over the underlying data, promoting SOLID design principles while being conducive to scalability and easy long-term maintenance.

In this chapter, we are going to explore two of the mainstream ORM frameworks – Entity Framework Core and Dapper. With these two technologies, we will be able to map the entities in our database and manage them as if the data was contained within the classes that make up our minimal API project.

We will cover the following main topics:

- Introduction to ORMs
- Configuring Dapper in minimal API projects
- Performing CRUD operations with Dapper
- Configuring Entity Framework in minimal API projects
- Performing CRUD operations with Entity Framework

Technical requirements

You will need the following software to be installed on your machine:

- Visual Studio 2022 or Visual Studio Code
- Microsoft SQL Server 2022 Developer Edition
- Microsoft SQL Server Management Studio

You will need to create a database in SQL Server (`MyCompany`). The SQL to create the required `Employees` table was provided in the previous chapter, but I will also include it in this chapter.

The code for this chapter is available in the GitHub repository at: `https://github.com/PacktPublishing/Minimal-APIs-in-ASP.NET-9`.

Introduction to ORMs

ORMs were first introduced in the 1990s to address the mismatch between the way data is modeled in relational databases such as SQL and **Object-Oriented Programming** (**OOP**) languages, often referred to as the **Impedance Mismatch**.

Data in a *relational database* is laid out in a series of tables, each with a number of columns defining the property of each record, which in turn is represented by a row in the table. The relationships between entities in a relational database are represented by *foreign keys* and *join* operations that occur during a query.

In contrast, data in an *OOP language* is represented as objects that have fields, properties, and operational logic such as methods and functions that can act on the data. Relationships between objects in OOP are more abstract, represented by pointer references and concepts such as inheritance and polymorphism.

An ORM bridges the gap between these two paradigms by providing a means of mapping the data, which allows us to work with database records as if they were objects. This provides a layer of abstraction that simplifies the complexities of SQL, making it easier to perform **Create**, **Read**, **Update**, **Delete** (**CRUD**) operations.

There are many, widely used ORMs on offer for various OOP languages and frameworks. The first widely used ORM was **TopLink**. Developed in 1994, it was designed to provide mapping for Java applications, influencing many of the ORM technologies we take for granted today, such as the two we will be exploring in this chapter – Dapper and Entity Framework.

ORMs are a significant accelerator to any project, but particularly to minimal API projects. They reduce boilerplate code in ASP.NET because they can be easily installed as a package, and configuration can be achieved centrally, with queries and commands requiring less ceremony than direct SQL connections that use classes such as `SqlConnection` and `SqlCommand`.

One of the most powerful aspects of ORMs is the ability for them to manage the schema of the underlying database. Objects can be of course mapped from an existing database, but ORMs provide the ability to manage the database structure in the same way classes are configured in code.. This makes schema management really simple and more efficient because developers would be altering class structures anyway. It prevents *double keying*, taking advantage of the work that has already been done in code to automate the dependent changes in the database.

If you read the previous chapter, you'll remember that we created a database called `MyCompany` to use as an example for connecting directly from our API. We will continue to use this database, but instead, we will map the objects within it using ORMs. Let's first do this using the ORM, Dapper.

Configuring Dapper in minimal API projects

I'm starting with Dapper because it is an ORM that is often referred to as a *Micro-ORM* when compared to Entity Framework. The reason for this is that it does away with a lot of ORM features such as result caching, change tracking, lazy loading, and database migrations. Instead, Dapper focuses on simplicity and performance. Being a more lightweight solution means that it could be preferable to Entity Framework, depending on the needs of your minimal API.

Dapper is a good starting point for learning ORMs because it still uses SQL queries, making it the perfect middle-ground between the direct connection method shown in the previous chapter and the more verbose ORM feature set provided by Entity Framework.

> **Database migrations and Dapper**
>
> The last differentiating feature (database migrations) is an important one because it relates to the ability to change the schema of a database. We will talk about migrations later in the chapter when we explore Entity Framework, but for now, know that database migrations change the database schema from our code, and Dapper does not support this via migrations. However, you can still change the table schema by sending SQL commands through Dapper. This is outside of the scope of this chapter.

Dapper works with many database providers, including SQL Server, Oracle, SQLite, MySQL, and PostgreSQL. It uses ADO.NET, meaning that it will work with any database platform that has a provider using ADO.NET. Because we are using the database we created in the previous chapter, we will be connecting to a SQL Server database.

Let's create a new (empty) ASP.NET project in Visual Studio so that we have a clean slate to work on.

Once you have created the project, navigate to `Program.cs`, which should have the template `Hello World` example.

To start with, we need a database to connect to. If you followed along with the previous chapter, you will have installed a SQL Server instance and created a database called `MyCompany`. If you haven't done this already, install SQL Server and create the database within SQL Server Management Studio.

Once you have a database, if you don't yet have the `Employees` table, you can use the following SQL to create one:

```sql
CREATE TABLE dbo.Employees
    (
    Id int NOT NULL IDENTITY (1, 1),
    Name varchar(MAX) NOT NULL,
    Salary decimal(10, 2) NOT NULL,
    Address varchar(MAX) NOT NULL,
    City varchar(50) NOT NULL,
    Region varchar(50) NOT NULL,
    Country varchar(50) NOT NULL,
    Phone varchar(200) NOT NULL
    PostalCode varchar(50) NOT NULL,
    )
```

Dapper uses providers to facilitate the connection to the target database platform. For SQL Server, the required providers are the same as for direct connections to SQL Server from C#: `Microsoft.Data.SqlClient`.

Install `Microsoft.Data.SqlClient`, either from the `NuGet` package manager GUI or in the Package Manager Console by running the following:

```
Install-Package Microsoft.Data.SqlClient
```

While we're installing `NuGet` packages, we also need to install the `Dapper` package. You can do this in the package manager console by running the following:

```
Install-Package Dapper
```

We could technically start writing queries now, directly within our minimal API endpoints, but for consistency and good practice, we should create a new service specifically for Dapper and register it for dependency injection. Create a class called `DapperService`. As we did in the previous chapter for `SQLService` and `MongoDbService`, we will register this class as a singleton in `Program.cs`. Ensure you register the service before `app.Run();`:

```
builder.Services.AddSingleton<DapperService>();
```

We have now configured the project to use Dapper on a SQL Server database using dependency injection with the relevant provider, and we have created a database to work with, meaning that we can proceed with performing our first CRUD operations from our minimal API.

Performing CRUD operations with Dapper

Let's work our way through each of the aspects of CRUD in Dapper with some examples. First of all, let's create an employee.

Creating an Employee record

First, we will create an endpoint that creates an employee. That means we'll be using the POST method:

1. Go to `Program.cs` and map a POST endpoint to the `employees` route. It should accept an `Employee` as a parameter, and it should inject `DapperService`:

   ```
   app.MapPost(
       "/employees",
       (Employee employee,
       [FromServices] DapperService dapperService) =>
   {

   });
   ```

2. Next, we can create a method within `DapperService` that handles the creation of the employee in the database (this is where we get to use Dapper).

3. Open `DapperService.cs` and create a method called `AddEmployee`:

   ```
   public async Task AddEmployee(Employee employee)
   {

   }
   ```

   Like the direct connection examples from the previous chapter, Dapper uses `SqlConnection` to connect to a SQL Server. Inside the scope of that connection, you need to write the appropriate query for the action you want to take. Because we're creating an `employee`, we will be adding a new record to the database and so we will write an `INSERT` statement.

4. Make a `using` statement to hold the connection to the database (remember, `using` statements allow the connection to be automatically disposed of) and add the connection string to your database.

5. Follow this up by defining a string that represents the `INSERT` statement:

   ```
   using (var sqlConnection = new
       SqlConnection("YOURCONNECTIONSTRING"))
   {
       var sql = "INSERT INTO Employees " +
                 "(Name, Salary, Address, City, " +
                 "Region, "Country, Phone) VALUES " +
                 "(@Name, @Salary, @Address, @City, " +
                 "@Region, @Country, @Phone)";
   }
   ```

   Notice how the `INSERT` statement must contain all the relevant columns and values as parameters for those columns.

6. Next, we will use Dapper to commit the database transaction against the instantiated `SqlConnection`. We can use `ExecuteAsync()`, a Dapper extension method that will execute the statement while mapping the properties from the `Employee` object that we passed into this the `AddEmployee()` method:

```
await sqlConnection.ExecuteAsync(sql, new
{
    employee.PostalCode,
    employee.Name,
    employee.Salary,
    employee.Address,
    employee.City,
    employee.Region,
    employee.Country,
    employee.Phone
});
```

We now have a method on `DapperService` that can receive an `Employee` parameter and commit it to the database via Dapper, as shown here:

```
public class DapperService
{
    public async Task AddEmployee(Employee employee)
    {
        using (var sqlConnection = new
            SqlConnection("YOURCONNECTIONSTRING"))
        {
            var sql = "INSERT INTO Employees " +
                (Name, Salary, Address, City, " +
                Region, Country, Phone) VALUES " +
                (@Name, @Salary, @Address, " +
                @City, @Region, @Country, @Phone)";

            await sqlConnection.ExecuteAsync(sql, new
            {
                employee.PostalCode,
                employee.Name,
                employee.Salary,
                employee.Address,
                employee.City,
                employee.Region,
                employee.Country,
                employee.Phone
```

```
            });
        }
    }
}
```

7. All that remains now is to call this method in the `POST` endpoint we started writing in `Program.cs`, before returning an `HTTP 201 CREATED` status code to the client:

```
app.MapPost(
    "/employees",
    async (Employee employee,
           [FromServices] DapperService dapperService)
        =>
{
    await dapperService.AddEmployee(employee);
    return Results.Created();
});
```

That's taken care of the *Create* part of CRUD.

> **Storing and referencing connection strings**
>
> In the previous chapter, I demonstrated how you can follow best practices by storing connection strings in a configuration file and then referencing them via `IConfiguration`.
>
> If you haven't already done so, please refer to this in the previous chapter so that you can implement it for Dapper and Entity Framework usage.

Let's move on to the *Read* part now.

Reading an Employee record

The *Read* part will entail having a `GET` endpoint on top of a `SELECT` query on the database:

1. Start by adding a `GET` endpoint to `Program.cs`, mapped to the `Employees` route. It should have a route parameter called `id` that is passed through the body of the lambda expression inside the endpoint, and it should inject `DapperService`:

```
app.MapGet(
    "/employees/{id}",
    (int id,
      [FromServices] DapperService dapperService) =>
{

});
```

2. Next, we're going to take the same approach we took in the last example by making a new function in `DapperService`, but this time, instead of inserting, it will run a `SELECT` query to get the employee for the specified `id`, before returning it to the endpoint:

```
public async Task<Employee>
    GetEmployeeById(int id)
{
    using (var sqlConnection = new
        SqlConnection("YOURCONNECTIONSTRING"))
    {
        var sql = "SELECT * FROM Employees
            WHERE Id = @employeeId";
        var result = await sqlConnection
            .QuerySingleAsync<Employee>(
                sql, new { employeeId = id });
        return result;
    }
}
```

`QuerySingleAsync<Employee>()` is where the Dapper code comes in. Like before, this is a Dapper extension method that allows us to execute a SQL query, with the expectation that one record will be returned, that record being an employee.

3. Notice the parameters being sent in. We passed the SQL query, but then we passed a new instance of an object array. This is the value for the `@employeeId` parameter that we declared in the SQL query. Dapper expects us to pass our parameter values in as an array of objects so that their values can be mapped to the relevant parameters in the query.

4. We also called a specific extension method – `QuerySingleAsync()`. The reason for this is obvious – we only want one record. If you want more, there are functions such as `Query()` that will return an `IEnumerable` containing many records.

5. Finally, we once again simply call the function in `DapperService` from the endpoint, returning the result to the client:

```
app.MapGet(
    "/employees/{id}",
    async (int id,
        [FromServices] DapperService dapperService)
        =>
{
    return Results.Ok(
        await dapperService.GetEmployeeById(id));
});
```

Next, let's look at how we can *update* an employee record.

Updating an Employee record

We're two letters into CRUD now. Let's take a look now at Update by taking the same approach – creating a PUT endpoint and connecting it to DapperService:

```
app.MapPut(
    "/employees",
     async (Employee employee,
            [FromServices] DapperService dapperService) =>
{
    await dapperService.UpdateEmployee(employee);
    return Results.Ok();
});
```

Then, we create a function that performs the update against the database:

```
        public async Task UpdateEmployee (
            Employee employee)
        {
            using (var sqlConnection = new
                SqlConnection("YOURCONNECTIONSTRING"))
            {
                var sql = "UPDATE Employees SET Name = " +
                @Name, Salary = @Salary, Address = " +
                @Address, City = @City, " +
                Region = @Region WHERE Id = @id";


                var parameters = new
                {
                    employee.Id,
                    employee.Name,
                    employee.Salary,
                    employee.Address,
                    employee.City,
                    employee.Region
                };

                await sqlConnection.ExecuteAsync(
                    sql, parameters);
            }

        }
```

Notice how the code we've added to update the record in `DapperService` is similar to the code we added to create a record. The main difference is the SQL string. Otherwise, we're still passing in an `Employee` object and mapping its properties to the record in the database via Dapper.

Deleting an Employee record

Finally, we've reached the final section of CRUD – `Delete`.

We'll follow the same principle we've applied in all the operations up to this point, but this time I'm going to start by adding the functionality to `DapperService` for deleting a record by ID:

```
public async Task DeleteEmployeeById(int id)
{
    using (var sqlConnection = new
        SqlConnection("YOURCONNECTIONSTRING"))
    {
        var sql = "DELETE FROM Employees WHERE Id =
            @employeeId";
        await sqlConnection.ExecuteAsync(
            sql,
            new { employeeId = id }
        );
    }
}
```

Now, we can add an endpoint to use the service for record deletion, returning a `NO CONTENT` result to the client on success:

```
app.MapDelete(
    "/employees/{id}",
    async (int id,
           [FromServices] DapperService
           dapperService) =>
{
    await dapperService.DeleteEmployeeById(id);
    return Results.NoContent();
});
```

We've covered enough of Dapper that you should now be able to use it to perform basic simple CRUD operations on SQL databases through this powerful yet lightweight (micro) ORM. You could also try swapping out the SQL provider for one that supports another database, such as MySQL or PostgreSQL, to improve your experience of using Dapper to manage data in SQL for incoming requests on your minimal APIs.

Dapper has its place, but Entity Framework is a more feature-rich alternative that is used for not only transacting data but also to manage the SQL database structure from code.

Let's take a look at how we can build the same functionality we've explored in the section, using Entity Framework.

Configuring Entity Framework in minimal API projects

Firstly, we need to use Microsoft's Entity Framework packages to configure the connection, referred to hereafter as the **context**. This wording already creates a layer of abstraction from the database as we start to consider our data as members of this context.

Start by installing the following packages via the package manager console in Visual Studio:

```
Install-Package Microsoft.EntityFrameworkCore
Install-Package Microsoft.EntityFrameworkCore.SqlServer
Install-Package Microsoft.EntityFrameworkCore.Tools
```

This ensures that all the libraries required to interact with SQL Server through Entity Framework are in place.

Next, we will **scaffold** the existing `MyCompany` database, again from the package manager console, using the connection string for the database:

```
Scaffold-DbContext "Your_Connection_String" Microsoft.
EntityFrameworkCore.SqlServer -OutputDir Models -Context
MyCompanyContext
```

Scaffolding means that Entity Framework looks at the schema of the database and maps the tables to objects in your code. The result is a `DbContext`, which wraps all of the different entities in the context. A series of models will also be created that are classes representing each of the entities. These are placed in the folder specified by the `OutputDir` switch used by the console command.

Because I stated that I want the context to be called `MyCompanyContext`, a new class called `MyCompanyContext` has been generated in the `Models` folder.

In this class, you can see that a `DbSet<Employee>` called `Employees` has been added. A `DbSet` represents all the current records in a given database table. This is a collection representing each of the records in `Employees`, and by adding to, retrieving from, updating, or removing from this collection, we can indirectly change the corresponding SQL table. Let's look at the generated code to further understand what is happening here.

`MyCompanyContext` is a class derived from `DbContext`. It represents the data source in use and provides a means of interacting with this source at a higher level of abstraction. When the class is instantiated, `DbContextOptions` is injected into it, which is then passed to the base `DbContext` class:

```
public partial class MyCompanyContext : DbContext
{
    public MyCompanyContext()
    {
    }

    public MyCompanyContext(
        DbContextOptions<MyCompanyContext> options)
        : base(options)
    {
    }

    public virtual DbSet<Employee> Employees { get; set; }
```

Entity Framework then generates the code required to build the context, mapping business objects to tables in the database, allowing a model to be created:

```
    protected override void OnConfiguring(
        DbContextOptionsBuilder optionsBuilder) =>
# warning To protect potentially sensitive information in
# your connection string, you should move it out of source
# code. You can avoid scaffolding the connection string by
# using the Name= syntax to read it from configuration -
# see https://go.microsoft.com/fwlink/?linkid=2131148. For
# more guidance on storing connection strings, see
# https://go.microsoft.com/fwlink/?LinkId=723263.
```

Entity Framework is instructed in this example to use SQL Server with the specified connection string to model the entities based on the database schema:

```
        optionsBuilder.UseSqlServer("YOURCONNECTIONSTRING");

    protected override void OnModelCreating(
        ModelBuilder modelBuilder)
    {
        modelBuilder.Entity<Employee>(entity =>
        {
            entity.HasNoKey();

            entity.Property(e => e.Address)
```

```
                .IsUnicode(false);
            entity.Property(e => e.City)
                .HasMaxLength(50)
                .IsUnicode(false);
            entity.Property(e => e.Country)
                .HasMaxLength(50)
                .IsUnicode(false);
            entity.Property(e => e.Id)
                .ValueGeneratedOnAdd();
            entity.Property(e => e.Name).IsUnicode(false);
            entity.Property(e => e.Phone)
                .HasMaxLength(200)
                .IsUnicode(false);
            entity.Property(e => e.PostalCode)
                .HasMaxLength(50)
                .IsUnicode(false);
            entity.Property(e => e.Region)
                .HasMaxLength(50)
                .IsUnicode(false);
            entity.Property(e => e.Salary)
                .HasColumnType("decimal(10, 2)");
        });

        OnModelCreatingPartial(modelBuilder);
    }

    partial void OnModelCreatingPartial(
        ModelBuilder modelBuilder);
}
```

Before we start looking at communicating with the database through Entity Framework from the API endpoints, we have another piece of configuration to explore.

It's important to understand how **migrations** are used by Entity Framework to change the database schema. A migration is a set of instructions to follow to make specific changes to a database. Whether to add a column to a table, add a new table, or remove a column, it can usually be done via a migration.

Migrations keep Entity Framework as the single source of truth for your data by outlining how a database's structural change should be managed, in addition to data.

Let's explore migrations by making a change to our `Employees` table. We're going to add a `Title` column to the table. First, open the `Employee` model that was generated in the `Models` folder and add `Title` as a `string` property:

```
public string Title { get; set; }
```

Then, we head back to the package manager console to input a command to add the migration. This command asks Entity Framework to look for any changes to any of the `DbSet` objects in the `DbContext`. It will then generate C# code that will eventually run SQL on the database to commit the changes.

Use the `Add-Migration` command in the package manager console, followed by a string that gives the migration a name:

```
PM> Add-Migration "Add_title_to_employees_table"
```

> **Migration names**
>
> When naming a migration, it is good practice to provide a summary of the changes these migrations make – for example, `changed_datatype_of_salary_column_to_decimal`.

Entity Framework will then build the project and add a new class for the migration in the `Migrations` folder, creating the folder if it does not yet exist:

```csharp
public partial class add_title_field_to_employees :
    Migration
{
    /// <inheritdoc />
    protected override void Up(
        MigrationBuilder migrationBuilder)
    {
        migrationBuilder.AddColumn<string>(
            name: "Title",
            table: "Employees",
            type: "nvarchar(max)",
            nullable: false,
            defaultValue: "");
    }

    /// <inheritdoc />
    protected override void Down(
        MigrationBuilder migrationBuilder)
    {
        migrationBuilder.DropColumn(
            name: "Title",
            table: "Employees");
    }
}
```

You can see that the migration specifies that a column is to be added called `Title`.

To commit this to the database, we can write another simple command in the package manager console:

```
Update-Database
```

If all went as expected, you'll see that the `Employees` table in the database has a `Title` column.

Now that we've covered the basics of its configuration, let's update the endpoints in `Program.cs` to use Entity Framework.

Performing CRUD operations with Entity Framework

We have a new dependency in the form of the `DbContext`. We should register it within the `Main` method in `Program.cs` for use during a request:

```
var builder = WebApplication.CreateBuilder(args);
builder.Services.AddScoped<MyCompanyContext>();
var app = builder.Build();
```

As we did in the previous examples using Dapper, we will create a new service for managing CRUD operations for `Employee` objects. This time, we will be more specific with the naming, and call it `EmployeeService`.

In `EmployeeService`, start by adding a constructor, to which we can pass the registered context:

```
public class EmployeeService
{
    private MyCompanyContext _companyContext;

    public EmployeeService(
        MyCompanyContext myCompanyContext)
    {
        _companyContext = myCompanyContext;
    }
}
```

Then, define all the functions that will be needed for CRUD operations using `MyCompanyContext`:

```
    public async Task AddEmployee(Employee employee)
    {
        await _companyContext.Employees
            .AddAsync(employee);
        await _companyContext
            .SaveChangesAsync();
    }

    public async Task<Employee> GetEmployeeById(int id)
    {
```

```csharp
            var result = await _companyContext.Employees
                .FirstOrDefaultAsync(x => x.Id == id);
            if(result == null)
            {
                throw new EmployeeNotFoundException(id);
            }
            return result;
        }

        public async Task UpdateEmployee(Employee employee)
        {
            var employeeToUpdate = await GetEmployeeById(
                employee.Id);
            _companyContext.Employees.Update(employeeToUpdate);
            await _companyContext.SaveChangesAsync();
        }

        public async Task DeleteEmployee(Employee employee)
        {
            _companyContext.Remove(employee);
            await _companyContext.SaveChangesAsync();
        }


}
```

Finally, we'll create a customer exception called `EmployeeNotFoundException`, which can we throw in the event a requested employee is not present in the data source:

```csharp
public class EmployeeNotFoundException : Exception
{
    public EmployeeNotFoundException(int id)
        : base(
            $"Employee with id {id} could not be found")
    {
    }
}
```

In each of these new functions within `EmployeeService`, we are interacting with the database via the `Employees` collection sitting within `MyCompanyContext`. We are then committing the changes we have made to this collection to the database using `SaveChangesAsync();`.

Take note of the reusability of one of the functions, `GetEmployeeById`. In most CRUD operations, we need to be able to target the affected `Employee` object, and we can reuse this function for this. To guard against the potential of an employee not being found in the collection, there is a custom exception that can be thrown. This is useful for the API endpoint because it means it can cater its response to a specific exception if it occurs, in this case, returning a `404 NOT FOUND` status code if necessary.

We've established that in Entity Framework, interacting with a database table means interacting with a collection in C#. This is apparent in `EmployeeService`, where LINQ queries are used in place of the SQL queries that would have been used in a direct SQL connection or a micro-ORM such as Dapper.

With the establishment of `EmployeeService`, the API endpoints in `Program.cs` can be altered to use Entity Framework rather than the previously used Dapper. But to what extent do they need to be changed?

The answer to this is – not very much at all, thanks to the abstraction we've created in the form of `EmployeeService`. We've used an injected dependency to manage the database interaction, with the functions within having the same name or **signature** as each other, meaning that we can just swap out the injected `DapperService` for the new `EmployeeService` that uses Entity Framework.

Head back to `Program.cs` and register `EmployeeService` for dependency injection:

```
var builder = WebApplication.CreateBuilder(args);
builder.Services.AddScoped<MyCompanyContext>();
builder.Services.AddScoped<EmployeeService>();
var app = builder.Build();
```

Double-click the parameter that currently passes in `DapperService` to any of the mapped endpoints. In Visual Studio, you can rename this object `EmployeeService` by holding *Ctrl* and pressing the *R* key twice.

After renaming, all other occurrences will also be updated. You shouldn't have any errors as long as the functions called by each endpoint have the same signature regardless of whether you're using `DapperService` or `EmployeeService`.

The following code shows the `POST` endpoint for creating an `employee` after it has been updated to use `EmployeeService`:

```
app.MapPost(
    "/employees",
    async (Employee employee,
        [FromServices] EmployeeService
        employeeService) =>
{
    await employeeService.AddEmployee(employee);
    return Results.Created();
});
```

This was a rather whirlwind introduction to Entity Framework, which has a great deal more in the way of features. However, the main focus is on a minimal API's interaction with databases in an abstracted manner, and this example is enough to get you started on your ORM journey.

Let's review the things we've learned about Dapper and Entity Framework in this chapter.

Summary

This chapter has introduced the use of Dapper and Entity Framework to provide an abstraction layer between minimal API endpoints and relational databases.

We opened with an introduction to ORMs, defining their role in simplifying database interactions in minimal APIs, before providing an overview of the various features available for interaction with data sources.

We then stepped through the configuration of Dapper, adding the relevant libraries and providing a dedicated `DapperService` that could be used on minimal API endpoints with dependency injection. Once we had configured Dapper, we created the SQL queries in `DapperService` and linked the endpoints to the service to provide an end-to-end link between API and database via Dapper.

Having established CRUD operations on the database with Dapper, we contrasted this by configuring Entity Framework, and then performed the equivalent setup of a service for completing CRUD operations.

Finally, the original `DapperService` was swapped out for the new `EmployeeService` using Entity Framework, demonstrating the versatility of injecting an abstraction as a dependency for data management.

There's no doubt that integrating data sources via ORMs is a significant aspect of building a minimal API. When managing data, depending on the way the data is requested, the potential for bottlenecks in performance can be significant. We will explore this concept and ways that these bottlenecks can be mitigated in the next chapter.

Part 3 - Optimal Minimal APIs

To build high-performing, scalable APIs, it's essential to fine-tune your system's performance and take advantage of advanced programming techniques. This part covers how to identify bottlenecks, employ asynchronous programming, and implement caching strategies to improve efficiency and user experience.

This part has the following chapters:

- *Chapter 10, Profiling and Identifying Bottlenecks*
- *Chapter 11, Utilizing Asynchronous Programming for Scalability*
- *Chapter 12, Caching Strategies for Enhanced Performance*

10
Profiling and Identifying Bottlenecks

As your minimal API project evolves, the potential for performance bottlenecks increases. Working with data, making connections over networks, and running business logic and calculations – all these activities have a performance cost. If configured the wrong way, these activities could incur a higher than necessary cost.

In this chapter, we are going to explore strategies for analyzing resource utilization, identifying common bottlenecks, and implementing them. We will cover the following:

- An introduction to profiling and performance monitoring
- Profiling tools and techniques
- Common performance bottlenecks

Technical requirements

You will need Visual Studio 2022 or Visual Studio code running, at minimum, a new ASP.NET core minimal API project. It is recommended to use the code from the previous chapter, as we will be working with performance examples within the context of the `MyCompany` API project. Because the examples in this chapter are run against the code examples in *Chapter 10*, you will need to have Entity Framework installed as per the instructions in the previous chapter. (See the *Configuring Entity Framework in minimal API projects* section in *Chapter 9*.)

An introduction to profiling and performance monitoring

At the beginning of this chapter, we established that the code we run in a minimal API application will incur performance costs, some of which could be presented as bottlenecks, hampering the efficiency of the overall system. To remedy this, we can leverage a profiling tool, also known as a profiler.

Introducing the profiler

A **profiler** is a piece of software that measures the cost of running code. While your API application runs, the profiler will provide telemetry that outlines how expensive certain areas of the code base are in terms of resource usage. This allows us to identify areas of inefficiency, which is critical to optimizing the performance of your minimal API applications. This is an important practice for many reasons, not limited to the following:

- **Scalability**: The ability to ensure that your code will be able to perform at an increasing rate of demand.
- **Availability**: Access to the API to outside clients is paramount. If clients cannot access the API because of a lack of available hardware resources, the application has lost availability.
- **Security**: The connection between the client and API should not be open for any longer than necessary. If your API takes a long time to complete a request, the connection is open for longer, leaving more opportunities for malicious activity to occur.
- **Cost**: The financial cost of not optimizing a system can be severe. If production servers frequently require upgrades because of software bottlenecks, each scale-up of the hardware incurs financial costs.
- **User experience**: Ensuring that your API runs as quickly as possible ensures that people will have a positive experience, securing repeat usage of the application.
- **Error detection**: While profiling allows for the detection of bottlenecks, it can also indirectly reveal other bugs in the code base that may not have been detected by unit or integration testing.

Along the same vein, the advantages of profiling minimal APIs are considerable:

- **Latency reduction**: With profiling, response times can be increased, resulting in a much more responsive API.
- **Optimal hardware usage**: Profiling can help you see where you are overconsuming resources such as CPU, memory, and I/O.
- **Preventative measures**: Running a profiler to identify potential optimizations allows developers to get ahead of potential future issues, letting them make planned changes rather than reactionary ones.
- **Maintenance**: Overall, a more performant code base is usually easier to maintain. If the minimal API application is easy to maintain, it will likely see a more frequent release cadence.

Next, let's look at some performance metrics.

Performance metrics

Before releasing an application for general use, it is difficult to predict how an API will cope under heavy load in an accurate way without performing stress testing and gathering the resulting data. **Performance monitoring** can help by providing insights into how your code is performing in specific scenarios. This data in the form of metrics can inform how you optimize your code as you approach release. One of the key things you need to understand from performance metrics is how the resources on the machine hosting the API handle a high volume of requests.

Profiling can monitor various resources within a minimal API and its dependencies, including the following:

- **Response times**: The amount of time it takes for a request to be handled by the API, with a response being returning the client.
- **Throughput**: The volume of data flowing through a connection at any given time.
- **CPU processing**: The amount of processing being completed by the API host's CPU during requests, or even on background tasks not related to a client request.
- **Memory**: The amount of RAM being consumed by the application at any given time.

Having access to metrics allows us to start identifying potential bottlenecks so that we can then take steps to address them in the minimal API code.

For example, the profiler might show a sudden increase in CPU usage during a particular operation. This may indicate that the operation is written in a sub-optimal way (e.g., an unnecessary loop or iteration over a collection).

With some understanding of profiling and performance monitoring, let's take a look at some tools and techniques for the former.

Profiling tools and techniques

There are many different profiling tools available, but for the purposes of developing minimal APIs in ASP.NET, we will be looking at two examples: the Visual Studio profiler and BenchmarkDotNet. The former is a GUI-based tool, whereas the latter is a library that we can add as a dependency to our project.

Each of these tools has its strengths in particular use cases, as shown here:

- **The Visual Studio profiler**: It is integrated into the IDE and provides live performance data and CPU and memory metrics. It is ideal for capturing a quick profile, performing basic performance analysis, and identifying areas of high CPU and memory usage.
- **BenchmarkDotNet**: It can be installed as a package within a .NET project and is adept at micro-benchmarking. It is used for establishing baseline performance and the fine-tuning of code.

There are several other potential choices that are not free, such as dotTrace by JetBrains, which is a very competent profiler that can provide the usual resource consumption metrics along with some very in-depth views of the call tree and events over a timeline. I can certainly recommend dotTrace, but as it is not free, we will keep things simple by exploring profiling examples in the Visual Studio profiler and BenchmarkDotNet.

Profiling in Visual Studio

Let us start by setting up profiling in Visual Studio:

1. Open the `MyCompany` API example in Visual Studio. Then, click **Debug**, and select **Performance Profiler**. You will see several different options on the screen for various kinds of profiling. For this example, we are going to profile CPU usage to demonstrate profiling.

2. Tick **CPU Usage** and click **Start**.

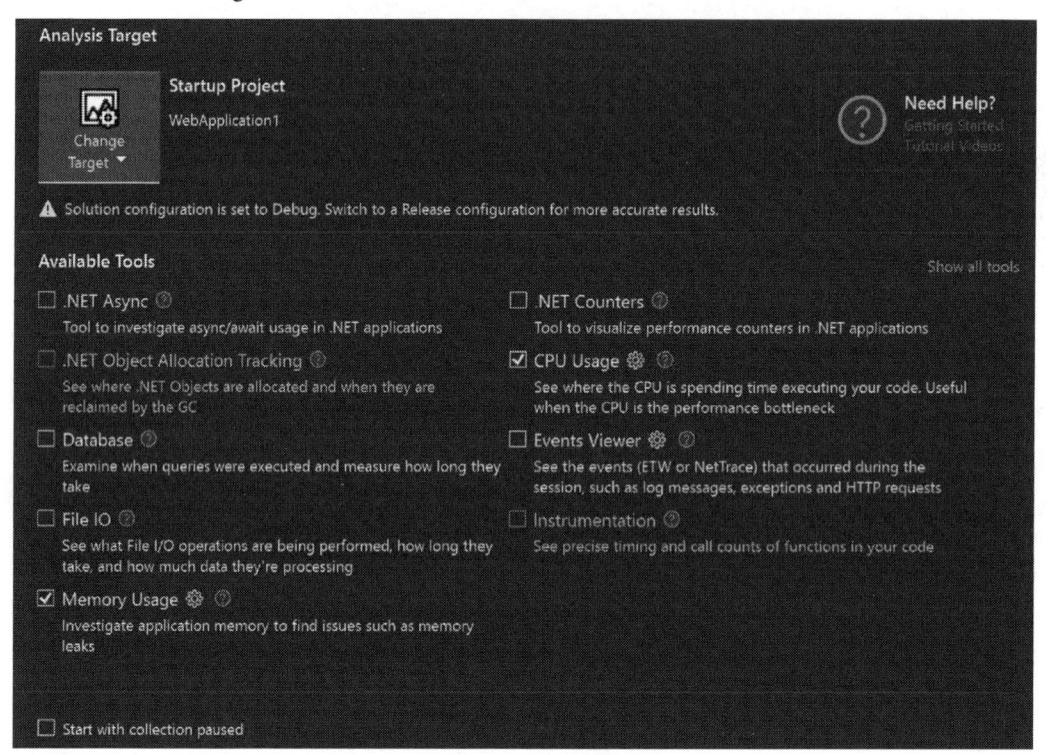

Figure 10.1: The profiling configuration screen

The aim will be to start profiling so that it is capturing CPU usage data in the background while we are interacting with the API. Once the application stops, a report will be generated that will give us a breakdown of CPU usage over time, which we can then track back to specific lines of code.

3. After starting the profiler (ensure that it is recording) your API project will also start running. Interact with the API by calling the `GetEmployeeById` endpoint, passing an ID value for an existing employee record. You will notice when you make the request that the profiler updates in real time. You should see an increase in CPU usage as soon as the request starts, which settles down again once the request has completed.

4. Once you have made some requests to the API, click the **Stop Collection** button in the top-left corner of the screen, and then click the **CPU Usage** tab (around a quarter of the way down the screen toward the left). The result should be a diagnostic report showing the peaks and dips in CPU usage across the time being profiled.

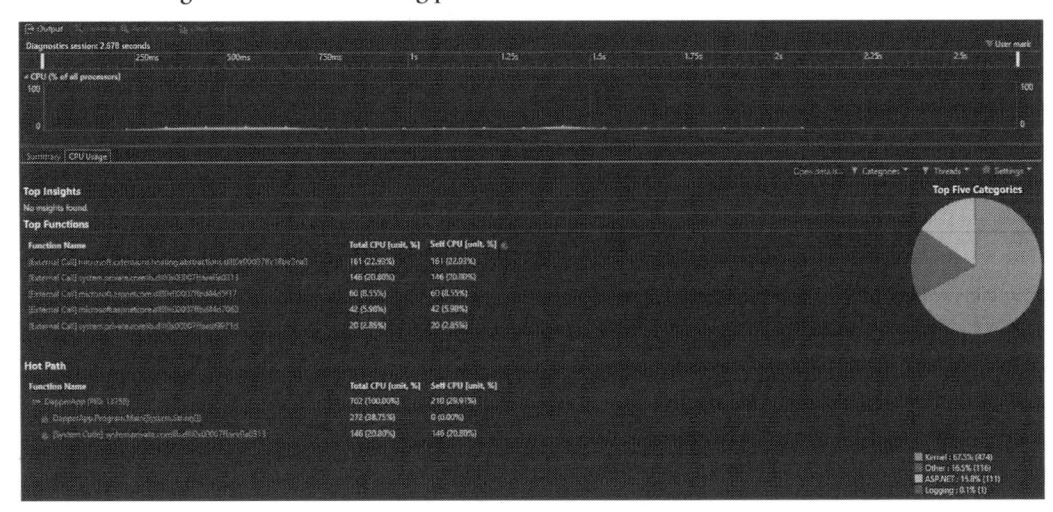

Figure 10.2: The profiler report for CPU usage

As you can see in *Figure 10.2*, there was a spike in CPU usage at the beginning of the profiling session. This was at the point that a `GET` request was made to the `employees` endpoint, with the API handling the request by returning an `Employee` object with the given ID.

There is a wealth of information that can be filtered in this view. Suffice it to say, a whole book could be written on profiling in .NET alone. However, by way of example, click the **Open Details** button toward the top-right corner of the **CPU Usage** pane.

The details shown on the screen following this will provide more detailed information about the code that consumes various percentage levels of CPU for the given time. There are several key views, such as the **Call Tree** view, which shows the nested relationships between function and method calls (i.e., *what called what*).

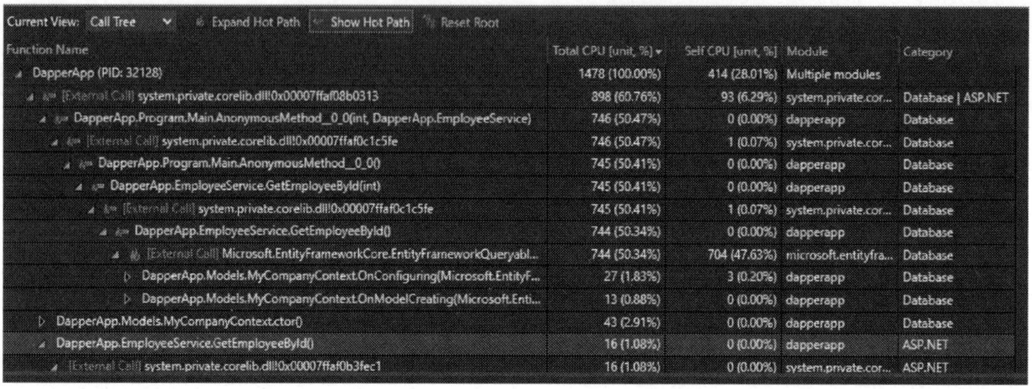

Figure 10.3: The Call Tree view, showing the CPU consumed by functions at each level of the tree

The **Functions** view is quite useful in the sense that it can be used to identify which specific lines of code are consuming higher amounts of CPU. By sorting this view by **Total CPU% descending**, you can quickly identify the top consumer of CPU. This can be beneficial when performing optimization on a minimal API, as you can gain insights into the underlying functions' impact on an endpoint's response time for example.

What is more, any of the entries in this view can be double-clicked to reveal the original source code, with the CPU usage annotated next to the function signature.

The **Caller/Callee** view, which demonstrated what functions are called by and what they themselves call, is particularly insightful in this request.

Take the example in *Figure 10.4*. We can see that for the current function in `EmployeeService`, `GetEmployeeById()`, the CPU resource was consumed at 51.42%. Going deeper, we can see that the function is called into a method within Entity Framework Core. In this case, the function was `FirstOrDefault()`.

`FirstOrDefault()` is a **Language Integrated Query** (**LINQ**) feature that will get the first item in a collection that meets the given condition, or it will return a default value, in this case, `null`.

What we can see in *Figure 10.4* is that of the 51.42% of CPU usage consumed by `GetEmployeeById()`, 50.34% of that usage was taken up by `FirstOrDefault()`; don't be surprised if the value you get for the same profiling differs. This value should and would vary between machines. The important thing is that you are able to see a spike in usage.

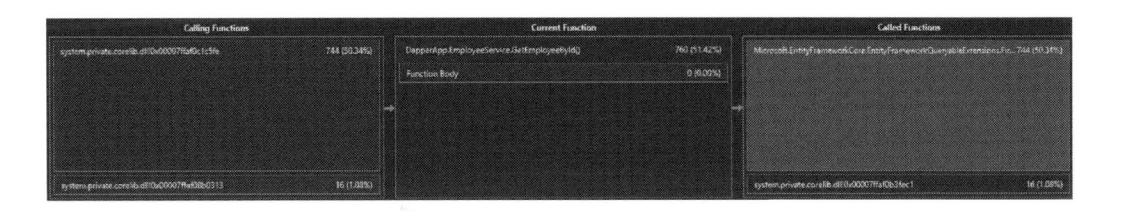

Figure 10.4: The Caller/Callee view, demonstrating the breakdown
of CPU usage for the GetEmployeeById() function

This result demonstrates the percentage of CPU usage spread across each function. On its own, this does not necessarily indicate a bottleneck, but it is useful information when troubleshooting performance or for general optimization.

We could dig into this further by replacing `FirstOrDefault()` with our own custom implementation of a loop for finding the first employee with the matching ID.

The loop would look like the example here:

```
foreach(var employee in _companyContext.Employees)
{
    if (employee.Id == id)
    {
        return employee;
    }
}
throw new EmployeeNotFoundException(id);
```

If we run this loop in place of `FirstOrDefault()`, we can check the same profiling capture and compare the CPU usage.

In this case, when running the updated code using a loop, we saw a minor increase in CPU usage compared to `FirstOrDefault()`. So, while `FirstOrDefault()` is not confirmed to be the most performant method of retrieving `Employee` for the calling API endpoint, it is confirmed that our alternative is not as performant. This is a process of elimination technique, which is an exercise worth practicing across your whole code base.

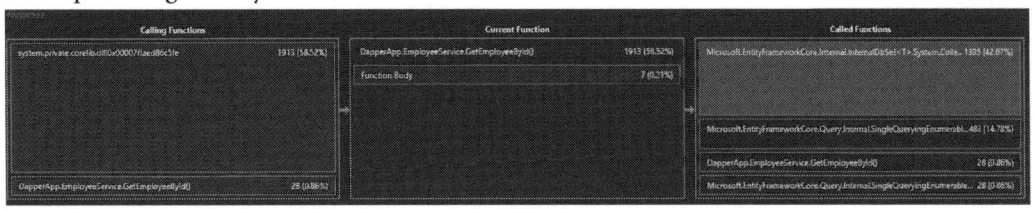

Figure 10.5: CPU usage for GetEmployeeById() using a foreach loop instead of FirstOrDefault()

As mentioned previously, we could go much further into the Visual Studio profiler, but that is beyond the scope of this book. With this foundation, you should now have at least one item in your toolset for optimizing minimal APIs. Let us look at another useful tool for analyzing API performance – BenchmarkDotNet.

Benchmarking with BenchmarkDotNet

BenchmarkDotNet is an open source .NET library designed to facilitate micro-benchmarking in .NET applications. It was created by software engineer, Andrey Akinshin, a prominent member of the .NET community specializing in software performance.

The project started around 2014 to provide developers with an easy-to-use tool for measuring and comparing the performance of different pieces of code.

The library is available as a NuGet package and will need to be installed in order for us to run performance benchmarking against the `MyCompany` API project.

To keep things clean, we will perform the benchmarking in another project. However, we can stay within the current Visual Studio setup by adding the new benchmarking project to the current solution.

In Visual Studio's Solution Explorer, right-click the current solution and select **Add | New Project**.

In the **New Project** screen there is a search box at the top of the window that allows you to search for a project template. Use this to search for **"C# Console App"**. Once you see it, select it and click **"Next"**. You will be asked to choose a .NET version. We are using version 9, so leave this selected and click **"Create"**.

Next, we will need to add the `BenchmarkDotNet` library package to the new project via the Package Manager Console:

```
dotnet add package BenchmarkDotNet
```

The new project is in our solution and has the required libraries installed, but how is it supposed to be able to reference the dependencies from the minimal API project?

The way to address this is to create a project reference. This allows us to reference object types across multiple .NET projects. This is especially easy when the projects are in the same solution as they are in this example.

To add the project reference, right-click your new benchmarking project and click **Add | Project Reference**.

You will be presented with a dialog box in which you can browse to the project location. Your ASP.NET project should have been compiled as a **Dynamic Link Library** (**DLL**) so you should be able to select that from the bin folder within your ASP.NET project directory.

Now that you have a project reference, you can add using statements to reference types in that project as if they had been created within the benchmarking project.

We can now move on to setting up our benchmarks and utilizing the dependencies that we would have normally injected, but first, the benchmarks need their own class; so, create one called `EmployeeBenchmarks`.

In this new class, create a private field to hold `EmployeeService`:

```
public class EmployeeBenchmarks
{

    private EmployeeService _employeeService;

}
```

Next, we can create a method that accesses the required dependencies. We will call this method `Setup()`. We need to annotate this method with an attribute – `[GlobalSetup]`

Having this attribute means that BenchmarkDotNet will run the logic inside `Setup()` before benchmarks run:

```
[GlobalSetup]
    public void Setup()
    {
        var services = new ServiceCollection();
        services.AddScoped<MyCompanyContext>();
        services.AddScoped<EmployeeService>();

        var serviceProvider =
            services.BuildServiceProvider();
        _employeeService =
            serviceProvider
                .GetRequiredService<EmployeeService>();
    }
```

This code uses `ServiceCollection`, which will require the `Microsoft.Extensions.DependencyInjection` package to be installed.

Inside `Setup()`, we have created the required dependencies and added them to `ServiceContainer` so that they are ready to be used at runtime.

We have also retrieved `EmployeeService` and stored it in the private field so that our benchmark can call the `GetEmployeeId()` function within it.

Finally, for this class, we add the benchmark itself, which is the important part. We want to create a benchmark for the activity running in Entity Framework so we will call the `GetEmployeeId()` function so that it interacts with the database via `MyCompanyContext`, and this activity will be recorded by BenchmarkDotNet. We are passing a hardcoded ID to `GetEmployeeById()`, because we know that the `Employee` record with ID 6 exists and that this is not going to change (obviously, you must ensure a record with this ID exists, or change the value from 6 to one you know to exist in the database):

```
[Benchmark]
public void GetEmployeeByIdBenchmark()
{
    var result = _employeeService
        .GetEmployeeById(6)
        .GetAwaiter()
        .GetResult();
}
```

Notice the presence of the `[Benchmark]` attribute decorating the `GetEmployeeByIdBenchmark()` method. This labels the method as being a relevant benchmark that should be run.

Now, this is where having a separate console application really helps. In the `Main()` method of the benchmark console application's `Program.cs` class, we can simply call the static `BenchmarkRunner` and tell it to run any of the benchmarks in the benchmark class, which it will detect based on the presence of the `[Benchmark]` attribute:

```
static void Main(string[] args)
{
    var result = BenchmarkRunner.Run<EmployeeBenchmarks>();
}
```

The benchmarking console application can now be run to provide results for any methods or functions in `EmployeeBenchmarks` that are annotated with the `[Benchmark]` attribute.

Before running the console application, right-click the console application project in Solution Explorer and select **Set as Startup Project**.

Once the console app has finished running, you will see the benchmark output in the console window, as well as a series of files published to the `bin` directory of the application in a folder called `BenchmarkDotNet.Artifacts`. Here, you will find the output to the console, as well as the results organized in HTML, Markdown, and Excel formats.

Let's look at the most important section of the output. In the result shown in the console, you'll notice a table. This table contains the benchmarking information for `GetEmployeeById()`:

Method	Mean	Error	StdDev
GetEmployeeByIdBenchmark	171.1 μs	3.37 μs	5.63 μs

This table shows the average time in microseconds that it took to run `GetEmployeeById()` out of several iterations.

The average time taken is displayed as a mean value, giving us a measurement we can use as a basis for performance analysis. It would be advisable to note this mean average, and then run benchmarking several more times with different inputs, to provide further re-enforcement of this average value.

The `Error` and `StdDev` columns provide some further supporting information. `StdDev` represents the **standard deviation**, which is the amount of variation from the average. A smaller standard deviation means that benchmark times were consistent. If you see a higher standard deviation, it implies more variability in average results.

The `Error` column represents the estimated standard deviation of the mean average result, which is an indication of how reliable the result is. The smaller the number, the more reliable the result.

Again, it makes sense to run several benchmarks with varying inputs. If you are seeing similar standard deviations and errors, you can be confident in the accuracy of the results.

> **Release mode**
> Your project will need to be built in Release mode for the preceding profiling to work. If you see the word **Debug** in a dropdown in the top ribbon of Visual Studio, change it to **Release** and then rebuild your project.

Common performance bottlenecks

Let's look at some common reasons that performance could be degraded and how you might address them. These are by no means applicable to every situation, but they are well-known bottlenecks:

- **Database access**: The bottleneck is caused by slow database queries or inefficient use of database connections. To mitigate this, do the following:

  - Use asynchronous database operations (`async`/`await`).
  - Optimize SQL queries and use proper indexing. Look at any WHERE clauses or JOIN operations that might be taxing the system.
  - Implement connection pooling to reduce the number of times new connections need to be opened.
  - Use a caching system such as ASP.NET's `IMemoryCache` for frequently accessed data.

- **I/O operations**: The bottleneck is due to blocking I/O operations, such as file or network access. To mitigate this, do the following:
  - Use asynchronous I/O operations.
  - Minimize disk and network I/O. Where possible, retrieve commonly required data from memory rather than from persistent storage or over a network.
  - Use efficient data formats (e.g., JSON instead of XML).
- **Serialization/deserialization**: The bottleneck arises from slow or inefficient serialization and deserialization of data. To mitigate this, do the following:
  - Use optimized serializers such as `System.Text.Json` instead of `Newtonsoft.Json`.
  - Minimize the size of the data being serialized.
- **Middleware pipeline**: The bottleneck is caused by excessive or inefficient middleware in the request pipeline. To mitigate this, do the following:
  - Review and optimize middleware components.
  - Remove unnecessary middleware.
  - Use lightweight middleware.
- **Logging**: The bottleneck results from extensive or synchronous logging. To mitigate this, do the following:
  - Use asynchronous logging.
  - Reduce the log verbosity level in production.
  - Use efficient logging frameworks such as Serilog.
- **Dependency injection (DI)**: The bottleneck is due to the inefficient use of dependency injection. To mitigate this, do the following:
  - Use scoped or singleton lifetimes where appropriate.
  - Avoid unnecessary injections of services. If there is a simpler alternative that avoids dependency injection, use it.
- **Garbage collection (GC) pressure**: The bottleneck results from excessive memory allocation, leading to frequent garbage collection. To mitigate this, do the following:
  - Reduce allocations by reusing objects.
  - Use value types instead of reference types where possible.
  - Optimize data structures and avoid large allocations of objects onto the heap (relates back to using value types over reference types where possible).

- **Network latency**: The bottleneck is caused by high latency in network calls. To mitigate this, do the following:

  - Minimize the number of network calls.

  - Implement retry policies with exponential backoff.

  - Investigate alternative network protocols, using benchmarking to see whether they are less resource-intensive.

By having a general understanding of the most common bottlenecks and how they can be mitigated, you will become more vigilant when debugging and reviewing code in minimal APIs.

We will now recap the various topics we have covered in this chapter.

Summary

In this chapter, we explored at a high level the various pitfalls and mitigation options for performance issues in minimal APIs.

We started by outlining the basics of performance analysis and why it is important within not just minimal APIs, but in general software engineering.

We then reviewed some of the different tools on offer, before narrowing the scope of the tools we would use to the Visual Studio profiler and BenchmarkDotNet.

Then, we started profiling the MyCompany API using the Visual Studio profiler, with a breakdown of the various metrics that are outputted into the diagnostic report produced by the profiler. This allowed us to find the overall CPU usage of a section of a code, but then also to break that down further by its called functions lower down in the call tree.

Moving on to BenchMarkDotNet, we implemented the same analysis example undertaken by the Visual Studio profiler, this time running a performance benchmark against the target method. We then reviewed the output to understand how best to secure an accurate benchmark based on the consistency of the error rate and the standard deviation.

Like many topics in this book, this is just a scratch of the surface, but it will provide a solid foundation for further optimization of minimal APIs and give you a good grounding in analyzing their efficiency.

Let's move on to the next chapter, in which we will be exploring ways to use asynchronous programming to scale minimal APIs.

11
Utilizing Asynchronous Programming for Scalability

Whenever we execute a function, we expect a result, but what happens between the request and the outputted result?

Imagine you're in town, and you have a bunch of errands to run, but you're also hungry and need to eat lunch. You walk into a pizza shop, situated within a shopping mall. The shop cooks fresh pizza to order. It takes around fifteen minutes for the pizza to be prepped and then cooked. You can wait around in the shop until the pizza is done, but you need to go to the bank, which has a branch across the road. The pizza store owner is a friend of yours and agrees to text you when your pizza is ready to pick up. You have an opportunity to get something else done while your pizza is cooking; that's a much better use of your time.

This is a simple analogy for an **asynchronous** function. The act of walking into the pizza shop is the function starting, and you running over to the bank while it is cooking is the function running. When your phone beeps with a text to say the pizza is ready, that is the function returning its output.

This example demonstrates the benefits of an asynchronous function, which allows for the execution of other tasks while waiting for a specific operation to complete. Cooking your pizza doesn't block your overall goal, which is to run your errands.

If the pizza shop owner was a lot less friendly and demanded that you wait in the shop until the pizza was done, that would be an example of a **synchronous** operation, the opposite of asynchronous. Synchronous operations block the progression of your overall goal (running your errands) until the current operation is complete.

Where possible, we want to reap the benefits of asynchronous programming for operations that are executing as part of minimal APIs.

In this chapter, we're going to cover the following main topics:

- Understanding and implementing asynchronous patterns in a minimal API
- Common pitfalls and challenges

Technical requirements

The code for this chapter is available in the GitHub repository at: https://github.com/PacktPublishing/Minimal-APIs-in-ASP.NET-9. Visual Studio with the .NET 9 SDK is required to run the code.

Understanding and implementing asynchronous patterns in a minimal API

The opening pizza analogy is hopefully a good, high-level illustration of the difference between asynchronous and synchronous programming. Asynchronous programming is significant in minimal APIs because it provides a lot of flexibility for managing the conversations between client and server. It is particularly beneficial to long-running operations, where the overall performance of a request would be compromised by operations running in a linear fashion, with each operation blocking the other.

Asynchronous programming also provides scalability benefits, allowing APIs to cope with high demand. This is achieved by ensuring that threads are not blocked. Operations in an asynchronous endpoint can register callbacks to ensure that the execution thread can continue running other tasks until that callback is resolved. This brings with it other resource benefits such as better management of the thread pool, lower CPU consumption, and decreased memory footprint. All of these things are crucial for minimal APIs, which are designed to be as straightforward and efficient as possible.

Task-based asynchronous pattern

.NET has seen the use of several different asynchronous programming patterns on its journey from .NET Framework to .NET core. In the .NET Framework days, the **Task-based Asynchronous Pattern** (**TAP**) was the preferred method for managing asynchronous execution. Introduced in the Task Parallel Library in .NET 4, it uses `Task` and `Task<T>` to represent asynchronous operations and to provide a way to handle their results or exceptions. The explicit implementation of the TAP is now obsolete in .NET 9, but the example is effective at demonstrating asynchronous operations. If we were to use it in a minimal API, it would be situated in the body of an endpoint, with the establishment of a `Task<T>`, which would execute a long-running task. We would then start the `Task` while at the same time telling it what logic it should call back to once it has finished. We can see this in this example, which runs a task to grab data from another API and then continues by checking the result before returning a response to the client:

```
app.MapGet("/fetch-data", (HttpContext httpContext) =>
```

```csharp
{
    HttpClient client = new HttpClient();
    string url =
        "https://jsonplaceholder.typicode.com/posts/1";

    // Initiate the asynchronous operation and return a
    // continuation task
    return client.GetStringAsync(url).ContinueWith(task =>
    {
        if (task.IsCompletedSuccessfully)
        {
            // Task completed successfully, return the data
            return httpContext.Response.WriteAsJsonAsync(
                new { data = task.Result }
            );
        }
        else if (task.IsFaulted)
        {
            // Task faulted, handle the exception
            var errorMessage =
                task.Exception.Flatten().InnerException
                    ?.Message ?? "An error occurred";
            httpContext.Response.StatusCode =
                StatusCodes.Status500InternalServerError;
            return httpContext.Response.WriteAsJsonAsync(
                new { error = errorMessage }
            );
        }
        else
        {
            // If task was cancelled or some other state,
            // handle accordingly
            httpContext.Response.StatusCode =
                StatusCodes.Status500InternalServerError;
            return httpContext.Response.WriteAsJsonAsync(
                new { error = "Unknown error occurred." }
            );
        }
    });
});
```

While this code can demonstrate asynchronous execution in an API endpoint, it could be a lot more readable. Fortunately, back in .NET Framework 4.5 and .NET 5, the `async/await` keywords were introduced.

TAP with async/await

The `async/await` keywords made asynchronous programming more accessible by allowing us to write asynchronous code that resembles synchronous code. This went a long way toward making asynchronous code more readable and therefore understandable. In a minimal API, where we're aiming to be economical with the real estate in our IDE, this is very valuable.

This is what the endpoint from the last example looks like when using `async/await` instead of using the original Task-based syntax:

```
app.MapGet(
    "/fetch-data-async-await",
    async (HttpContext httpContext) =>
{
    HttpClient client = new HttpClient();
    string url =
        "https://jsonplaceholder.typicode.com/posts/1";

    try
    {
        // Asynchronously fetch data from the external
        // service
        string data = await client.GetStringAsync(url);
        await httpContext.Response.WriteAsJsonAsync(
            new { data}
        );
    }
    catch (HttpRequestException ex)
    {
        // Handle error (e.g., network issues, server
        // problems)
        httpContext.Response.StatusCode =
            StatusCodes.Status500InternalServerError;
        await httpContext.Response.WriteAsJsonAsync(
            new
            {
                error =
                    "Error fetching data: " + ex.Message
            });
    }
    catch (Exception ex)
```

```
        {
            // Handle any other exceptions
            httpContext.Response.StatusCode =
                StatusCodes.Status500InternalServerError;
            await httpContext.Response.WriteAsJsonAsync(
                new
                {
                    error =
                        "An unexpected error occurred: " +
                            ex.Message
                });
        }
});
```

It's hopefully clear to see that the section of code in the second example, which starts the asynchronous call to the other API, is much cleaner and shorter than its counterpart in the first example.

In minimal APIs, we don't need to do much to make an API endpoint compatible with `async/await`. Notice how, in the second example that uses `async/await`, the endpoint has the `async` keyword preceding the lambda expression defined after the route. This, like in regular .NET functions and methods, allows for the use of the `await` keyword in the body of the function. Without the `async` keyword, `await` is not supported.

The first example did not use the `async` keyword, but it was ultimately still able to create an asynchronous operation. This may look like a contradiction until we consider that as well as `async`, `await` is notably absent from the first example. So, it's important to remember that the `async` keyword is not a pre-requisite for any asynchronous code in a minimal API, but it allows for the use of `await`, and therefore a simpler implementation of asynchronous operations that resemble synchronous ones.

By using `async/await`, we can implement the TAP in a streamlined fashion.

Asynchronous processing pattern

There is another well defined pattern that achieved asynchronous execution known as the **Asynchronous Processing Pattern**.

Sometimes referred to as **deferred processing**, this pattern can be somewhat complex compared to the TAP, but the principle is the same. The flow of control is returned to the consumer of the function while other long-running operations are completed. However, in this pattern, the consumer of the function is not the API application's main thread, but the client making the request to the API endpoint.

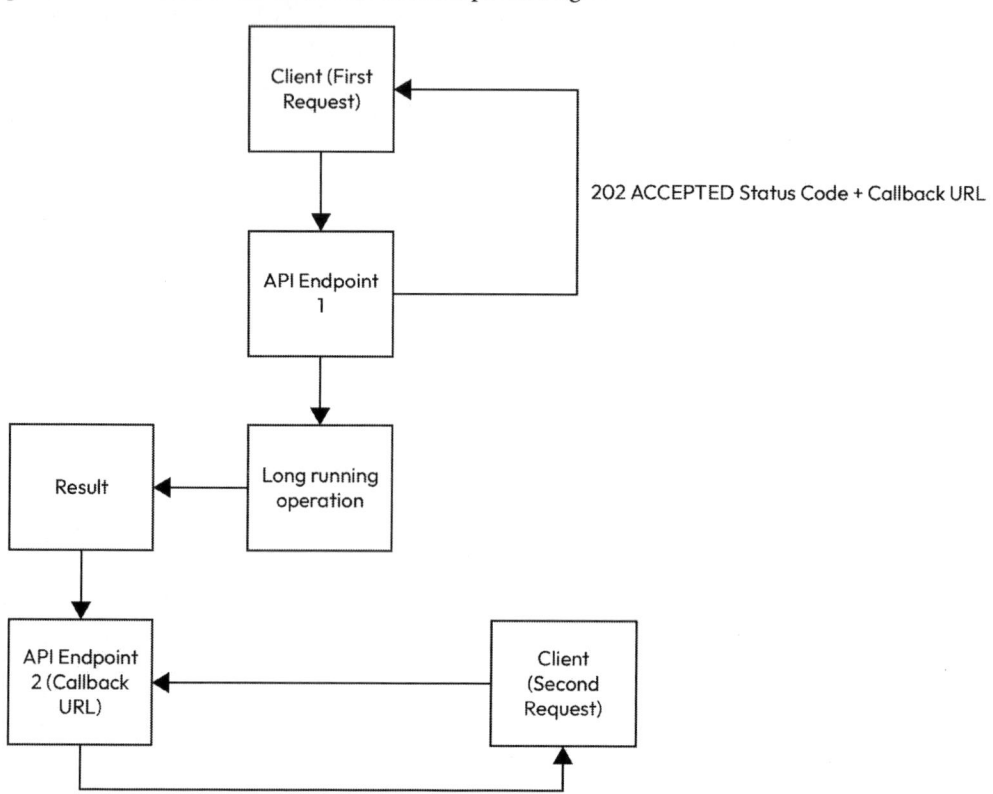

Figure 1.1 demonstrates execution via deferred processing:

Figure 11.1: Deferred processing spanning two client requests

We can turn the current example into a version that uses deferred processing relatively easily. First, we would need to make an endpoint that starts execution of the long-running task, but then immediately acknowledges the caller by returning a status code. However, a status code on its own will not suffice. We must return a callback URL for the client. This URL will route to another endpoint, which will check to see whether our long-running operation has completed. If it has, it will retrieve the relevant data before returning it to the client as a response. If the operation has not been completed, it will still respond to the client, indicating that the operation is still running.

Let's start by creating the first endpoint, which will acknowledge the client's request for the long-running operation to start. We'll also create a dictionary to hold responses waiting to be collected by clients via callbacks:

```
var results = new ConcurrentDictionary<Guid, string>();

// Endpoint to start the long-running background task
```

```
app.MapPost("/start-process", async () =>
{
});
```

The dictionary has been added as a `ConcurrentDictionary` because it is thread-safe, meaning that .NET will automatically manage scenarios where it is accessed by multiple concurrent threads. An example would be if there are multiple requests to the API.

Next, inside the body of the `POST` endpoint, we generate a `GUID` to represent the pending request, as well as a string version of the `GUID` that can be referenced in the callback response:

```
var requestId = Guid.NewGuid();
var requestIdStr = requestId.ToString();
```

All that remains now is to start the long-running task, before returning the `GUID` to the client so that they can use it in the callback request to see whether their result is ready for retrieval:

```
// Start the long-running task
_ = Task.Run(async () =>
{
    await Task.Delay(10000); // Simulate a long-running
                             // task (10 seconds)
    results[requestId] = $"Result for {requestIdStr}";
    // Store result in dictionary
});

// Respond with the request ID
return Results.Ok(new { RequestId = requestIdStr });
```

Now that the client has a unique identifier in the form of the returned `GUID`, it can be used in a second request to get the result.

Let's create a `GET` endpoint for this purpose. The endpoint will be a lot simpler than the first. It will simply attempt to find an entry in the dictionary that has a key matching the passed-in `GUID` parameter. If the dictionary contains the requested key-value pair, the original long-running operation is completed. Otherwise, it must still be running or was never initiated. The `GET` endpoint must handle both of these scenarios:

```
// Endpoint to get the result based on the request ID
app.MapGet("/get-result/{requestId}", (string requestId) =>
{
    if (Guid.TryParse(requestId, out var guid) &&
        results.TryGetValue(guid, out var result))
    {
        return Results.Ok(new { Result = result });
```

```
        }
        return Results.NotFound(new { Error =
            "Result not found or not yet completed."
        });
    });
});
```

Go ahead and try calling these two endpoints, one after the other. If you request the second endpoint within less than ten seconds of the first one, you should get a `404 NOTFOUND` result with the **Result not found or not yet completed** message and then get the expected `GUID` result after ten seconds. This will have demonstrated deferred processing in a simple way.

To expand your practice of this execution pattern, you should attempt more elaborate use cases, such as running complicated mathematical calculations or making database or network requests in the background.

Common pitfalls and challenges

Asynchronous programming brings with it a series of pitfalls and challenges. Let's go through some examples of things that you should be vigilant about when writing asynchronous code in a minimal API:

- **Deadlocks**: A deadlock occurs when concurrent operations cannot complete due to blocking. In a minimal API, this can be seen when the main thread is blocked. In the following example, the use of `Task.Run` can cause a deadlock because it blocks the main thread:

    ```
    // Deadlock-prone code
    public async Task<IActionResult> GetData()
    {
        var data = Task.Run(() =>
            GetDataFromDatabase()).Result; // Blocking
                                            // call
        return Ok(data);
    }
    ```

    The way to avoid deadlocks would simply be to use `await` when running the task, to ensure that the call does not block the main thread:

    ```
    public async Task<IActionResult> GetData()
    {
        var data = await Task.Run(() =>
            GetDataFromDatabase());
        return Ok(data);
    }
    ```

- **Resource Management**: Where possible, minimal API code that manages resources such as database connections or file handles should be disposed of appropriately in an asynchronous context.

Any resource that implements `IDisposable` can make use of a `using` statement to automatically dispose of the resource when no longer in use. However, when writing asynchronous code for resources, try to use `IDisposableAsync` where available. This means you use `await` in conjunction with a `using` statement:

```
public async Task<IActionResult> GetData()
{
    await using (var dbContext = new DbContext())
    {
        var data = await dbContext.GetDataAsync();
        return Ok(data);
    }
}
```

- **Race conditions**: A race condition is the result of multiple threads accessing and modifying shared data concurrently. For example, if you have a static field in your minimal API, and an endpoint that accesses it for modification, you must remember that requests can execute concurrently, with multiple clients potentially running the endpoint logic at the same time. This would cause the static field in your API to become inconsistent and therefore inaccurate. You must ensure that each operation against shared data is *atomic* – a single operation must complete before another occurs:

```
private static int _counter = 0;

public async Task<IResult> IncrementCounter()
{
    var newCounterValue = _counter + 1;
    await Task.Delay(100); // Simulate async work
    _counter = newCounterValue;
    return Results.Ok(_counter);
}
```

In this example, multiple requests to `IncrementCounter` can lead to an inconsistent state of `_counter`.

The solution to this problem is to use a synchronization mechanism to manage the state of a shared value. The most common synchronization mechanism is `lock`, which uses an `object` to block execution against a particular value while a thread is accessing it. This means *locking* it from access by other threads, forcing them to wait their turn:

```
private static int _counter = 0;
private static readonly object _counterLock =
    new object();
public async Task<IActionResult> IncrementCounter()
{
    lock (_counterLock)
```

```
        {
            var newCounterValue = _counter + 1;
            _counter = newCounterValue;
        }
        await Task.Delay(100); // Simulate async work
        return Ok(_counter);
    }
```

This example shows the establishment and execution of a `lock` to ensure that `_counter` is updated by one thread at a time, eliminating the possibility of race conditions occurring within the API.

Asynchronous programming can add a new layer of complexity to any minimal API project, but we've demonstrated in this chapter that with careful attention, it can be a powerful tool in optimizing API efficiency. Let's recap the areas covered in this chapter.

Summary

We opened this chapter with the pizza store analogy. We introduced asynchronous programming by likening it to a takeout food order that you don't simply wait for, but instead continue your ongoing tasks until the pizza is ready for you to collect.

We then laid the foundations for understanding how asynchronous code can benefit a minimal API, with its optimal use of hardware resources and scope for application scalability.

We explored some common asynchronous programming patterns, namely the TAP and deferred execution patterns, with examples of how the use of `async`/`await` can make asynchronous code more readable by making it look more like synchronous code. We explored how Deferred Execution can make an API asynchronous at the client level, allowing the client to receive an acknowledgment that their request has been received, along with a unique identifier for them to reference, stretching the overall end-to-end execution across multiple API requests.

Finally, we addressed the common challenges asynchronous programming presents, particularly in minimal APIs, with three common examples. The first was deadlocks, in which execution can no longer be continued on a global scale due to contention between multiple threads or operations. Next was poor resource management, in which the code does not account for the asynchronous context when disposing of connections to external resources. Lastly, we looked at race conditions, the classic example of multiple operations competing to update the state of a shared value or resource, causing inconsistent behavior and the creation of inaccurate data.

No software developer can easily escape the need to manage asynchronous execution, especially in a .NET minimal API. Thus, practicing vigilance, combined with good testing and the profiling techniques learned earlier in the book, can go a long way to making the experience as painless as possible.

Next, we will explore a critical method for optimizing the performance of any minimal API – caching.

12
Caching Strategies for Enhanced Performance

It's been frequently mentioned how minimal APIs should be just that, minimal. For the most part, this minimalism has been based on minimizing real estate – trying to keep the visible footprint of our code on the page as minimal as possible. But minimalism in APIs also extends to the resource footprint, meaning that, where possible, we should minimize the strain put on the system by overusing database/network connections and CPU.

Enhancing the performance of APIs through minimalism is the goal, and this can be achieved in part by caching.

When data is cached, it is stored following its first use for reuse in future operations. By doing this, we can reduce the latency or overhead incurred when fetching that data.

In this chapter, we're going to cover the following main topics:

- Introduction to caching in minimal APIs
- In-memory caching techniques
- Distributed caching strategies
- Response caching

Technical requirements

Visual Studio 2022 or Visual Studio Code will be required to run the code in this chapter. You will also need SQL Server 2022 installed on your system, with a working database you can query as an example. It is recommended that you complete *Chapter 9* before this chapter so that you have the example employee database configured for use.

The code for this chapter is available in the GitHub repository at: `https://github.com/PacktPublishing/Minimal-APIs-in-ASP.NET-9`.

This chapter demonstrates distributed caching strategies that require an in-memory caching provider – in this example's case, Redis. Installing Redis is not within the scope of this book, but documentation on how to install Redis or host it in Azure can be found at `https://learn.microsoft.com/en-us/azure/azure-cache-for-redis/quickstart-create-redis` and `https://redis.io/docs/latest/operate/oss_and_stack/install/install-redis/`.

The way to use Redis on your local Windows machine would be to install it through **Windows Subsystem for Linux** (**WSL**) and host it on your local WSL instance. More information on installing WSL can be found here: `https://learn.microsoft.com/en-us/windows/wsl/install`.

Introduction to caching in minimal APIs

APIs execute operations, and operations (usually) rely on data or state. Data needs to be retrieved or calculated as it either exists *at rest* (i.e., in a database or in a remote file location) or it exists as *data in use* (i.e., data that is yet to be calculated to produce other data).

Whichever way we look at it, there is overhead in retrieving data, whether it is retrieved as-is or whether it is the result of a computation. Caching aims to reduce that overhead by making use of data or state that has already been produced from its original source.

It could be argued that computing is so fast now that the overhead should be minimal to the point that caching is no longer needed. This would, however, be woefully inaccurate. Looking at a single operation in isolation, such as retrieving a record from a SQL database, may seem extremely quick, but at scale, the benefits of caching become more apparent.

Let's take a working example of how caching can be beneficial. A start-up has built a system that can be used to send alerts to mobile devices, accessible via a minimal API. They must ensure that requests are allowed to be processed by calling clients, so they require an API key to be sent in the request headers for validation during each request.

To validate the key, the start-up's developers decided to outsource the key validation to a cloud company that manages the key and the encryption algorithms to be used – hosting an API itself for this purpose. The start-up is charged per request for validating the key.

In the early days, the cost of validating keys went relatively unnoticed because they had a low number of sporadic requests. However, as soon as their business started to grow, so did the number of requests. Soon, they had a scary invoice from their cloud partner for a huge amount of API validations, charged per request.

Caching could have been used to mitigate the cost of validating API keys. An initial request could be made to validate the key, and then the result could be cached. From then on, when requests using that key are received, there would be an initial check against the cache first. If there is a record in the cache that validates the key, there is no need to call the paid API to validate it. Each cached record has an expiration date, meaning that it can be refreshed by calling the paid API again. This dramatically reduces the financial effects of validating API keys.

We've established that caching is good for performance, reducing latency, and supporting overall application scalability, but what type of caching should we use? To answer this, we will explore three key caching methods available in minimal API development: in-memory caching, distributed caching, and response caching.

In-memory caching techniques

Out of the various caching techniques supported by ASP.NET Core, **in-memory caching** is probably the simplest. This type of caching stores its contents in the memory of the machine hosting the minimal API.

The implementation of the cache is based on `IMemoryCache`, included within the `Microsoft.Extensions.Caching.Memory` package, which is usually included by default in ASP.NET Core projects.

Like other core services, `IMemoryCache` is available using dependency injection, so we can quite easily inject it as needed within various areas of a minimal API.

Using this cache type, we can store an object, which is our minimal requirement, but we can also very easily specify an expiration time, which is a best practice as periodically recycling the cache keeps it running smoothly.

Let's explore a simple example within a minimal API. I'm going to use the API project from *Chapter 9* (which is available on GitHub) as a foundation for this example project. Our aim is to mitigate the latency and overhead incurred when communicating with a database.

In this API, we have an endpoint that allows clients to get an employee with a specific ID. The API will use Entity Framework to run a SQL query against the database, returning the result in the request response.

Using an in-memory cache, we can add some optimization logic to this operation. Here are the steps we are going to work through:

1. Run the operation as requested, fetching the data from the database.
2. Check the in-memory cache to see whether the employee with this ID is currently cached.
3. If it isn't, add the retrieved employee to the cache.
4. Return the employee in the request response.
5. Create a request for the same employee (same ID).
6. Get the employee from the cache instead of the database.
7. Return the cached employee to the client.

Before we can achieve this goal, we need to reference `IMemoryCache` in the project.

First, add `IMemoryCache` to the dependency injection container in `Program.cs`:

```
builder.Services.AddMemoryCache();
```

Then, you can create the `GET` endpoint, injecting this `IMemoryCache` object along with `DapperService`:

```
app.MapGet(
    "/employees/{id}",
    async (int id,
           [FromServices] DapperService dapperService,
           IMemoryCache memoryCache) =>
{
});
```

Now that you have a cache, you can add code for retrieving values from it:

```
if(memoryCache.TryGetValue(id, out var result))
{
    return result;
}
```

By first running a check, we can avoid unnecessary execution of code and get the required object to the client much quicker, also avoiding a call into the database via Dapper.

Assuming that the item doesn't exist, we will use our original logic of looking up the `Employee` record from the database using `DapperService`. However, instead of returning the item straight away, we will first add it to the cache:

```
var employee = await dapperService.GetEmployeeById(id);
memoryCache.Set<Employee>(employee.Id, employee);
```

This works well but, ideally, we don't want this to stay in the cache forever. It's a good idea to refresh the cache periodically because data may change, and we want to ensure we are getting the most up-to-date data where possible while balancing this with reducing latency from database transactions.

We can strike this balance by imposing an expiration on cached objects. This needs to be done after the retrieval of the `Employee` object but before it is added to the cache. Let's set an expiry of 30 seconds as an example:

```
var cacheEntryOptions = new MemoryCacheEntryOptions()
    .SetSlidingExpiration(TimeSpan.FromSeconds(30));
```

By creating an instance of `MemoryCacheEntryOptions`, we have defined some cache configuration parameters that can be passed into the cache when we add a new object to it. Update the `cache.Set()` method to include this parameter:

```
memoryCache.Set<Employee>(
    employee.Id,
    employee,
    cacheEntryOptions);
```

Your endpoint should now look like this:

```
app.MapGet("/employees/{id}",
async (int id,
    [FromServices] DapperService
    dapperService, IMemoryCache memoryCache)
    =>
{
    if(memoryCache.TryGetValue(id,
        out var result))
    {
        return result;
    }

    var employee = await
        dapperService.GetEmployeeById(id);
    var cacheEntryOptions = new
        MemoryCacheEntryOptions()
            .SetSlidingExpiration(
                TimeSpan.FromSeconds(30));
    memoryCache.Set<Employee>(
        employee.Id,
        employee,
        cacheEntryOptions);

    return Results.Ok(employee);
});
```

There you go! You've successfully introduced caching to your minimal API endpoint using `IMemoryCache`.

In-memory caching is most likely the default caching strategy when starting an API project, but if your system has growth in adoption, then scalability and high availability will become increasingly important measurements of success. When looking to scale, distributed caching strategies can be adopted with the use of a reputable caching framework. Let's look at one of the most famous caching technologies, Redis.

Distributed caching strategies

A **distributed caching strategy** uses methods such as `IMemoryCache` within an architecture that supports scalability. In contrast to `IMemoryCache`, distributed caching involves a connection between the ASP.NET application hosting your minimal API and the caching provider.

In this example, the caching provider I will be using is **Redis**.

Redis is an in-memory caching provider that can also be used as an in-memory database. It is available as an open source product for installation on-premises or in the cloud.

For the purposes of this demonstration, I installed Redis on an Ubuntu machine as a basic service. I then updated the Redis configuration so that Redis binds to `0.0.0.0`, listening on the default port of `6379`. This should only be relevant to you if your Redis service is running on a separate machine like mine is.

With a Redis instance available, I can add the required NuGet packages to the API project for interacting with Redis as a cache.

Add the `NRedisStack` package to the project:

```
dotnet add package NRedisStack
```

We will still be interacting with the cache in `Program.cs`, so we need to reference namespaces from `NRedisStack` here:

```
using StackExchange.Redis;
```

Now, we can update the endpoint for retrieving employees by `Id` with a new cache, replacing the `IMemoryCache` implementation with Redis.

We start by creating `ConfigurationOptions`, which can be passed as a parameter when connecting to the Redis instance:

```
ConfigurationOptions options = new ConfigurationOptions
{
    EndPoints = { { "REDIS IP", 6379 } },
};

ConnectionMultiplexer redis =
    ConnectionMultiplexer.Connect(options);
IDatabase db = redis.GetDatabase();
```

Following this, we should now have a Redis connection that can be referenced in the db variable. Next, we will add the equivalent logic for caching from the IMemoryCache example, where we first check for a cache entry with a key (the Employee ID as a string, in this case) and return that if it exists, returning the Employee instance from the cache if it does:

```
var employeeIdKey = id.ToString();
var cachedEmployee = db.StringGet(employeeIdKey);

if (cachedEmployee.HasValue)
{
    return Results.Ok(
        JsonSerializer.Deserialize<Employee>(cachedEmployee)
    );
}
```

When calling `StringGet()` to retrieve a relevant entry from Redis, if it doesn't exist already, an object will be returned with HasValues set to false. Assuming that the Redis cache doesn't contain the Employee record we're looking for, we fetch it from the database and cache it before returning it to the client:

```
var employee = await dapperService.GetEmployeeById(id);
db.StringSet(
    employeeIdKey,
    JsonSerializer.Serialize(employee));
```

Please note that Redis doesn't natively support the insertion of strongly typed .NET objects, so we need to convert the Employee object to a JSON string through serialization when saving it and deserialize it from a JSON string to an Employee object when retrieving it.

Your updated Redis-connected endpoint should now look like this:

```
app.MapGet(
    "/employees/{id}",
    async (int id,
          [FromServices] DapperService dapperService) =>
{
    ConfigurationOptions options = new ConfigurationOptions
        {
          EndPoints = { { "192.168.2.8", 6379 } },
        };
        ConnectionMultiplexer redis =
            ConnectionMultiplexer.Connect(options);
        IDatabase db = redis.GetDatabase();
        var employeeIdKey = id.ToString();
        var cachedEmployee = db.StringGet(employeeIdKey);
```

```
            if (cachedEmployee.HasValue)
            {
                return Results.Ok(
                    JsonSerializer.Deserialize<Employee>(
                        cachedEmployee));
            }
            var employee = await
                dapperService.GetEmployeeById(id);
            return Results.Ok(employee);
});
```

Implementing a cache in a separately hosted environment using something such as Redis has introduced more flexibility to our minimal API. I encourage you to take this simple example further by creating a generic service that can facilitate the interactions between ASP.NET and the Redis cache so that you are ultimately decoupling the API from its caching system. In the future, should you wish to move away from Redis to a different caching technology, you need to be able to do this without affecting the original API code.

We've covered two examples of caching strategies so far. Let's wrap up with a third technique, focusing on the caching of request responses.

Response caching

Response caching works within the same logical principles as the previous two caching strategies, but instead of caching database objects in memory, it caches responses at the HTTP level.

Like `IMemoryCache`, minimal APIs can leverage ASP.NET's native middleware by enabling response caching as a feature in `Program.cs`:

```
var builder = WebApplication.CreateBuilder(args);
builder.Services.AddResponseCaching();
var app = builder.Build();
app.UseResponseCaching();
```

Once enabled, response caching is very simple to add to a `GET` endpoint. We can add `HttpContext` to the parameters, and then, whenever we have the `Employee` object and are ready to return it, we can set the response to be cached for a certain amount of time, meaning that requesting the same data within that time will simply return the cached HTTP response instead of touching the database:

```
    app.MapGet(
        "/employees/{id}",
        async (int id,
            [FromServices] DapperService dapperService,
```

```
            HttpContext context) =>
{
    var employee = await
        dapperService.GetEmployeeById(id);
    context.Response.GetTypedHeaders().CacheControl =
        new Microsoft.Net.Http.Headers
            .CacheControlHeaderValue()
{
    Public = true,
    MaxAge = TimeSpan.FromSeconds(60)
};
    context.Response.Headers[Microsoft.Net.Http.Headers
        .HeaderNames.Vary] =
            new string[] { "Accept-Encoding" };

    return Results.Ok(employee);
});
```

As you can see, this is a remarkably straightforward way to cache frequent responses, and the expiry time can, of course, be adjusted as needed. You could even combine the caching approaches, having an in-memory cache that retrieves the data and then caching the response.

With three working examples of caching in a minimal API under our belt, let's review what we've learned in this chapter.

Summary

In this chapter, we have explored caching using three different strategies: ASP.NET in-memory, distributed, and response caching.

We started by defining caching as a concept, relating it to the context of minimal APIs, before exploring a hypothetical scenario of a company looking to save on the cost of retrieving data via APIs with a cache.

Following this, we explored the ASP.NET native method of caching in memory, learning about `IMemoryCache` and how it can be implemented within an endpoint to limit the overhead produced by database transactions. We also learned how to make cached data expire.

Then, we took this knowledge and expanded on it, following similar caching principles within a distributed cache in the form of Redis.

Finally, we reviewed an example of response caching, allowing us to take frequently sent requests and bypass the database by resending a previously sent HTTP request.

In the next chapter, we will explore the best practices you can observe to increase the readibility, scalability and maintainability of your minimal APIs.

Part 4 - Best Practices, Design, and Deployment

In the final part, we shift our focus to the principles of robust API design and deployment. You'll learn about best practices for shipping production-ready minimal APIs, as well as strategies for testing and maintaining compatibility across different environments.

This part has the following chapters:

- *Chapter 13, Best Practices for Minimal API Resiliency*
- *Chapter 14, Unit Testing, Compatibility, and Deployment of Minimal APIs*

13
Best Practices for Minimal API Resiliency

Like any software system, minimal APIs can be built in many ways. By carefully choosing and applying different patterns and following some set practices, an application can be greatly enhanced.

There are several good reasons to build patterns into the design of your minimal API, the first being readability. Since most of us are part of a team and may have other developers to delegate or hand over code, making it as accessible as possible is paramount. By ensuring that your endpoints are tidy, that code is as *self-documenting* as possible, and that the naming conventions are consistent, it will be relatively straightforward for another developer to support the maintenance of an API project.

Next is scalability. If the volume of requests grows, so will the need to optimize an application. Consistency and good design make meeting demands simple. Whether adding a load balancer to manage traffic flow or changing the data storage method, it is essential to design APIs in such a way that modifications to the system—whether adding or removing components—do not break functionality across the application.away parts of the system does not break functionality across the application.

Finally, security is equally important. By following best security practices such as encryption at rest and in transit, password hashing and salting, and scoped access, sensitive data can be managed securely, reducing the risk of a breach and the ensuing legal challenges that present themselves as a result.

Ultimately, achieving these goals depends on applying practices that concern the way a code base is structured for readability, the way unexpected and fatal scenarios are dealt with in error handling, and the considerations applied from a cybersecurity perspective.

Let's realize some of these benefits in your minimal API projects by exploring some design practices and coding conventions that can improve the quality of your code.

In this chapter, we're going to cover the following main topics:

- Code organization and structure
- Error handling
- Security considerations

Let's get into it!

Technical requirements

Visual Studio 2022 or the latest version of Visual Studio code is recommended to run the code from this chapter. The code examples for this chapter are available in the GitHub repository at: `https://github.com/PacktPublishing/Minimal-APIs-in-ASP.NET-9`.

One of the examples uses code from *Chapters 9* and *12*, both of which have a dependency on Entity Framework Core. It is recommended that you complete those chapters before this one.

Code organization and structure

Perhaps the most important thing to understand about organizing and structuring code in any system is that there is no one correct way to do it. While there are some widely accepted structural patterns, this can be quite a personal topic, as a structure must serve the maintainer. However, as we have previously confirmed, most minimal API systems in a commercial or open-source setting will have multiple maintainers, so a consistent structure will make it as easy as possible for developers to collaborate on the code base.

We will explore two examples of ways that a project can be organized, both sharing one key theme – modularity.

Modularity is the practice of organizing and structuring your code into smaller, self-contained, and reusable units or modules. Let's break down some of the benefits of this practice:

- **Separation of concerns**: By grouping together code containing similar functionality, we create contexts within the code base that mirror the business domains they serve. For example, code that is solely based on the context of managing users is separate from code that is solely based on managing products. Establishing clear boundaries between these contexts ensures that dependencies are minimized.

- **Reusability**: Adopting a modular design allows you to create components such as the ones we explored in this book – for example, services and middleware. In a system where separation of concerns is the aim, having reusable components can help bridge contexts as necessary in a way that reduces the creation of dependencies.

- **Ease of maintenance**: Modules can be developed and tested independently of each other, making parallel development between multiple developers easier. Modularization also supports the open-closed principle, which states, "*Software entities (classes, modules, functions, etc.) should be open for extension, but closed for modification.*"

This means that, in an ideal world, whenever we want to extend our minimal API with new functionality, we *do* not need to change the existing code base to enable the change.

Effective organization of code is often dominated by architectural design patterns. While this is certainly important, simply reorganizing the folder structure of a project goes a long way to making code readable and simpler to maintain.

Let's explore some example folder structures.

Exploring folder structures

Most of the time, simple consideration of the way a project's folders are arranged within a project can significantly improve the readability and maintainability of a minimal API. We're looking for a consistent system to lay out classes and interfaces. Let's look at some specific folder structures that we can apply to our projects to achieve this.

Feature-based modular structure

In this structure, the minimal API project is organized by features, with each feature having its own folder, containing everything related to that feature, regardless of what kind of component is used. Here's an example of such a structure:

```
/src
  /MyMinimalApiProject
    /Modules
      /Users
        UserEndpoints.cs
        UserService.cs
        UserRepository.cs
        User.cs
        UserDto.cs
        UserValidator.cs
      /Products
        ProductEndpoints.cs
        ProductService.cs
        ProductRepository.cs
        Product.cs
        ProductDto.cs
        ProductValidator.cs
```

```
      /Middleware
        ErrorHandlingMiddleware.cs
        AuthenticationMiddleware.cs
      /Configuration
        SwaggerConfig.cs
        DependencyInjectionConfig.cs
      /Utils
        DateTimeHelper.cs
        LoggingHelper.cs
      Program.cs
      appsettings.json
```

In this structure, the developer is expected to adopt a feature-based mindset. For example, if you want to add an endpoint relating to user management, you would head to a folder based on users rather than one dedicated to endpoints.

As mentioned earlier in the chapter, folder structures can be a personal and somewhat polarizing topic. Some may not prefer to mix component types under the banner of a feature set, while others enjoy the domain-based nature of this structure and are less concerned with what kind of component acts within each domain.

Layered modular structure

This structure is the one I prefer personally because I tend to think about the type of component before I think about the feature or business domain. In a layered modular structure, the project is first grouped by components (e.g., endpoints and services) and then further broken down into business modules/features.

If you are like me and tend to think about the kind of class or file that I am looking to create or edit before I think about the domain in which it lives, this folder structure will work better for you. However, it's important to note that while this kind of structure prioritizes component types when creating folders, there is still a dedicated `Domain` folder that exists to hold entity models and **Data Transfer Objects** (**DTOs**), which describe the business domain. Here is an example of a layered modular file structure in a minimal API project:

```
/src
  /MyMinimalApiProject
    /Endpoints
      /Users
        UserEndpoints.cs
        UserValidator.cs
      /Products
        ProductEndpoints.cs
        ProductValidator.cs
```

```
/Services
    /Users
        UserService.cs
    /Products
        ProductService.cs
/Repositories
    /Users
        UserRepository.cs
    /Products
        ProductRepository.cs
/Domain
    /Entities
        User.cs
        Product.cs
    /DTOs
        UserDto.cs
        ProductDto.cs
/Middleware
    ErrorHandlingMiddleware.cs
    AuthenticationMiddleware.cs
/Configuration
    SwaggerConfig.cs
    DependencyInjectionConfig.cs
/Utils
    DateTimeHelper.cs
    LoggingHelper.cs
Program.cs
appsettings.json
```

Now that we've explored some simple examples of how folders can be structured within a minimal API project, let's look at some repeatable patterns that can be adopted when structuring a project's code. These patterns are referred to as *design patterns*, and like folder structure, there is debate around which patterns constitute best practice.

Design patterns

This book is not designed to tell you which patterns are the best; rather, it is designed to give you some guidance on how you can structure your code consistently to create a consistent API system. Here are some example patterns.

The factory pattern

A **factory pattern** is designed to create objects without specifying the exact class of object that will be created. Earlier, I mentioned the open/closed principle, and factory patterns help minimal APIs adhere to this principle by closing the code for modification while making it open for extension.

Let's consider an example use case in which you want to create logs in different locations. One location is via a database, and another is in a text file.

In the future, you may want to add more log sources, such as a Webhook or third-party API. A factory could help you retrieve the correct logger for your use case while making it simple to add new loggers without changing the old ones.

Let's look at an example of how we can improve logging by implementing a factory pattern:

1. First, create an interface called `ILogger`, which will be implemented by all loggers, regardless of the specific log they execute when saving a log to their respective source. `ILogger` is an interface that will represent an object that implements logic for the purposes of writing logs to different sources:

   ```
   public interface ILogger
   {
       void Log(string message);
   }
   ```

2. Next, create two classes that each implement `ILogger`. One of the classes, `FileLogger`, will be used to log to a file, and another, `DatabaseLogger`, will log to a database:

   ```
   public class FileLogger : ILogger
   {
       public void Log(string message)
       {
           // Logic to log to a file
       }
   }

   public class DatabaseLogger : ILogger
   {
       public void Log(string message)
       {
           // Logic to log to a database
       }
   }
   ```

   These classes may have different names, but they are both an `ILogger` object meaning that they must implement the `Log()` method.

3. Furthermore, we can create a function that returns `ILogger`, as shown here:

```
public static class LoggerFactory
{
    public static ILogger CreateLogger(
        string loggerType
    )
    {
        return loggerType switch
        {
            "File" => new FileLogger(),
            "Database" => new DatabaseLogger(),
            _ => throw new ArgumentException(
            "Invalid logger type")
        };
    }
}
```

In this example, we created a `LoggerFactory` class with a function that returns the relevant logger class, depending on the contents of a string that was entered by the caller. If the `loggerType` parameter is not valid, an exception is thrown, allowing the error to be handled.

The main benefit to this is that to add another logger, we simply create a new class that implements `ILogger` before adding a new entry to the `switch` statement in `CreateLogger()`. We haven't had to introduce any breaking changes to extend the types of loggers that are supported in the API.

The repository pattern

This pattern creates an abstraction layer for data access logic, providing a more general API to access data from a database for the minimal API.

Earlier in the book, we explored Entity Framework Core to access data from a database. Simply by using Entity Framework Core, your code already uses a repository pattern because it provides an implementation of the repository pattern that utilizes the built-in `DBContext`.

However, it is still worth implementing a custom repository pattern to handle data so that you further generalize the solution, meaning that Entity Framework Core could be swapped out of the minimal API application without affecting the overall data access logic.

To create a repository pattern on top of Entity Framework Core, we can simply create a class for each entity in the database. Each repository class receives the Entity Framework context via dependency injection, and then the generic **Create, Read, Update, Delete** (**CRUD**) operations for this entity can be added. Following this, each repository can be also registered for dependency injection for use elsewhere in an application.

In the following example, `EmployeeRepository` reflects the available data operations available for an employee entity. As described, the Entity Framework context is injected as the data access layer to be used within the repository:

```csharp
public class EmployeeRepository : IEmployeeRepository
{
    private readonly MyCompanyContext _context;

    public EmployeeRepository(MyCompanyContext context)
    {
        _context = context;
    }

    public async Task<Employee> GetByIdAsync(int id)
    {
        return await _context.Employees.FindAsync(id);
    }

    public async Task<IEnumerable<Employee>> GetAllAsync()
    {
        return await _context.Employees.ToListAsync();
    }

    public async Task AddAsync(Employee employee)
    {
        await _context.Employees.AddAsync(employee);
        await _context.SaveChangesAsync();
    }

    public async Task UpdateAsync(Employee employee)
    {
        _context.Employees.Update(employee);
        await _context.SaveChangesAsync();
    }

    public async Task DeleteAsync(int id)
    {
        var employee = await
            _context.Employees.FindAsync(id);
        if (employee != null)
        {
            _context.Employees.Remove(employee);
            await _context.SaveChangesAsync();
        }
```

```
        }
    }
```

Going forward, if a decision is made to replace Entity Framework Core, the only thing that needs to change is the repository. The consumers of the repository would not be affected because the methods and functions they call within the repository would maintain their original signatures, despite their underlying logic changing.

The strategy pattern

The **Strategy pattern** allows us to define a family of algorithms, each one represented by a class. This pattern is very powerful in situations where there are multiple ways of executing an operation, as you can seamlessly switch between them in a dynamic fashion.

Let's look at an example involving a minimal API endpoint that calculates how much annual leave an employee has. In this example, there are different ways to calculate leave based on various factors, such as which country the employee is in, whether they are in their probationary period, and how many years they have served at the company.

Here is an example outline of the logic to calculate leave (not related to any specific labor laws in any country!):

- If the employee is in their probationary period, the following applies:
  - The minimum amount of leave awarded is 10 days
  - If the employee is based in the United Kingdom, they get an extra three days
- If the employee is not on probation, the following applies:
  - The minimum amount of leave awarded is 16 days
  - If the employee is based in the United Kingdom, they get an extra three days
  - For each year of service, an extra day is awarded

There are a lot of factors in play here, but to start with, we can narrow down the operations required to calculate leave based on whether the employee is or is not on probation. This means we have two strategies to calculate leave, which we can switch to automatically. How do we achieve this?

1. First, we create an interface to represent a strategy. It stipulates that we require a `CalculateLeaveAllowance()` function taking a parameter of type `Employee` and returning an integer:

    ```
    public interface IAnnualLeaveStrategy
    {
        int CalculateLeaveAllowance(
    ```

```
            Models.Employee employee
    );
}
```

2. Then, we'll create `ProbationaryAnnualLeaveStrategy`, which implements the interface. Within this class, `CalculateLeaveAllowance` will encapsulate the logic to calculate the total leave available for a probationary employee:

```
public class ProbationaryAnnualLeaveStrategy
    : IAnnualLeaveStrategy
{

    public int CalculateLeaveAllowance(
        Models.Employee employee
    )
    {
        var leaveTotal = 10;
        if(employee.Country == "United Kingdom")
        {
            leaveTotal += 3;
        }
        return leaveTotal;
    }
}
```

3. Then, the same can be done for an employee who is not on probation:

```
public class PostProbationaryAnnualLeaveStrategy
    : IAnnualLeaveStrategy
{
    public int CalculateLeaveAllowance(
        Models.Employee employee
    )
    {
        var leaveTotal = 16;
        if(employee.Country == "United Kingdom")
        {
            leaveTotal += 3;
        }
    leaveTotal += employee.YearsOfService;
        return leaveTotal;
    }
}
```

4. The two strategies should be registered for dependency injection in `Program.cs`:

   ```
   builder.Services
       .AddScoped<
           ProbationaryAnnualLeaveStrategy
       >();
   builder.Services
       .AddScoped<
           PostProbationaryAnnualLeaveStrategy
       >();
   ```

5. Finally, an endpoint can be created to calculate the annual leave for a given `Employee` ID. Within the endpoint, we create the strategy based on whether or not the employee is on probation. We then retrieve `Employee` using the ID sent by the client and call the `CalculateLeaveAllowance()` function to get the result. This way, the appropriate strategy is automatically used to execute the correct logic, based on the data that was sent by the client in the request:

   ```
   app.MapGet(
       "/calculate-employee-leave-allowance/
           {employeeId}",
       async (int employeeId,
           bool employeeOnProbation,
           [FromServices]
           EmployeeService employeeService) =>
   {
       IAnnualLeaveStrategy annualLeaveStrategy =
           employeeOnProbation
               ? new ProbationaryAnnualLeaveStrategy()
               : new PostProbationaryAnnualLeaveStrategy();
       var employee = await
           employeeService.GetEmployeeById(employeeId);
       return annualLeaveStrategy
           .CalculateLeaveAllowance(employee);
   });
   ```

By separating logic into individual strategies, the Strategy pattern allows minimal APIs to conform to the open/closed principle. It does that by allowing us to extend the code base with new functionality, rather than alter the existing code.

It also offers self-containment, meaning that ways of performing similar tasks do not cross-contaminate each other, which reduces the potential for bugs.

Design patterns alone do not make a resilient system. Resiliency is achieved through a good understanding of where and how errors occur.

> **Years of service property required**
>
> The example in this section will work with the original `Employee` object used in *Chapter 9* if you add an `int` property, called `YearsOfService`. We assume that you will have done this before attempting to follow this strategy pattern example.

With that in mind, let's move on to explore good practices around error handling in minimal APIs.

Error Handling

When it comes to the topic of error handling and resilience, the first is the method and the second is the outcome. By implementing effective error handling, we achieve resilience.

So, while using `try/catch` across the code base is important, a standardized manner of handling errors at the top level is still critical. For a minimal API, middleware is an effective way to handle errors from the top level. Let's explore an example.

> **Note**
>
> This section assumes that you read *Chapter 5* or that you already have an in-depth understanding of how to write middleware in ASP.NET.

Implementing middleware ensures that we have a global solution to error handling in a minimal API. Think of it as a giant `try/catch` that wraps around all of your minimal API's endpoints.

As we explored middleware extensively in *Chapter 5*, we do not need to go through the specifics of how middleware is built, so we shall dive straight into an example of an error-handling middleware class, as shown in the upcoming code blocks.

First, we create a class for the middleware, along with a constructor and an `InvokeAsync` method that can be used to initiate the middleware's logic:

```
public class ErrorHandlingMiddleware
{
    private readonly RequestDelegate _next;
    private readonly ILogger<ErrorHandlingMiddleware> 
        _logger;

    public ErrorHandlingMiddleware(
        RequestDelegate next,
        ILogger<ErrorHandlingMiddleware> logger
    )
    {
        _next = next;
        _logger = logger;
```

```csharp
    }

    public async Task InvokeAsync(HttpContext context)
    {
        try
        {
            await _next(context);
        }
        catch (Exception ex)
        {
            _logger.LogError(
                ex, "An unhandled exception occurred."
            );
            await HandleExceptionAsync(context, ex);
        }
    }
}
```

Following this, we can add a method that takes in the current `HttpContext` to handle any detected errors:

```csharp
    private static Task HandleExceptionAsync(
        HttpContext context, Exception exception)
    {
    If (context.Response.HasStarted) return;
    context.Response.ContentType = "application/json";
    context.Response.StatusCode =
        (int)HttpStatusCode.InternalServerError;

        var response = new
        {
            message =
                "An unexpected error occurred. Please try
                again later.",
            details = exception.Message
        };

        return context.Response.WriteAsJsonAsync(response);
    }
}
```

It is worth noting that this middleware example for error handling could easily replace the similar error handling example in *Chapter 5*.

This middleware will catch an exception thrown higher up in the request pipeline, ensuring that the error is returned to the requesting client via `HttpContext`. This ensures a consistent error response to the client regardless of the endpoint that was called.

As you will be aware from earlier in the book, middleware, such as services for dependency injection, must be registered in `Program.cs`. Register this middleware class as the first piece of middleware to be registered, and then create an example endpoint that throws an exception:

```
app.UseMiddleware<ErrorHandlingMiddleware>();
app.MapGet(
    "/error",
    () => {
        throw new InvalidOperationException(
            "This is a test exception");
    });
```

You should find that not only the message from the exception is returned but also a generic message, consistently, like the one shown here:

```
{
    "message": "An unexpected error occurred. Please try
        again later.",
    "details": "This is a test exception"
}
```

Another practice that should be consistent when developing any API is that of secure development. Let's explore some good security practices that you can apply when authorizing requests to your minimal API.

Security considerations

There are two critical areas of security within a minimal API – authentication and authorization. Regardless of their differences, the attitude toward their implementation should be largely the same – *don't roll your own*.

This mantra serves as a warning that a proven security framework will usually be safer than one you devise yourself.

Let's first look at the difference between authentication and authorization, as well as how you can achieve a good degree of security using the well-known technology **JSON Web Tokens (JWTs)**.

Authentication

Authentication verifies the identity of users or systems accessing your API. It allows you to allow only legitimate requests to enter a system.

JWTs are widely used for their stateless authentication capabilities in minimal APIs. Users authenticate once and receive a token, which is included in subsequent requests to access protected resources.

Authorization

Authorization is a means of checking to see whether an authenticated user is accessing resources within their specific permissions. In JWT, these permissions are known as **claims**.

A claim can be the name of a resource or type of user, or it can be a role. Either way, JWT has built-in functionality to define and validate claims against specific endpoints in a minimal API:

1. To get started with this authorization framework, we first need to add the `Microsoft.AspNetCore.Authentication.JwtBearer` NuGet package. Do this via the NuGet Package Manager Console, accessible via **Tools | NuGet Package Manager | Package Manager Console**:

    ```
    dotnet add package Microsoft
        .AspNetCore.Authentication.JwtBearer
    ```

2. We then need to ensure that `Program.cs` has the relevant namespaces:

    ```
    using Microsoft.AspNetCore.Authentication.JwtBearer;
    using Microsoft.IdentityModel.Tokens;
    using System.Text;
    using System.IdentityModel.Tokens.Jwt;
    using System.Security.Claims;
    using Microsoft.AspNetCore.Authorization;
    ```

3. JWT can be implemented as a middleware, so it should first be set up in `Program.cs`:

    ```
    builder.AddAuthorization();
    builder.Services.AddAuthentication(
        JwtBearerDefaults.AuthenticationScheme)
        .AddJwtBearer(options =>
        {
            options.TokenValidationParameters =
                new TokenValidationParameters
                {
                    ValidateIssuer = true,
                    ValidateAudience = true,
                    ValidateLifetime = true,
                    ValidateIssuerSigningKey = true,
                    ValidIssuer = "https://yourdomain.com",
                    ValidAudience = "https://yourdomain.com",
                    IssuerSigningKey =
                        new SymmetricSecurityKey(
                            Encoding.UTF8.GetBytes(
    ```

```
                            "A_Not_Very_Secret_Key_1234567
                                         890"
                        )
                    )
            };
        });

        var app = builder.Build();
        app.UseAuthentication();
        app.UseAuthorization();
```

4. This registration specifies how your tokens are validated. Next, we need to provide a means of generating a token. We can do this by creating a dedicated API endpoint:

```
        app.MapGet("/generate-token", () =>
        {
            var tokenHandler =
                new JwtSecurityTokenHandler();
            var key = Encoding.UTF8.GetBytes(
                " A_Not_Very_Secret_Key_1234567890"
            );

            var tokenDescriptor =
                new SecurityTokenDescriptor
            {
                Subject = new ClaimsIdentity(new[]
                {
    new Claim(ClaimTypes.Name, "TestUser"),
    new Claim(ClaimTypes.Role, "Admin")
}),
                Expires = DateTime.UtcNow.AddHours(1),
                Issuer = "https://yourdomain.com",
                Audience = "https://yourdomain.com",
                SigningCredentials =
                    new SigningCredentials(
                        new SymmetricSecurityKey(key),
                            SecurityAlgorithms
                                .HmacSha256Signature
                    )
            };

            var token =
                tokenHandler.CreateToken(tokenDescriptor);
            var tokenString =
```

```
            tokenHandler.WriteToken(token);

        return Results.Ok(tokenString);
});
```

5. Finally, now that we have a means of creating a JWT token, we can create an endpoint that requires it. Let's again create a simple GET endpoint, but this time, we add an [Authorize] attribute and chain RequireAuthorization() to it:

```
app.MapGet(
    "/secure",
    [Authorize] () => "This is a secure endpoint")
    .RequireAuthorization();
```

6. To test this, we can make a GET request to this endpoint and add the returned JWT token as a bearer token. With an example JWT token, the header would look something like this:

```
"Authorization: Bearer eyJhbGciOiJIUzI1NiIsInR5cCI6IkpXVCJ9.
eyJ1bmlxdWVfbmFtZSI6IlRlc3RVc2VyIiwicm9sZSI6IkFkbWluIiwibm-
JmIjoxNjQyNzE2MzY0LCJleHAiOjE2NDI3MTk5NjQsImlhdCI6MTY0MjcxN-
jM2NCwiaXNzIjoiaHR0cHM6Ly95b3VyZG9tYWluLmNvbSIsImF1ZCI6Imh0dH-
BzOi8veW91cmRvbWFpbi5jb20ifQ.-Ym30PjdvWl5eYdltZd0yA5XQ1ikf5D-
4KrDlmHMIj0s"
```

ASP.NET core will then authenticate the request, based on the validation parameters you specified when you registered the JWT middleware.

7. Taking this further, if we wanted to create a more restricted endpoint, which can only be accessed by users with the role claim, Admin, we can add a parameter to the [Authorize] attribute:

```
app.MapGet(
    "/admin",
    [Authorize(Roles = "Admin")] () =>
{
    return Results.Ok("Welcome, Admin!");
});
```

Using JWT tokens, our minimal APIs are provided with protection against unauthorized activity. However, this alone will not guarantee that authorized use is not abused.

In truth, it is impossible to guarantee this, but an extra step you can take to ensure that a minimal API is not abused is to limit the number of requests that can be made during a specified period. This practice is called **rate limiting**.

Rate limiting

By controlling the number of requests a client can make to your minimal API within a specific timeframe, rate limiting can help prevent a system from being overwhelmed by too many requests, whether the requests are legitimate or not.

Let's explore a simple example of rate limiting in an ASP.NET core minimal API.

First, add the `AspNetCoreRateLimit` package from NuGet via the Package Manager Console. You can open this in Visual Studio by clicking **Tools | Manage NuGet Packages | Package Manager Console**. This will open the console, in which you can type the following:

```
dotnet add package AspNetCoreRateLimit
```

Then, add rate limiting (along with memory caching) via `Program.cs`:

```csharp
using AspNetCoreRateLimit;

var builder = WebApplication.CreateBuilder(args);
builder.Services.AddMemoryCache();
builder.Services.Configure<IpRateLimitOptions>(options =>
{
    options.GeneralRules = new List<RateLimitRule>
    {
        new RateLimitRule
        {
            Endpoint = "*",
            Limit = 10,
            Period = "1m"
        }
    };
});
builder.Services
    .AddSingleton<IRateLimitConfiguration,
        RateLimitConfiguration>();
builder.Services.AddInMemoryRateLimiting();

var app = builder.Build();
app.UseIpRateLimiting();

app.MapGet("/", () => "Hello, World!");

app.Run();
```

This configuration will limit all endpoints to a maximum of 100 requests per minute, per IP address. If the limit is exceeded, the client will receive a `429 Too Many Requests` response.

To try this example out, change the maximum number of requests per minute to 2 and see what the results look like.

> **AspNetCoreRateLimit versus Microsoft.AspNetCore.RateLimiting**
>
> There is another option for rate limiting besides `AspNetCoreRateLimit`, shown in the preceding example. `Microsoft.AspNetCore.RateLimiting` can also be used to manage the rate of allowed requests. `AspNetCoreRateLimit` is a third-party library, while `Microsoft.AspNetCore.RateLimiting` is built-in middleware. For configuration, `AspNetCoreRateLimit` uses JSON or programmatic configuration, whereas `Microsoft.AspNetCore.RateLimiting` uses programmatic configuration with `RateLimiterOptions`.
>
> `AspNetCoreRateLimit` offers more flexibility with different strategies and distributed rate limiting, while `Microsoft.AspNetCore.RateLimiting` focuses on built-in algorithms and endpoint-specific policies.

We've only scratched the surface of the practices that can be implemented to improve resilience in minimal APIs, but the examples we have explored are a good starting point to improve their design. Let's recap the practices that we've seen in this chapter.

Summary

We started by observing the justification for implementing effective design practices – namely, for an increase in resiliency from a maintained scalability and security perspective.

We then looked at folder structures, with personal preferences discussed and a couple of folder structure examples outlined for use in a fresh project.

We then explored three design patterns in the form of factory, repository, and strategy, providing a solid foundation to arrange minimal API code in a scalable manner.

Then, we briefly reviewed an example of how middleware can act as a "global catch," standardizing the way error responses are returned to a client, before finally exploring some simple ways of authenticating requests and limiting the rate at which they can be processed.

We're moving closer to the end of the book, which means we will need to learn how to manage a minimal API that is deployed and active in a user base. With that in mind, the next chapter will cover the things we need to consider most when making our minimal API available to the wider world – testing, deployment, and documentation.

14
Unit Testing, Compatibility, and Deployment of Minimal APIs

It's an exciting time when you're preparing to deploy an application to production. Before that can happen, there are many questions to be answered, namely, "Is this quality code?", "Is everything going to work as intended?", and "Will it be sustainable over a long period of time?".

To help set our minimal APIs up for success, testing is required before they go into the hands of users or become responsible for any critical business operations.

This statement is *really* obvious. Of course we need to test, but in some cases, what is less obvious is *how* we will be testing. Unit and integration testing can help us in this area, offering an automated solution to testing our acceptance criteria, checking for new bugs introduced by code changes, often referred to as **regression**, and giving us (in some IDEs literally) a red or green light for deployment.

There is also compatibility to consider before deployment. What operating system are we deploying to? What kind of web server will be in use? Are we hosting in the cloud or on-premises?

Finally, the appropriate method of deployment can be dictated by all of the preceding considerations. It seems like a lot, but it will be worth it when we inevitably deploy our minimal APIs with confidence that they will bring the intended value, and hopefully more.

In this chapter, we will cover the following:

- Unit testing and integration testing for minimal APIs
- Compatibility and migrating minimal APIs to .NET 9
- Deploying minimal APIs

Technical requirements

Visual Studio 2022 or the latest version of Visual Studio code is recommended in order to run the code from this chapter. The code examples for this chapter are available in the GitHub repository at: `https://github.com/PacktPublishing/Minimal-APIs-in-ASP.NET-9`.

To follow along with all deployment methods in this chapter, you will need to have access to an Azure subscription and be able to install Docker.

Unit testing and integration testing for minimal APIs

It's highly likely that you've come across the terms unit testing and integration testing, but by way of a refresher, let's briefly define them.

Unit testing involves testing individual components of functions of a code base in isolation, whereas integration testing checks how different components of modules of a system interact. In a minimal API, a unit test may simply test that a service does what it should, while an integration test would confirm that an HTTP request to the endpoint uses the services and other components together correctly.

In short, you're either testing a single unit of code, or you're testing how different units interact with each other.

Let's create a unit test for a service that does something very simple: calculate the sum of given numerical values. Here is the service as it looks in `Program.cs`, where it is registered for dependency injection and used as part of a POST endpoint:

```
public class Program
{
    public static void Main(string[] args)
    {
        var builder = WebApplication.CreateBuilder(args);
        builder.Services.AddTransient<CalculatorService>();
        var app = builder.Build();


        app.MapPost(
            "/SumIntegers",
            (int[] integers,
             CalculatorService calculatorService) =>
        {
            var result = calculatorService.Sum(integers);
            return Results.Ok(result);
        });
```

```
        app.Run();
    }
}
```

There are several testing frameworks we can implement, but to keep things simple, I'm going to use xUnit:

1. Right-click your solution in Visual Studio and select **Add | New Project...**.

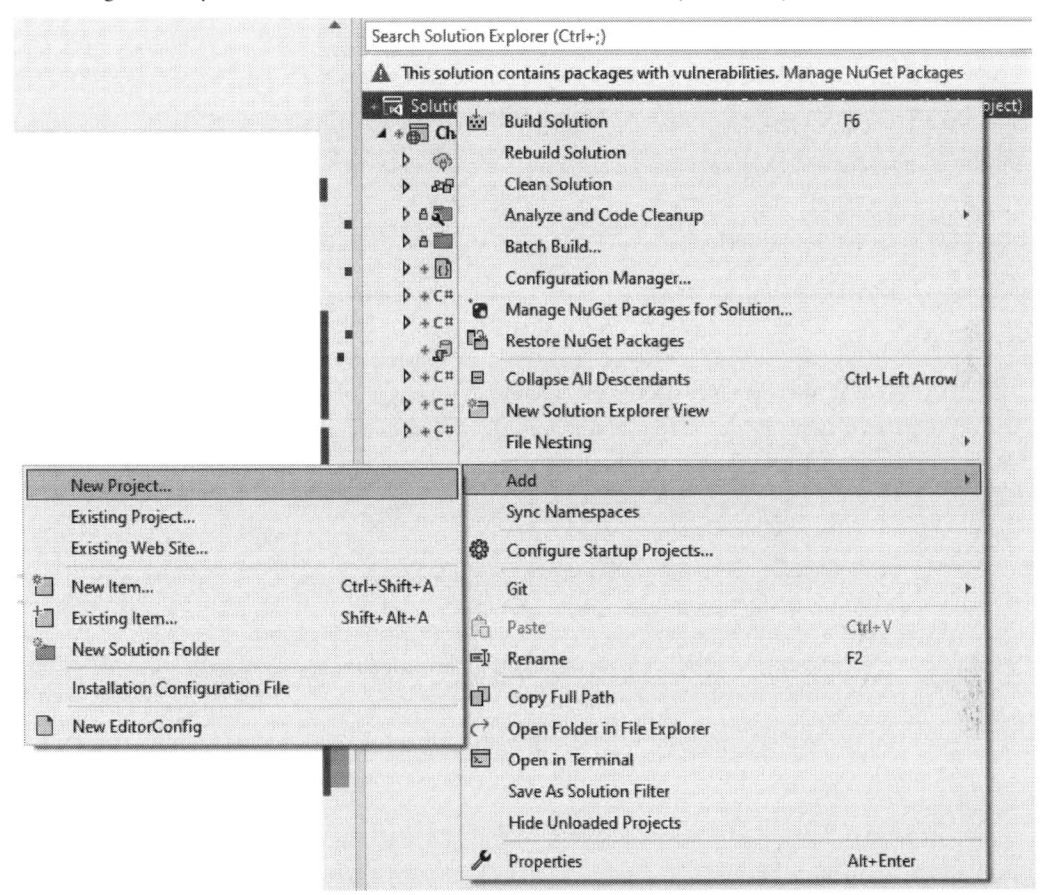

Figure 14.1: Add a new project from within Solution Explorer

2. Then search for **xUnit** (or your preferred testing framework if you don't wish to follow along exactly).

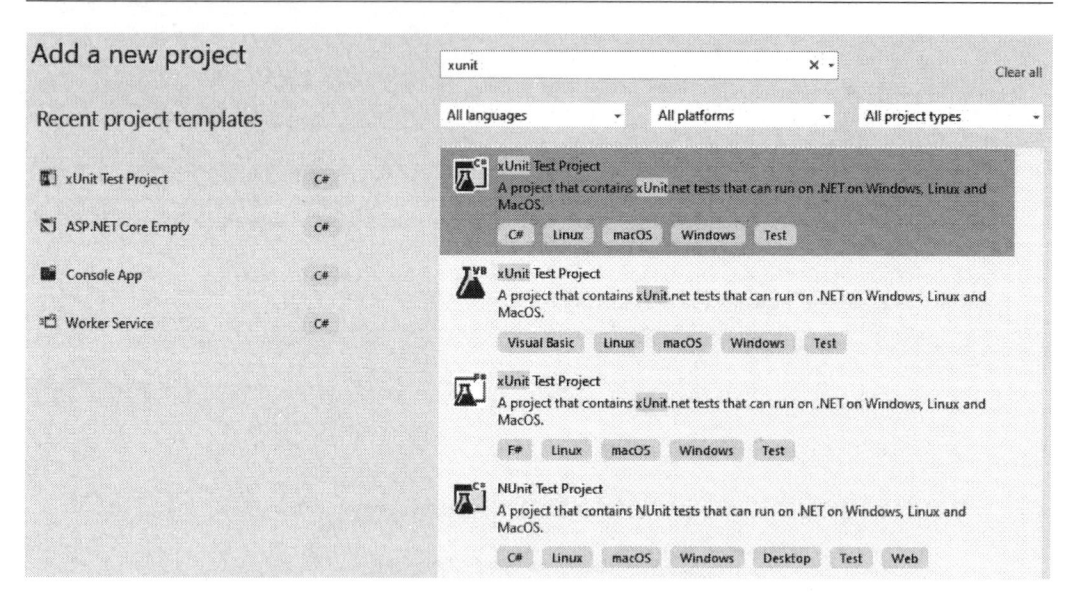

Figure 14.2: Creating a new xUnit project

3. If the **Do not use top-level statements** option is shown, I recommend unchecking it so that you can clearly see the namespaces you're using in each class. It is a personal preference but it will make it easier for you to follow along with this example.

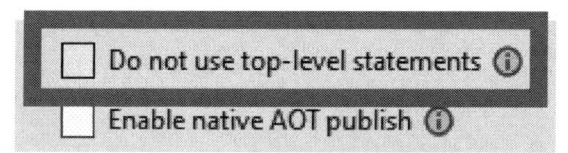

Figure 14.3: Unchecking the Do not use top-level statements box

4. Once you've created your test project within the solution, right-click **Dependencies** for the test project and add a project reference to your API project.

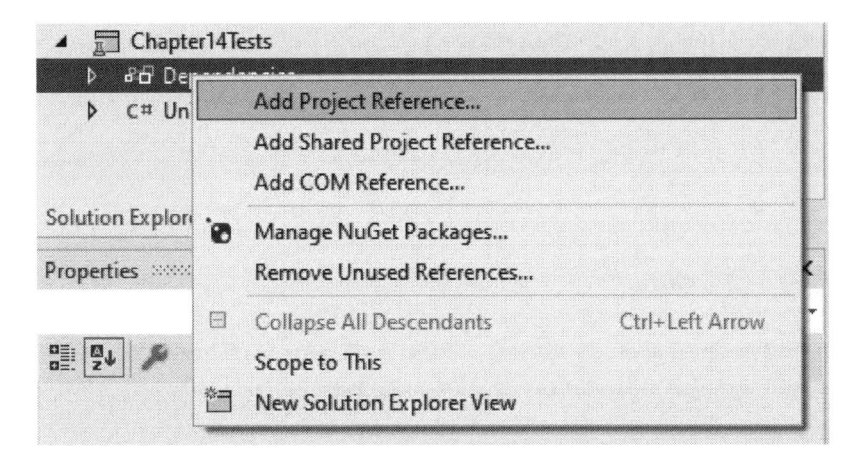

Figure 14.4: Adding a reference to another project

You now have two projects in your solution. One is a minimal API project and the other is a testing project linked to the former.

We can now start writing some tests. Let's start with a simple unit test against `CalculatorService`

In our test project, create a new class called `CalculatorTests`. Then, update the code so that a method called `Sum_Test()` exists, with an attribute above the method signature, `[Fact]`:

```
[Fact]
public void Sum_Test()
{

}
```

The `[Fact]` attribute is what xUnit uses to mark a method as a test. I like to think of it in the sense that we are stating that the method represents something that should be fact; it should be objective. In this case, we want a test that proves the fact that the sum of a given collection of integers is equal to the value we are expecting it to be. Let's explore this in more detail by writing the test logic.

In the body of `Sum_Test()`, instantiate a new instance of `CalculatorService` and create an array of integers that we can use during our test:

```
var calculatorService = new CalculatorService();
int[] integers = [ 1, 1, 8 ];
```

Because we kept this simple, it is easy to see at a glance that the expected result for the sum of the values in `integers` must be `10`.

Add a call to the `Sum()` function within `CalculatorService` and store it in a variable. Also, add a hardcoded variable of `10` for the expected result:

```
var result = calculatorService.Sum(integers);
var expectedResult = 10;
```

In unit testing, there is a principle known as the *three As*, which stands for arrange, act, and assert:

1. The first step, arrange, forces us to gather data and resources in a particular state so that testing is possible. We have achieved this by creating an instance of `CalculatorService`, an array of integers we know should add up to 10, which we have also hardcoded into a variable for reference. Finally, we make the call to the `Sum()` function to obtain the actual result.
2. The second step is act. This simply means that action is taken to enable the test to be evaluated. For example, if you're testing a calculation between two integer values, the actual calculation would take place at this point.
3. The final step is assert. An assertion is the test itself. In this, we will assert that our `[Fact]` is true. If the assertion is correct, `[Fact]` is true and the test will pass. If the assertion is incorrect, the test will fail.

Different testing frameworks have their own implementation of an assertion, but the principle remains the same. In xUnit, a static class, `Assert`, holds various types of assertions that can be used during testing. For example, an assertion that something is null or not null is represented via `Assert.Null()` and `Assert.NotNull()`, respectively. Likewise, we can assert that a statement is true with `Assert.True()`.

We want to assert that the expected result of `Sum()` is equal to the actual result. For this, we can use `Assert.Equal()`:

```
[Fact]
public void Sum_Test()
{
    var calculatorService = new CalculatorService();
    int[] integers = { 1, 1, 8 };
    var result = calculatorService.Sum(integers);
    var expectedResult = 10;
    Assert.Equal(result, expectedResult);
}
```

Running this test is as simple as right-clicking the method signature and selecting **Run Tests**. The test will run, and the test result will be shown by Visual Studio in Test Explorer. You should see a green circle next to the test to indicate success.

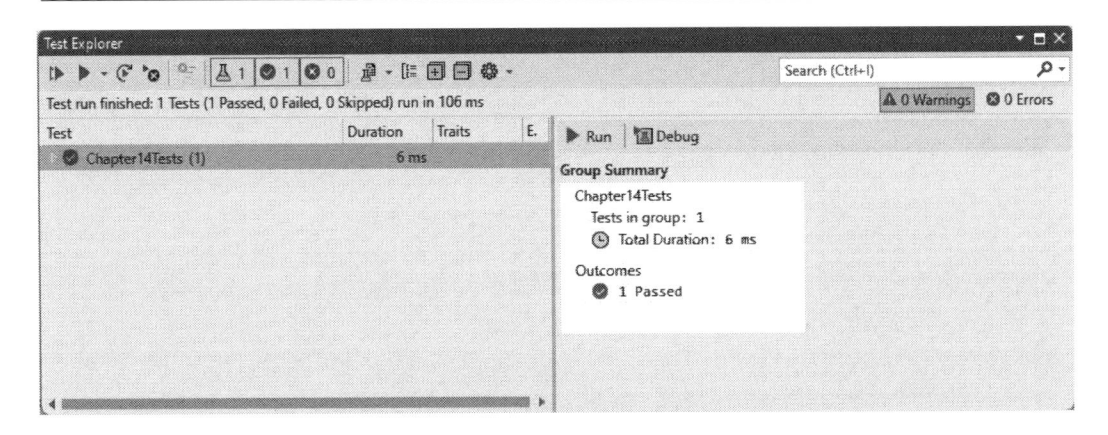

Figure 14.5: The Test Explorer screen, showing available tests and their results

A similar approach to writing tests can be taken for integration tests, the main difference being the scope of the test. For this example, a minimal API, a simple integration test's scope could cover a whole endpoint. Let's put this into practice by writing an integration test for the `/sumintegers` API endpoint that checks the resulting status code.

To run this test, we will need to be able to access an `HttpClient` object and run `WebApplication` in the test project, because the test needs to make a request against an endpoint. To make this possible, you can make your test class implement `IClassFixture` of type `WebApplicationFactory`.

> **IClassFixture usage in a test class**
>
> `IClassFixture` is an interface that allows objects to share scope across a class. In this case, we want to share the scope of a `WebApplicationFactory` object so that an `HttpClient` instance can be created for tests within the class.

Because `WebApplicationFactory` needs `Microsoft.AspNetCore.Mvc.Testing` to be installed, use the NuGet package manager console to install this package:

```
dotnet add package Microsoft.AspNetCore.Mvc.Testing
```

Update the `CalculatorTests` class so that it implements `IClassFixture`:

```
public class CalculatorTests :
    IClassFixture<WebApplicationFactory<Program>>
```

This will require you to add a constructor for the class, in which you can inject `WebApplicationFactory`. You can also use this `WebApplicationFactory` to create a new `HttpClient` for use during tests. Let's store this in a `readonly` field so that we can keep things clean by not reinitializing it after the constructor has run:

```csharp
private readonly HttpClient _httpClient;

public CalculatorTests(
    WebApplicationFactory<Program> applicationFactory)
{
    _httpClient = applicationFactory.CreateClient();
}
```

Finally, we can write our tests. Let's *arrange* our test data by creating the required parameters as an array of integers and then serializing them to a JSON string so that they can be added to the body of the request:

```csharp
[Fact]
public async Task SumIntegers_ShouldReturnOk()
{
    //Arrange
    var integers = new[] { 2, 4, 4 };
    var jsonContent = new
        StringContent(JsonSerializer.Serialize(integers),
        Encoding.UTF8,
        "application/json"
    );
}
```

Next, we can *act* by making the POST request to the target endpoint:

```csharp
// Act
var response = await _httpClient.PostAsync(
    "/SumIntegers", jsonContent);
```

Finally, we can *assert* that the response code is the one we were expecting, in this case, 200 OK:

```csharp
Assert.Equal(HttpStatusCode.OK, response.StatusCode);
```

You could also assert that the result is the expected one by checking the response content:

```csharp
Assert.Equal(10, JsonSerializer.Deserialize<int>(await response.
Content.ReadAsStringAsync()));
```

This integration test may look pretty similar to the original unit test we wrote earlier in this chapter, but it differs in the sense that it has a wider scope.

By calling this test, we not only make a request to the target endpoint, but we also cover the testing of the encapsulated `CalculatorService`.

In both of these examples, integration and unit testing were conducted on pre-existing logic. If we were to adopt **Test-Driven Development** (**TDD**), we would augment our practices by writing the tests before any logic. Obviously, we expect the tests to fail initially, but our goal is to write code that allows the tests to pass. Assuming your tests make the same assertions as your acceptance criteria from an API requirements perspective, TDD is widely considered the optimal way to apply automated testing to a code base.

TDD or not, however you approach unit and integration testing, having test coverage will help to increase the quality of your minimal API code, and hopefully reduce the number of reported bugs post-release.

When it comes to the quality and stability of an API, testing the code's logic is one aspect; but before moving to deployment, there is another aspect to be considered: that of compatibility. Let's explore compatibility, with a particular focus on the latest version of .NET at the time of writing – .NET 9.

Compatibility and migrating minimal APIs to .NET 9

Let's assume that you have already created a minimal API project, but the .NET version is not the latest. You wish to deploy the API, but before you do so, you intend to bring the code base to the latest .NET version, which at the time of writing this book is 9. What factors do we need to consider to be confident that our application will run efficiently on this new version, and how can we migrate to it?

Before any .NET migration, it is critical that you consult Microsoft's documentation, where any known breaking changes are outlined.

.NET breaking changes fall into three categories:

- **Binary incompatible**: Existing binaries may fail to load and may need to be recompiled.
- **Source incompatible**: Code may require change in order to compile.
- **Behavioral change**: Code and binaries may behave differently after update, meaning code changes would be required.

While Microsoft is usually pretty effective in avoiding major breaking changes, checking the documentation at `https://learn.microsoft.com/en-us/dotnet/core/compatibility/9.0` ahead of time will provide valuable insight into any potential issues you may face. On top of this, if a breaking change does find its way into the minimal API post-update, unit and integration tests will increase the chances of the breaking changes being caught.

Microsoft outlines breaking changes for different areas of .NET. For minimal APIs, you will be most concerned with changes in the area of ASP.NET, but ensure you review other areas, such as core .NET libraries, deployment, networking, SDK, MSBuild, and serialization, as these are secondary areas that are all relevant to minimal APIs.

At the time of writing, there are only two breaking changes outlined in ASP.NET for .NET 9, which are summarized here:

- `DefaultKeyResolution.ShouldGenerateNewKey`: There is a different meaning behind Boolean (true/false) result returned in previous versions. This breaking change is caused by a redefinition of the `true/false` result returned by `ShouldGenerateNewKey`. Let's delve into this in more detail:

  - When managing keys in your minimal API, if you're using ASP.NET's default implementation to generate the key, there is a Boolean that is provided to tell you whether a new key should be generated.

  - Previously, the result of the Boolean was produced based on whether the default key was within two days of expiration.

  - It was decided that "within two days" of expiration was not appropriate on its own, as there are other factors that could influence whether the key should be regenerated. Now, the result of `ShouldGenerateNewKey` is based on several factors related to `IdefaultKeyResolver` as well as whether or not a default key exists in the first place, rather than an arbitrary meaning based on whether the key is two days away from expiry.

- When a minimal API application starts, you can specify in `UseDefaultServiceProvider` whether validation should be run on registered services and service scopes. Previously, validation was always turned off by default. Let's break down this change a little further to see whether it affects your existing code:

  - The validation of services ensures that all services can be created at startup.

  - The validation of scopes checks that scoped services are not resolved from the root provider, which would violate their scope.

  - Overall, this meant that no validation was performed by default. You had to turn on the previous validation for it to be executed when the application is loaded. However, validation is now performed by default.

Based on this, there are no major breaking changes when moving a minimal API to .NET 9 (at least where ASP.NET Core is concerned). However, it is still important to be prepared for any potential change. With that in mind, how would we mitigate these changes?

- For `DefaultKeyResolution.ShouldGenerateNewKey` affecting key resolution, you only really need to act if you have written logic that is now redundant thanks to the way .NET 9 checks for an expired key.

  For example, if previously you were checking that a default key exists, you no longer need to do this, because .NET 9 does this for you. The impact of this change is therefore fairly minimal.

- For `UseDefaultServiceProvider`, the required changes are simple. If by updating your minimal API to .NET 9 you start to see errors on startup owing to the fact that validation of services and scope is now enabled by default, you must address the outputted validation errors.

For most basic scenarios, it is unlikely that your minimal API is configured in such a way that services could not be resolved or scoped services are being incorrectly resolved from the root provider, but it is still important to be aware of these factors.

> **Accuracy at the time of writing and other affected areas of .NET**
>
> It is important to emphasize that these changes were reported before the release of .NET 9, during its preview. Developers must consult Microsoft's documentation before any migration to see whether any further breaking changes have been reported. Moreover, the summary provided in this book is only targeting ASP.NET Core, which is the main area we are concerned with when writing minimal APIs. However, other areas mentioned, such as the .NET SDK, networking, and serialization, could all affect minimal API projects depending on the use case.

Now that we've explored the potential compatibility issues we face when publishing a minimal API application to .NET 9, let's look at the various methods of deployment we have at our disposal.

Deploying minimal APIs

There are many different ways to deploy a minimal API project, and exploring them all would be way out of the scope of this book. However, we can look at some of the most common deployment targets.

Deploying to Microsoft Azure App Service (cloud deployment)

Deploying to Azure App Service is very straightforward and can be achieved using a publish profile in Visual Studio. A publish profile is a configuration object that specifies how a project should be deployed. It contains metadata about the type of runtime in play, the target architecture (x86, ARM, etc.), and the target host, which in this example will be Azure.

For the purposes of this example, I'm assuming that an Azure App Service instance exists in your Azure subscription, to which you are allowed to deploy. If an App Service instance does not exist in Azure, you will need to create one.

The pricing for Azure app services can be calculated via Microsoft's pricing calculator at https://azure.microsoft.com/en-gb/pricing/calculator/. At the time of writing, there is a free tier that allows for basic testing which will probably be suitable for most people reading this book to practice their deployment. A basic tier app service currently costs approx $55-60 per month, but this can increase depending on the use case and the required specification.

The creation of an App Service instance is out of the scope of this book:

1. First, right-click on the project you wish to deploy in **Solution Explorer** in Visual Studio and then click **Publish...**:

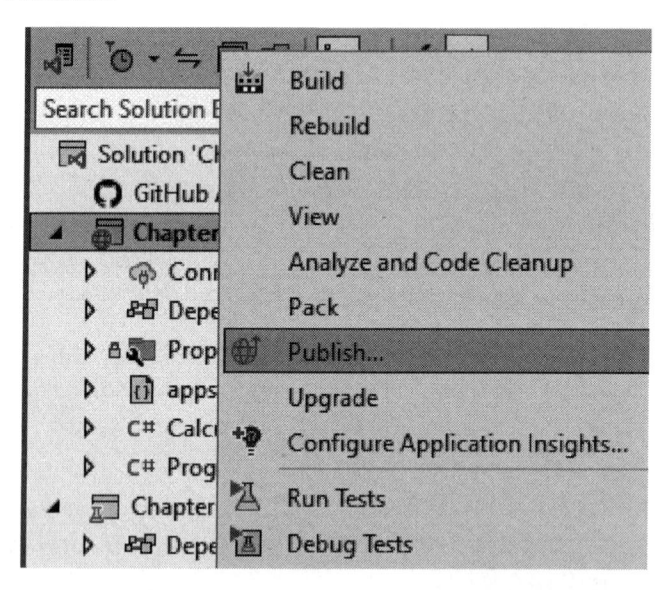

Figure 14.6: Publishing from Solution Explorer in Visual Studio

If you don't have any publish profiles already set up, you will see the **Publish** dialog. If you don't see this, it's because you do already have a publish profile for another deployment. You can select **Add a publish profile** to open the **Publish** dialog if this is the case.

2. Once you see the **Publish** dialog, select **Azure**:

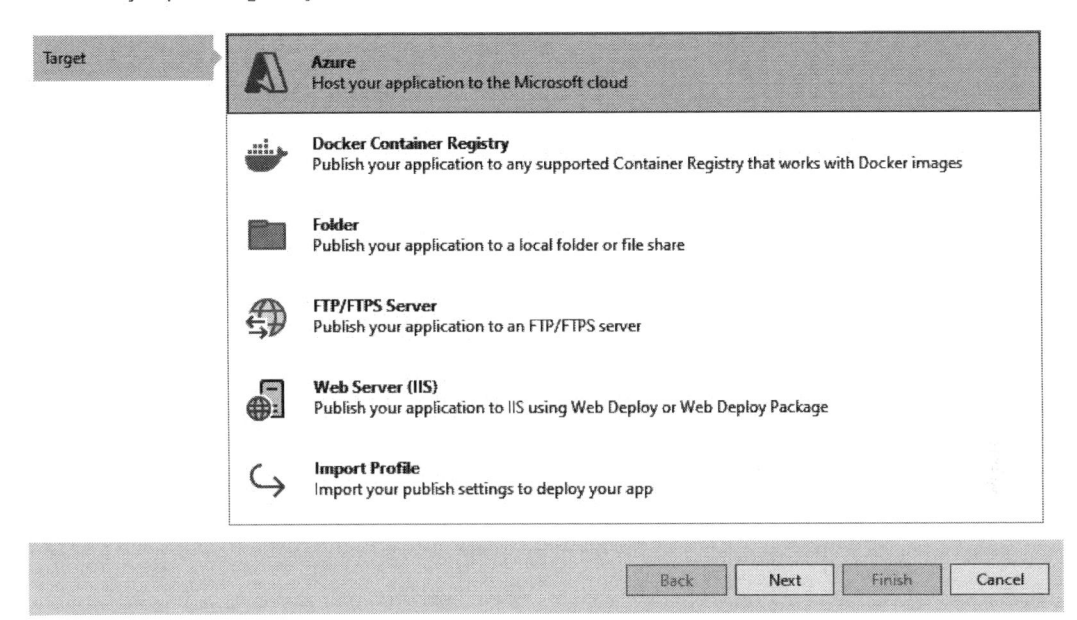

Figure 14.7: Selecting a publish target in Visual Studio

3. Then select **Azure App Service**, ensuring that you select the correct operating system running on the target App Service in Azure (Windows or Linux).

   The next screen will then request that you choose your Azure subscription. If you're not already logged in to Azure, you can connect using the option at the top right of the dialog.

4. Once connected, you should see your Azure subscription in the dropdown, along with the available App Service instances to deploy to. Select the service you wish to target and click **Next**:

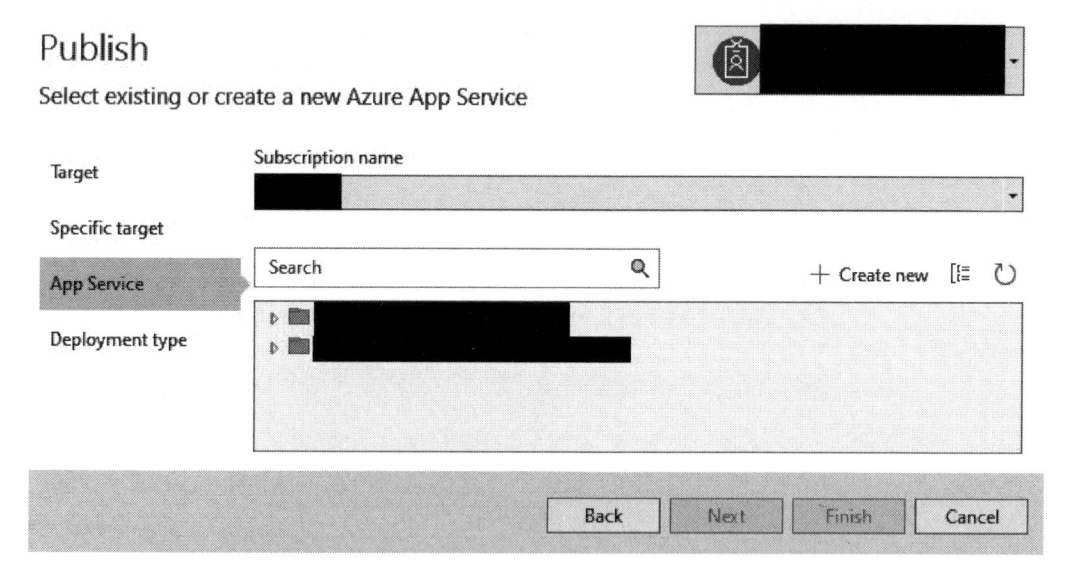

Figure 14.8: Choosing the target Azure App Service resource

5. Finally, you will be asked whether you wish to publish using a `.pubxml` file or via GitHub Actions. We won't be covering continuous integration/continuous delivery pipelines such as GitHub Actions in this book, so select **Publish**.

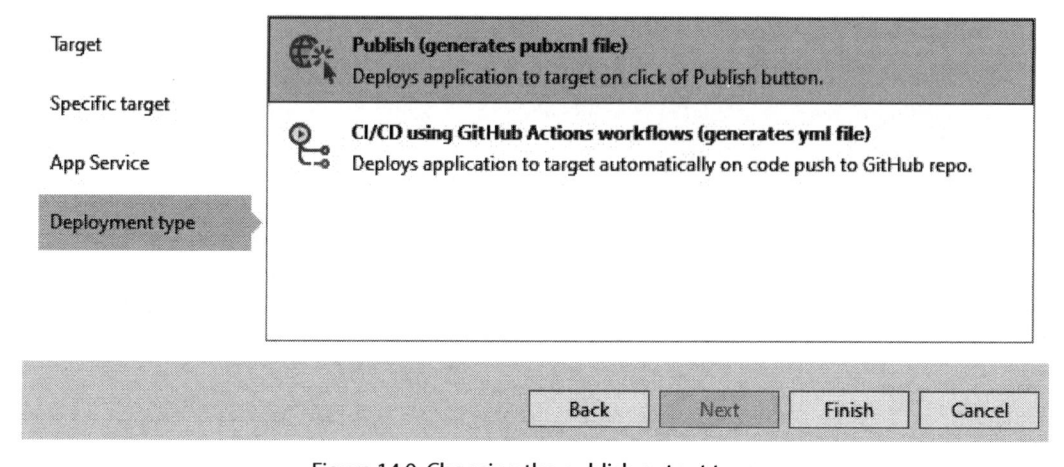

Figure 14.9: Choosing the publish output type

Once this is complete, the dialog will close and your new publish profile is created. From there you can see and change the publish settings, such as what configuration you will be publishing (almost always **Release**), the framework which in our example is .NET9, the deployment mode, which is either **Framework - dependent** or **Self - contained** (More on that below) and the target runtime which in my example is **64bit Linux**.

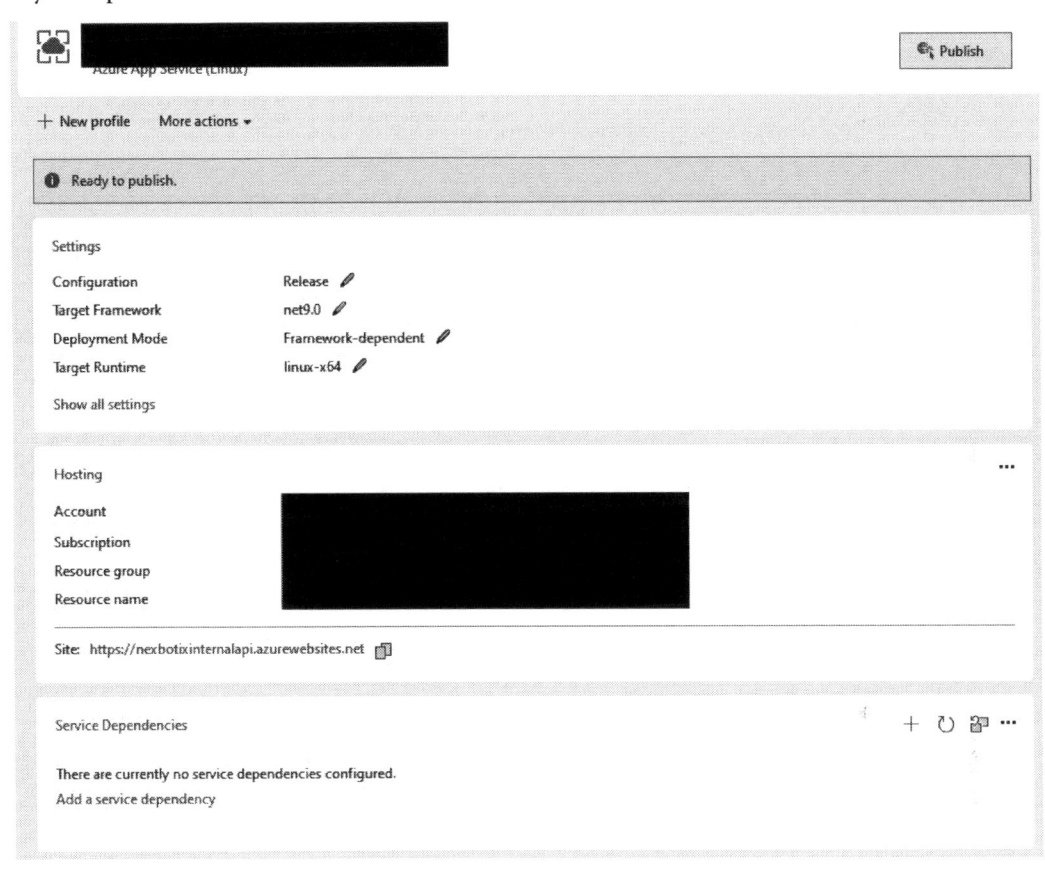

Figure 14.10: The newly created publish profile

Do this and your application will be built before being deployed to the target App Service. Once completed, Visual Studio will automatically open a browser window and navigate to the minimal API's URL.

> **Framework-dependent versus self-contained deployment modes**
>
> You have two choices of deployment mode. **Framework-dependent** requires that .NET 9 (or whichever version you are using) is installed on the target machine. **Self-contained** will package the runtime with the application. The former produces a smaller set of output files but has the drawback of requiring the specific .NET version to be installed on the target machine, whereas the latter has a larger output but has fewer prerequisites for the target machine for the application to run, making it more portable.

Next, let's move on to deploying to a Docker container.

Deploying to a Docker container

ASP.NET and .NET Core are already well positioned to offer cross-platform functionality, but there are still subtle differences in configuration depending on the host operating system. Containerizing your minimal API application with Docker can make it agnostic, meaning that it doesn't care what operating system it's running on.

Firstly, you must ensure that Docker is installed on your system. Documentation outlining this is available at `https://docs.docker.com/engine/install/`. For Windows, you will need to install Docker Desktop, documentation for which can be found here at `https://docs.docker.com/desktop/install/windows-install/`, whereas for Linux, simply running Docker Engine should suffice.

Once you have completed the install, you need to create a Dockerfile, which will describe how your minimal API project should be packaged into a Docker container as well as how it should run on the host machine.

You can create this file within your project as a new item in Visual Studio:

1. Select the button at the top left of **Solution Explorer** to change the view:

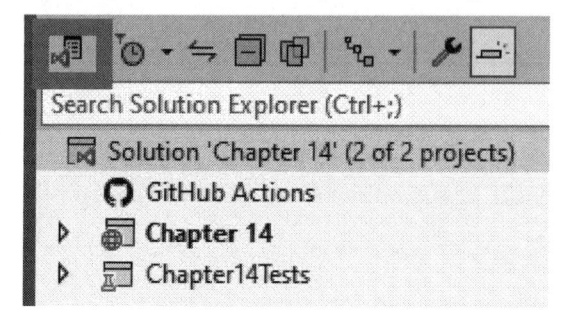

Figure 14.11: Changing view options in Solution Explorer

2. Select **Folder View**:

Figure 14.12: Switching to Folder View

3. Then, right-click your project folder and select **Add | New File**.

Figure 14.13: Creating a new file in the project within Folder View

4. A Docker file has no name, just an extension of `.dockerfile`. Create this file. It should then open as a tab in Visual Studio. (There are reports of issues with Docker files not working unless they are called `Dockerfile`, so you can try this if you are having similar issues.)

Now we can write the Docker file.

First, we need to specify a base image to be used for the runtime environment of the minimal API application. We can pull the official .NET 9 ASP.NET runtime image from Microsoft's container registry like so:

```
FROM mcr.microsoft.com/dotnet/aspnet:9.0 AS base
```

Then, we can tell Docker that we want to set the working directory inside the container to `/app`, so that any subsequent commands will be executed relative to this directory. We will also specify that we wish to expose port `80` on the container:

```
WORKDIR /app
EXPOSE 80
```

Next, we add a section that downloads the .NET 9 SDK, which will be required as the full runtime necessary for compiling the minimal API application. We then set the working directory again, this time to a folder of our choice; we'll choose `/src`.

Following this, the entire content of the current directory is copied into the /src directory inside the container so that it can be built, dotnet restore is executed to add any NuGet packages required as dependencies, and the app is compiled in release mode to the /app folder:

```
FROM mcr.microsoft.com/dotnet/sdk:9.0 AS build
WORKDIR /src
COPY . .
RUN dotnet restore
RUN dotnet publish -c Release -o /app
```

At this point in the execution, the container will have been built. Finally, we can add a section to the Docker file that runs the built container by copying the container assemblies and running from the DLL output by .NET after compilation:

```
FROM base AS final
WORKDIR /app
COPY --from=build /app .
ENTRYPOINT ["dotnet", "MyminimalAPIProject.dll"]
```

So far, we have specified how the image for the container should be built, but we haven't yet triggered the build. To do this, open a terminal or command prompt window running from your project directory and run the following command, replacing MYAPINAME with a suitable image name:

```
docker build -t MYAPINAME .
```

In this command, we are creating a tag for the image being built with the given name, and then we use . to indicate that the build context for the image is the current directory where the Docker file is located.

Once built, you can run the container to start the app, which should be available to receive requests on a port of your choosing:

```
docker run -d -p 8080:80 --name MYCONTAINERNAME MYAPINAME
```

In this command, we have told Docker Engine to run the container with -d (detached mode), which allows it to run in the background. We then used -p to specify that port 80 on the container should be mapped to port 8080 on the host machine. This means your minimal API will be available at http://localhost:8080.

Finally, there is one other method you can use that is extremely simple: deploying to the built-in Kestrel web server.

Deploying on-premises with Kestrel

If you simply want to host your minimal API as an ASP.NET Core application on a Windows machine, you can create a new publish profile and then follow the publish profile wizard in Visual Studio outlined earlier in this chapter. However, instead of choosing Azure as the target, choose **Folder**.

Publish

Where are you publishing today?

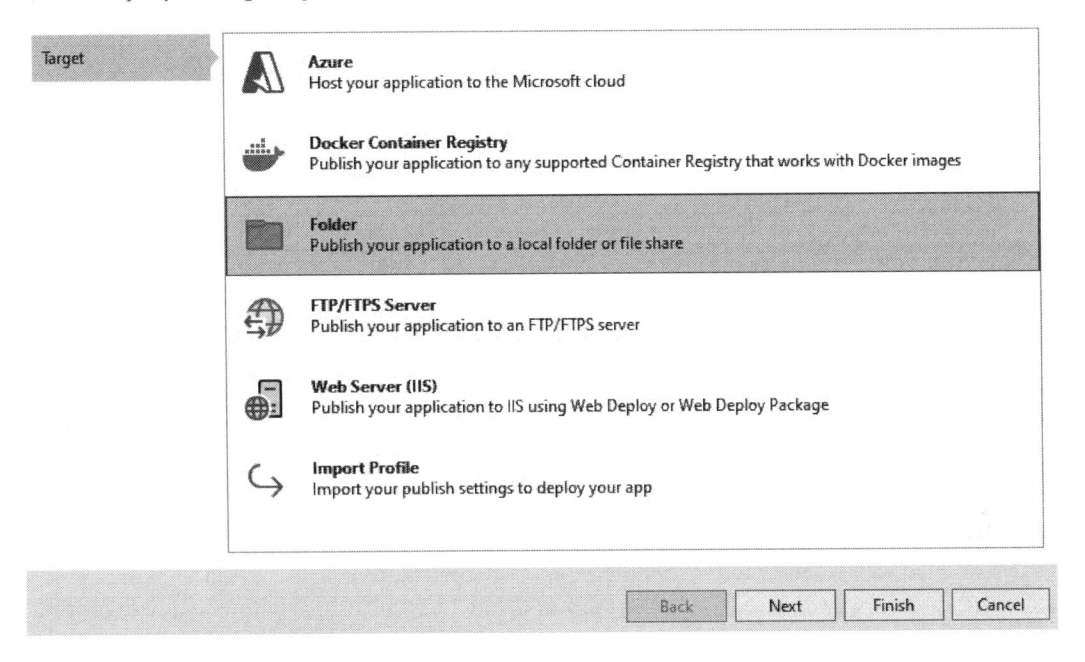

Target

- **Azure**
  Host your application to the Microsoft cloud

- **Docker Container Registry**
  Publish your application to any supported Container Registry that works with Docker images

- **Folder** *(selected)*
  Publish your application to a local folder or file share

- **FTP/FTPS Server**
  Publish your application to an FTP/FTPS server

- **Web Server (IIS)**
  Publish your application to IIS using Web Deploy or Web Deploy Package

- **Import Profile**
  Import your publish settings to deploy your app

[Back] [Next] [Finish] [Cancel]

Figure 14.14: Choosing Folder as the publish target

On selection, the wizard will ask you to specify a target folder to deploy to. This folder can be local, or it can be a network path on a remote server.

Once published, the resulting .EXE file can be double-clicked and the application will run using the Kestrel web server, which listens on port 5000 by default.

If you wish to change the port, you can do so via the appsettings.json file in your project by adding the following (e.g., change to port 8080):

```
"Kestrel": {
    "Endpoints": {
        "Http": {
            "Url": "http://*:8080"
        }
    }
}
```

We've explored a high-level overview of how we can prepare our minimal APIs for their inevitable deployment and consumption by end users. Now, we're nearing the end of our journey. Let's summarize what we've learned in this final chapter.

Summary

In this chapter, we've navigated through the crucial steps required to prepare minimal APIs for production, focusing on testing, compatibility with .NET 9, and deployment strategies. Each of these aspects plays a pivotal role in ensuring that your APIs are robust, compatible, and seamlessly delivered to end users.

We explored unit testing, which isolates and validates individual components, and integration testing, which ensures that different parts of the system work together correctly. Through practical examples with xUnit, we demonstrated how to set up and execute these tests to validate functionality and performance. The key takeaway is that thorough testing—whether through unit tests or integration tests—helps catch potential issues early, reducing the likelihood of bugs slipping into production and ensuring that your API meets its acceptance criteria.

Compatibility with .NET 9 is crucial for maintaining the longevity and efficiency of your minimal APIs. We discussed the importance of understanding breaking changes and adapting your code base accordingly. By keeping abreast of Microsoft's documentation on .NET 9 changes, and leveraging unit and integration tests, you can mitigate the impact of any breaking changes. This proactive approach ensures that your APIs continue to function correctly with the latest .NET version and provides a smoother transition during migrations.

Deployment encompasses several methods tailored to different environments and needs. We covered deployment to Microsoft Azure App Service, which offers a straightforward, scalable solution for cloud environments. We also explored containerization with Docker, providing a portable, cross-platform deployment option. For on-premises deployments, running minimal APIs directly with Kestrel offers a simple and effective approach. Each deployment method has its own set of configurations and considerations, such as choosing between framework-dependent and self-contained deployments or managing container ports and environment settings.

Ensuring that your minimal APIs are well tested, compatible with the latest .NET versions, and deployed using the most suitable method empowers you to deliver high-quality, reliable software. By applying the practices outlined in this chapter, you set a solid foundation for successful deployment and long-term maintenance of your APIs, contributing to both immediate operational success and future scalability.

We're now at the end of our minimal API journey, and as the book ends, I hope you've gained a solid understanding of how to create minimal APIs in various use cases and that you've found the experience enjoyable.

The book has been a joy for me to write as someone who is passionate about the use of minimal APIs in varying use cases and contexts. APIs are critical to nearly all modern software systems, and I think a good knowledge of minimal APIs and their advantages will give any .NET developer an edge in their programming career.

Thanks for reading. Now go and build some more minimal APIs!

Index

A

API endpoints
  database transactions, executing
    from 114, 115
API request lifecycle 34, 35
Application Programming Interface (API) 3
arrange, act, and assert (AAAs) 208
ASP.NET 87
ASP.NET, built-in lifetime options
  scoped 90
  singleton 90
  transient 90
ASP.NET Identity provider 28
async/await keywords
  TAP 164, 165
asynchronous function 161
asynchronous patterns
  Asynchronous Processing Pattern 165-168
  implementing 162
  TAP, with async/await 164, 165
  Task-based Asynchronous
    Pattern (TAP) 162, 163
asynchronous programming
  pitfalls and challenges 168-170
attributes 78

authentication 196
authorization 197-199

B

BenchmarkDotNet 149, 154
  benchmarking with 154-156
best practices, DI 100
  sensible service lifetimes, using 102
  service locator pattern, avoiding 100, 101
  services, registering with
    extension method 101

C

caching 172
  distributed caching strategies 176-178
  in-memory caching 173-175
  response caching 178, 179
claims 197
connection string
  reference link 108
container 88
context 137
contract 109
controller-based APIs 5
Controllers 18

Create, Read, Update, Delete (CRUD) 19, 105, 128, 189
  performing, with Entity Framework 141-144
cross-site request forgery (CSRF) protection 8
CRUD operations, with Dapper
  Employee record, creating 131-133
  Employee record, deleting 136, 137
  Employee record, reading 133, 134
  Employee record, updating 135, 136
  performing 130
custom binding logic
  creating 82-84
custom middleware 61
  error-handling middleware 61
  implementing 62-64
  IP-blocking middleware 62
  logging middleware 61
  request-timing middleware 62
  validation middleware 61

D

Dapper
  configuring, in minimal API projects 129, 130
database transactions
  executing, from API endpoints 114, 115
data integration 106, 107
Data Transfer Objects (DTOs) 186
deadlock 168
default middleware 61
deferred processing 165
DELETE method 22
dependencies 87
dependency hell 87
dependency injection (DI) 87, 88
  best practices 100-102
  case 88, 89
  configuring, in minimal APIs 89
design patterns 187
  factory pattern 188, 189
  repository pattern 189-191
  Strategy pattern 191-193
DI container 88
distributed caching strategy 176-178
Docker container
  minimal APIs, deploying to 218-220
don't repeat yourself (DRY) principle 57
Dynamic Link Library (DLL) 154

E

employee management API
  building 23-25
  endpoint, testing with OpenAPI 28
  first endpoint, creating 25-27
Employee record
  creating 131-133
  deleting 136, 137
  inserting 113
  reading 133, 134
  updating 135, 136
endpoints 18
  defining, in Todo API 41
Entity Framework
  configuring, in minimal API projects 137-141
  CRUD operations, performing with 141-144
error handling 194-196
error-handling middleware 61
explicit binding
  with attributes 78, 79

F

factory pattern 188, 189
feature-based modular structure 185, 186
folder structures
   feature-based modular structure 185, 186
   layered modular structure 186, 187
form values 77
framework-dependent 218

G

GET methods 20
Graphical User Interface (GUI) 77, 115

H

headers 76
hooks 33
HTTP methods
   DELETE 22
   GET 20
   PATCH 21
   POST 20
   PUT 21
HTTP requests
   handling 28, 29
   Typed Results 29

I

Impedance Mismatch 128
inline middleware 59, 60
in-memory caching 173-175
integration testing
   for minimal APIs 204-211
IP-blocking middleware 62

J

JSON Web Tokens (JWTs) 196

K

Kestrel
   used, for on-premises deployment 220, 221

L

Language Integrated Query (LINQ) 152
   query 44
layered modular structure 186, 187
Linux
   Visual Studio Code, installing for 11
logging middleware 61, 64

M

Mac
   Visual Studio Code, installing for 11
mainstream database platforms
   examples 107
Microsoft Azure App Service
   (cloud deployment)
   minimal APIs, deploying to 213-217
middleware 56
   default middleware 61
   example 58
   inline middleware 59, 60
   order, maintaining 60, 61
   pipeline flow, example 56, 57
   terminal middleware 64-67
middleware classes 59
middleware pipeline
   errors, handling 67-69
migrations 139

minimal API application
   application lifecycle 33
   components 32
   configuration 33
   middleware 33
   routing 33
   services 33

minimal API projects
   Dapper, configuring 129, 130
   Entity Framework, configuring 137-141

minimal API resiliency, best practices
   code organization and structure 184
   design patterns 187
   error handling 194
   folder structures 185
   security considerations 196

minimal APIs 4
   anatomy 31, 32
   compatibility 211-213
   contrasting, with traditional API approaches 5-7
   deploying 213
   DI, configuring 89
   features 3
   history 3
   integration testing 204-211
   migrating, to .NET 9 211-213
   significance, in modern development 8
   tools and dependencies, installing 8, 9
   unit testing 204-211

models 18
Model-View-Controller (MVC) 5, 18
modularity 184
   benefits 184

MongoDB 115
   connecting to 115-124

MongoDB Compass 115

N

.NET breaking changes, categories
   behavioral change 211
   binary incompatible 211
   source incompatible 211

.NET SDK installer 9
NoSQL 106
   databases 107
   versus SQL 106

O

object binding 76
   strongly typed object binding 76, 77

Object-Oriented Programming (OOP) 128
Object Relation Mapping (ORM) 91, 105, 127-129
   CRUD operations, performing with Dapper 130
   Dapper, configuring in minimal API projects 129, 130
   Entity Framework, configuring in minimal API projects 137-141

on-premises
   deploying, with Kestrel 220, 221

order of precedence 81

P

Package Manager Console 118
parameter binding 71
   logic, creating 82-84
   precedence 81, 82
   through dependency injection 79-81

parameter binding, sources 71
   attributes 78, 79
   form values 77

headers 76
  optional query string parameters 74, 75
  query strings 73, 74
  route values 72, 73
  strongly typed object binding 76, 77
PATCH methods 21
performance bottlenecks 157
  database access 157
  dependency injection (DI) 158
  garbage collection (GC) pressure 158
  I/O operations 158
  logging 158
  middleware pipeline 158
  network latency 159
  serialization/deserialization 158
performance metrics 149
performance monitoring 147, 149
  CPU processing 149
  memory 149
  response times 149
  throughput 149
POST methods 20
profiler 148
profiling 147
  advantages 148
  setting up, in Visual Studio 150-153
profiling tools
  BenchmarkDotNet 149
  Visual Studio profiler 149
project
  creating, in Visual Studio 12, 13
  creating, in Visual Studio Code 13, 14
PUT methods 21

Q

query strings 73, 74
  optional parameters 74, 75

R

race condition 169
rate limiting 199
Redis 176
regression 203
relational databases 107
repository pattern 189-191
requests
  handling 40
request-timing middleware 62
request validation
  manual validation 48
  with data annotations 49-52
  with filters 52, 53
  with model binding 49-52
resource management 168
response caching 178, 179
route parameters 45
  constraints 46-48
  managing 45-47
routes 19
  value 72, 73

S

scaffolding 137
scoped DI project
  setting up 90-95
security considerations 196
  authentication 197
  authorization 197-199
  rate limiting 200, 201
self-contained 218
separation of concerns 184

service lifetimes
  scoped 102
  singleton 102
  transient 102
service locator pattern 100
short-circuiting 64
single responsibility 89
singleton 109
singleton DI project
  creating 95-100
SOLID principles 89
SQL 106
  versus NoSQL 106
SQL databases
  connecting to 107-113
  connection string 108
standard deviation 157
store 3
storefront 3
Strategy pattern 191-193
synchronous operation 161

T

Task-based Asynchronous Pattern (TAP) 162, 163
  with async/await 164, 165
terminal middleware 64-67
Test-Driven Development (TDD) 211
tight coupling 89
Todo API
  endpoints, defining 41
todo items
  creating 42, 43
  obtaining 41, 42
  updating 43-45
TopLink 128

U

unit testing
  for minimal APIs 204-211
User Interface (UI) 3

V

validation middleware 61
Visual Studio
  installing, for Windows 10
  profiling, setting up 150-153
  project, creating 12, 13
Visual Studio Code
  installing, for Mac and Linux 11
  project, creating 13, 14
Visual Studio profiler 149

W

Windows
  Visual Studio, installing for 10
Windows Subsystem for Linux (WSL) 172

‹packt›

www.packtpub.com

Subscribe to our online digital library for full access to over 7,000 books and videos, as well as industry leading tools to help you plan your personal development and advance your career. For more information, please visit our website.

Why subscribe?

- Spend less time learning and more time coding with practical eBooks and Videos from over 4,000 industry professionals
- Improve your learning with Skill Plans built especially for you
- Get a free eBook or video every month
- Fully searchable for easy access to vital information
- Copy and paste, print, and bookmark content

Did you know that Packt offers eBook versions of every book published, with PDF and ePub files available? You can upgrade to the eBook version at packtpub.com and as a print book customer, you are entitled to a discount on the eBook copy. Get in touch with us at customercare@packtpub.com for more details.

At www.packtpub.com, you can also read a collection of free technical articles, sign up for a range of free newsletters, and receive exclusive discounts and offers on Packt books and eBooks.

Other Books You May Enjoy

If you enjoyed this book, you may be interested in these other books by Packt:

Web API Development with ASP.NET Core 8

Xiaodi Yan

ISBN: 978-1-80461-095-4

- Build a strong foundation in web API fundamentals
- Explore the ASP.NET Core 8 framework and other industry-standard libraries and tools for high-performance, scalable web APIs
- Apply essential software design patterns such as MVC, dependency injection, and the repository pattern
- Use Entity Framework Core for database operations and complex query creation
- Implement robust security measures to protect against malicious attacks and data breaches
- Deploy your application to the cloud using Azure and leverage Azure DevOps to implement CI/CD

ASP.NET 8 Best Practices

Jonathan R. Danylko

ISBN: 978-1-83763-212-1

- Explore the common IDE tools used in the industry
- Identify the best approach for organizing source control, projects, and middleware
- Uncover and address top web security threats, implementing effective strategies to protect your code
- Optimize Entity Framework for faster query performance using best practices
- Automate software through continuous integration/continuous deployment
- Gain a solid understanding of the .NET Core coding fundamentals for building websites
- Harness HtmlHelpers, TagHelpers, ViewComponents, and Blazor for component-based development

Packt is searching for authors like you

If you're interested in becoming an author for Packt, please visit `authors.packtpub.com` and apply today. We have worked with thousands of developers and tech professionals, just like you, to help them share their insight with the global tech community. You can make a general application, apply for a specific hot topic that we are recruiting an author for, or submit your own idea.

Share Your Thoughts

Now you've finished *Minimal APIs in ASP.NET 9*, we'd love to hear your thoughts! Scan the QR code below to go straight to the Amazon review page for this book and share your feedback or leave a review on the site that you purchased it from.

`https://packt.link/r/1-805-12912-0`

Your review is important to us and the tech community and will help us make sure we're delivering excellent quality content.

Download a free PDF copy of this book

Thanks for purchasing this book!

Do you like to read on the go but are unable to carry your print books everywhere?

Is your eBook purchase not compatible with the device of your choice?

Don't worry, now with every Packt book you get a DRM-free PDF version of that book at no cost.

Read anywhere, any place, on any device. Search, copy, and paste code from your favorite technical books directly into your application.

The perks don't stop there, you can get exclusive access to discounts, newsletters, and great free content in your inbox daily

Follow these simple steps to get the benefits:

1. Scan the QR code or visit the link below

    https://packt.link/free-ebook/978-1-80512-912-7

2. Submit your proof of purchase
3. That's it! We'll send your free PDF and other benefits to your email directly

Printed in Dunstable, United Kingdom